A VOICE AND NOTHING MORE

A Voice and Nothing More

Mladen Dolar

THE MIT PRESS   CAMBRIDGE, MASSACHUSETTS   LONDON, ENGLAND

MIT Press books may be purchased at special quantity discounts for business or sales promotional use. For information, please email special_sales@mitpress.mit.edu or write to Special Sales Department, The MIT Press, 55 Hayward Street, Cambridge, MA 02142.

This book was printed and bound in the United States of America.

Library of Congress Cataloging-in-Publication Data

Dolar, Mladen.
    A voice and nothing more / Mladen Dolar.
        p. cm. — (Short circuits)
    Includes bibliographical references and index.
    ISBN 0-262-54187-4 (pbk. : alk. paper)
    1. Voice (Philosophy) I. Title. II. Series.

B105.V64D65   2006
128—dc22

                                                    2005054457

Contents

A short circuit occurs when there is a faulty connection in the network—faulty, of course, from the standpoint of the network's smooth functioning. Is not the shock of short-circuiting, therefore, one of the best metaphors for a critical reading? Is not one of the most effective critical procedures to cross wires that do not usually touch: to take a major classic (text, author, notion), and read it in a short-circuiting way, through the lens of a "minor" author, text, or conceptual apparatus ("minor" should be understood here in Deleuze's sense: not "of lesser quality," but marginalized, disavowed by the hegemonic ideology, or dealing with a "lower," less dignified topic)? If the minor reference is well chosen, such a procedure can lead to insights which completely shatter and undermine our common perceptions. This is what Marx, among others, did with philosophy and religion (short-circuiting philosophical speculation through the lens of political economy, that is to say, economic speculation); this is what Freud and Nietzsche did with morality (short-circuiting the highest ethical notions through the lens of the unconscious libidinal economy). What such a reading achieves is not a simple "desublimation," a reduction of the higher intellectual content to its lower economic or libidinal cause; the aim of such an approach is, rather, the inherent decentering of the interpreted text, which brings to light its "unthought," its disavowed presuppositions and consequences.

And this is what "Short Circuits" wants to do, again and again. The underlying premise of the series is that Lacanian psychoanalysis is a privileged instrument of such an approach, whose purpose is to illuminate a standard text or ideological formation, making it readable in a totally new way—the long history of Lacanian interventions in philosophy, religion, the arts (from the visual arts to the cinema, music, and literature), ideology, and politics justifies this premise. This, then, is not a new series of books on psychoanalysis, but a series of "connections in the Freudian field"—of short Lacanian interventions in art, philosophy, theology, and ideology.

"Short Circuits" intends to revive a practice of reading which confronts a classic text, author, or notion with its own hidden presuppositions, and thus reveals its disavowed truth. The basic criterion for the texts that will be published is that they effectuate such a theoretical short circuit. After reading a book in this series, the reader should not simply have learned something new: the point is, rather, to make him or her aware of another—disturbing—side of something he or she knew all the time.

Slavoj Žižek

A Voice and Nothing More

INTRODUCTION

CHE BELLA VOCE!

A man plucked a nightingale and, finding but little to eat, said: "You are just a voice and nothing more."

Plutarch, *Moralia: Sayings of Spartans* [Apophthegmata Laconica] 233a

There is a story which goes like this: In the middle of a battle there is a company of Italian soldiers in the trenches, and an Italian commander who issues the command "Soldiers, attack!" He cries out in a loud and clear voice to make himself heard in the midst of the tumult, but nothing happens, nobody moves. So the commander gets angry and shouts louder: "Soldiers, attack!" Still nobody moves. And since in jokes things have to happen three times for something to stir, he yells even louder: "Soldiers, attack!" At which point there is a response, a tiny voice rising from the trenches, saying appreciatively "*Che bella voce!*" "What a beautiful voice!"

This story can serve as a provisional entry into the problem of the voice. On the first level, it is a story of a failed interpellation. The soldiers fail to recognize themselves in the appeal, the call of the other, the call of duty, and they do not act accordingly. Surely the fact that they are Italian soldiers plays some role in it; they act according to their image of not being the most courageous soldiers in the world, as the legend has it, and the story is certainly not a model of political correctness—it indulges in tacit chauvinism and national stereotypes. So the command fails, the addressees do not recognize themselves in the meaning being conveyed, they concentrate instead on the medium, which is the voice. The attention paid to the voice hinders the interpellation and the assumption of a symbolic mandate, the transmission of a mission.

But on a second level, another interpellation works in the place of the failed one: if the soldiers do not recognize themselves in their mission as soldiers in the middle of a battle, they do recognize themselves as addressees of another message; they constitute a community as a response to a call, the community of people who can appreciate the aesthetics of a beautiful voice—who can appreciate it when it is hardly the moment, and especially when it is hardly the moment, to do so. So if in one respect they act as stereotypical Italian soldiers, they also act as stereotypical Italians in this other respect, namely as Italian opera lovers. They constitute themselves as the community of "the friends of the Italian opera" (to take the immortal line from *Some Like It Hot*), living up to their reputation as connoisseurs, people of refined taste who have amply trained their ears with *bel canto*, so they can tell a beautiful voice when they hear one, even amid the cannon fire.

From our biased perspective the soldiers did the right thing, at least in an incipient way, when they concentrated on the voice instead of the message—and this is the path I propose to follow. Although, to be sure, they did it for the wrong reasons: they were seized by a sudden aesthetic interest precisely when they should have attacked, they concentrated on the voice because they grasped the meaning all too well. If, in a prolongation of the stereotype, we imagine the Italian commander saying: "Soldiers, the town is full of beautiful girls, you can have the afternoon off," then we can perhaps doubt that they would prefer the medium of the voice to the call for action. Their selective aesthetic interest was based on a "I don't hear well,"[1] but with a twist: usually one hears the meaning and overhears the voice, one "doesn't hear [the voice] well" because it is covered by meaning. Yet, quite apart from their feigned artistic inclination, the soldiers also bungled the voice the moment they isolated it; they immediately turned it into an object of aesthetic pleasure, an object of veneration and worship, the bearer of a meaning beyond any ordinary meanings. The aesthetic concentration on the voice loses the voice precisely by turning it into a fetish object; the aesthetic pleasure obfuscates the object voice, which I will try to pursue.

I will try to argue that apart from those two widespread uses of the voice—the voice as the vehicle of meaning; the voice as the source of aesthetic admiration—there is a third level: an object voice which does not go up in smoke in the conveyance of meaning, and does not solidify in an object of fetish reverence, but an object which functions as a blind spot in the call and as a disturbance of aesthetic appreciation. One shows fidelity to the first by running to attack; one shows fidelity to the second by running to the opera. As for fidelity to the third, one has to turn to psychoanalysis. Army, opera, psychoanalysis?

Let me take as the second—and more precise—entry into our problem one of the most notorious and widely discussed passages, the first of Walter Benjamin's "Theses on the Philosophy of History," the last text he completed shortly before his death in 1940.

> The story is told of an automaton constructed in such a way that it could play a winning game of chess, answering each move of an opponent with a winning countermove. A puppet in Turkish attire and with a hookah in its mouth sat before a chessboard placed on a large table. A system of mirrors created the illusion that this table was transparent from all sides. Actually, a little hunchback who was an expert chess player sat inside and guided the puppet's hand by means of strings. One can imagine a philosophical counterpart to this device. The puppet called "historical materialism" is to win all the time. It can easily be a match for anyone if it enlists the service of theology, which today, as we know, is wizened [klein und hässlich] and has to keep out of sight. (Benjamin 1987, p. 253)

I am almost embarrassed to revisit this legendary and heavily interpreted text,[2] but let me try to use it as a prolegomenon to a theory of the voice. Admittedly, the connection is by no means evident.

Benjamin used the story as if it were widely known, and indeed it has been popular at least since the time of Edgar Allan Poe's curious piece "Maelzel's Chess-Player," written in 1836.[3] Poe's story is actually a piece of research journalism combined with Dupin-like detective "ratiocination"—when Johann Nepomuk Mälzel made his American tour with the alleged chess automaton in the 1830s, Poe took the trouble of attending many presentations, meticulously noting all the peculiarities, and the purpose of his piece was to show, by empirical observation and deductive reasoning, that this could not possibly be a thinking machine, as it pretended to be, but was clearly a hoax. There must be a ghost in this machine, a ghost in the shape of a human dwarf chess player.[4]

What exactly did Benjamin mean by that strange parable or metaphor (if it is one)? Leaving aside historical materialism and theology, the following mystery remains: how can a puppet enlist the services of the one who is operating it, who is literally pulling its strings? The puppet appears to be controlled by the hunchback, but in the second stage it is endowed with its own intentionality; it is supposed itself to pull the strings of its master, enlist his services for its own purpose.

The metaphor itself, like the automaton, seems to be redoubled, but maybe the secret of its double nature is to be sought in a very literal doubling.

The chess automaton was constructed in 1769 by one Wolfgang von Kempelen, an Austrian court official,[5] for the benefit of the Empress Maria Theresa (of course). It consisted of a Turkish puppet, a hookah in one hand and making the moves with the other, and of a box containing a complicated system of mirrors, entrapments, and contraptions which permitted the alleged hunchback to move around and remain invisible while the inside of the machine was displayed to the audience before the game started. The automaton achieved great notoriety; it beat many famous opponents (among whom was Napoleon, in a famous game which was recorded, although the record is doubtful—Napoleon had the reputation of being a very strong chess player, but this game did not do him credit: solo escapades with the queen, neglect of the defense—no wonder he was heading for Waterloo). After Kempelen's death in 1804 the automaton was taken over by Mälzel, who eventually took it for the long American tour. Mälzel's claim to historical fame otherwise rested on his construction of the first metronome, in 1816—the first person to use the metronome tempo indication was Beethoven in his Eighth Symphony (1817), a connection which was no coincidence, since Mälzel also constructed Beethoven's hearing aid—so there is an immediate voice relation.

But for Kempelen, the constructor made famous by his invention, the chess automaton was not at the center of his interest. He had another big obsession, a far more ambitious one: to construct a speaking machine, a machine which could imitate human speech. That was a problem which aroused some lively curiosity in the eighteenth century: in 1748 La Mettrie suggested that Vaucanson, the great constructor of automata, should try to build un parleur (1981, p. 143); and Leonhard Euler, the greatest mathematician of the century, drew attention to a serious problem in physics: how to construct a machine which could imitate the acoustic productions of the human mouth?[6] The mouth, the tongue, the vocal cords, the teeth—how is it that this simple panoply can produce a wide variety of specific sounds of such complexity and distinctiveness that no acoustic machine can emulate them? Euler himself entertained the fantasy of constructing a piano or an organ where each key would represent one of the sounds of speech, so that one could speak by pressing the succession of keys, like playing the piano.

The Royal Academy of Sciences in St. Petersburg issued a prize assignment in 1780: to construct a machine which could reproduce the vowels, and to explain their physical properties. Many people tried their hand at this strenuous task,[7] among them Kempelen, who constructed die Sprech-Maschine (still to be seen today in the Deutsches Museum in Munich, and still in working order). The machine was composed of a wooden box which was connected on one side to bellows (rather like bagpipes) which served as "lungs," and on the other to a rubber funnel which served as "mouth," and had to be modified by hand while "speaking." In the box there was a series of valves and ventricles which had to be operated by the other hand, and with some exercise one could produce astounding effects. As one witness put it in 1784:

> You cannot believe, my dear friend, how we were all seized by a magic feeling when we first heard the human voice and human speech which apparently didn't come from a human mouth. We looked at each other in silence and consternation and we all had goose-flesh produced by horror in the first moments. (Quoted by Felderer 2002, p. 269)

In 1791,[8] Kempelen meticulously described his invention in a book, Mechanismus der menschlichen Sprache nebst Beschreibung einer sprechenden Maschine ("The mechanism of the human speech with the description of a speaking machine"). The book laid down the theoretical principles, and the guidelines for practical realization. Yet, no matter how much the thing was described for everybody to study, the machine nevertheless kept producing effects which can only be described with the Freudian word "uncanny." There is an uncanniness in the gap which enables a machine, by purely mechanical means, to produce something so uniquely human as voice and speech. It is as if the effect could emancipate itself from its mechanical origin, and start functioning as a surplus—indeed, as the ghost in the machine; as if there were an effect without a proper cause, an effect surpassing its explicable cause—and this is one of the strange properties of the voice to which I will keep returning.

The imitative powers of the machine were somewhat limited. It could not "speak" German; apparently French, Italian, and Latin were much easier. We have some examples of its vocabulary: *"Vous êtes mon ami—je vous aime de tout mon Cœur—Leopoldus Secundus—Romanorum Imperator—Semper Augustus—papa, maman, ma femme, mon mari, le roi, allons à Paris,"*[9] and so on. If we were presented with this as a list of free associations, what would we make of the machine's unconscious? There are, to be sure, two basic functions of this speech: the declaration of love and the praise for the ruler, both all the more compelling since the anonymous speaking device mechanically produces affection implied in the form of address. The minimal vocabulary has the purpose of displaying the posture of devotion; the machine's voice is used to declare its submission, be it to the abstract beloved or to the actual ruler. It is as if the voice could subjectify the machine, as if there were an effect of exposure—something becomes exposed, an unfathomable interiority of the machine irreducible to its mechanical functioning, and the first use of subjectivity would be to throw itself at the mercy of the Other, something one can best do with the voice, or can do only in one's own voice. This immediately turns the voice into a pivotal point—voice as a pledge, a declaration, a gift, an appeal, but here brought about mechanically, impersonally, thus causing perplexity and bringing to light the curious link between subjectivity and voice.

Here we come to the point of this story. Kempelen toured the major European cities in the 1780s, and he often presented a double attraction, a double bill: on the one hand the speaking machine, on the other the chess automaton. The sequence of the two is crucial. The speaking machine was used as the introduction to the other wonder, and presented its counterpart, its foretaste, as it were, as if there were a double device, a double creature composed of the speaking and the thinking machine as the two Platonic halves of the same being. The difference between the two was ostentatious and didactic: first of all, the chess automaton was constructed in such a way as to appear as human-like as possible—it made the pretense of being engrossed in deep thought, it rolled its eyes, and so on—while the speaking machine was as mechanical as possible: it did not try to hide its mechanical nature; on the contrary, it exhibited it conspicuously. Its main attraction was the enigma of how something so utterly non-human could produce human effects. The anthropomorphic thinking machine was counterbalanced by the non-anthropomorphic speaking machine.

Second, Kempelen ultimately admitted that the chess automaton was based on a trick, but a trick he did not wish to disclose (and he carried its secret to his grave). The speaking machine, on the other hand, was no hoax, it was a mechanism that everybody was free to inspect and whose principles were carefully explained in a book, so that anybody could make one. The Turkish chess player was unique and shrouded in mystery, while the speaking machine was intended for replication on the basis of universal scientific principles. It so happened that in 1838, one Charles Wheatstone constructed a version of it, following Kempelen's instructions, and this machine made such a deep impression on the young Alexander Graham Bell that his pursuit of it eventually led him to nothing less than the invention of the telephone.[10]

Third, there was a teleology in the link between the two machines. Teleology in the weak sense that the speaking machine was presented as the introduction to the thinking machine, thus the former made the latter plausible, acceptable, endowed with an air of credibility; for if the first was demonstrated as actual, then the second was presented as a possibility, although admittedly based on a trick. But there was also teleology in a stronger sense: the second machine appeared as the fulfillment of the promise given by the first. A perspective was opened in which the thinking machine was but an extension of the speaking machine, so that the speaking machine, presented first, would reach its telos in the thinking machine, or, even more, that there was a quasi-Hegelian transition between the two machines from "in itself" to "for itself"—what the speaking machine was "in itself" had to be made "for itself" in the thinking machine. The point of this sequence could be read in such a way that speech and voice present the hidden mechanism of thought, something that has to precede thought as purely mechanical and something which thinking has to conceal under the disguise of anthropomorphism. Thinking is like the anthropomorphic puppet concealing the real puppet, which is the speaking puppet; so that the secret to be disguised by the Turkish puppet, hookah and all, was not the supposed human dwarf in its bosom, its homunculus mastermind, but, rather, the speaking machine, the voice machine which preceded the automaton and was displayed for all to see. That was the true homunculus pulling the strings of the thinking machine. The first machine was the secret of the second, and the second, the anthropomorphic puppet, had to enlist the services of the first if it was to win.

There is a paradox: the dwarf within the puppet himself turns out to be another puppet, the mechanical puppet within the anthropomorphic one, and the secret of the thinking machine is itself thoughtless, just a mechanism emitting voice, but thereby producing the most human of effects, an effect of "interiority." It is not simply that the machine is the true secret of thought, for there is already a certain split in the first machine: it endeavors to produce speech, some meaningful words and minimal sentences, but at the same time it actually produces the voice in excess of speech and meaning, the voice as an excess, and that was the point of fascination: the meaning was hard to decipher, given the poor quality of reproduction,[11] but the voice was what immediately seized everyone and inspired universal awe, precisely with the impression it made of quintessential humanity. Yet this voice-effect was produced not by a seamless mechanical causality but by a mysterious jump in causality, a breach, a limping causality, an excess of the voice-effect over its cause, where the voice came to occupy the space of a breach, a missing link, a gap in the causal nexus. Lacan, with his incomparable knack for slogans, says: "There is a cause only in something that doesn't work / Il n'y a de cause que de ce qui cloche." (Lacan 1979, p. 22) The cause appears only at the point of a hitch in causality, a limp, a troubled causality—and this is precisely where

Lacan situated the object, the object-cause. But this can perhaps also be seen as the lever of thought, as opposed to the anthropomorphic masquerade of thinking. There is a good line by Giorgio Agamben: "The search for the voice in language, this is what is called thought" (quoted by Nancy 2002, p. 45)—the search for what exceeds language and meaning.

For our present purpose, we could bend or transform Benjamin's thesis: *if the puppet called historical materialism is to win, it should enlist the services of the voice.* Hence the need for a theory of the voice, the object voice, the voice as one of the paramount "embodiments" of what Lacan called *objet petit a.*

CHAPTER 1

THE LINGUISTICS OF THE VOICE

The voice appears to be the most familiar thing. When I say "voice," when I use this word without further qualification, then the most immediate thing that comes to mind is no doubt the most usual one: the omnipresent use of the voice in our everyday communication. We use our voices, and we listen to voices, at every moment; all our social life is mediated by the voice, and situations where reading and writing actually take over as the medium of our sociability are, all things considered, much less common and limited (the Internet notwithstanding), even though, in a different and less tangible sense, our social being depends very much on the letter, the letter of the law—we will come back to that. We constantly inhabit the universe of voices, we are continuously bombarded by voices, we have to make our daily way through a jungle of voices, and we have to use all kinds of machetes and compasses so as not to get lost. There are the voices of other people, the voices of music, the voices of media,[1] our own voice intermingled with the lot. All those voices are shouting, whispering, crying, caressing, threatening, imploring, seducing, commanding, pleading, praying, hypnotizing, confessing, terrorizing, declaring . . .—we can immediately see a difficulty into which any treatment of the voice runs: namely, that the vocabulary is inadequate. The vocabulary may well distinguish nuances of meaning, but words fail us when we are faced with the infinite shades of the voice, which infinitely exceed meaning. It is not that our vocabulary is scanty and its deficiency should be remedied: faced with the voice, words structurally fail.

All those voices rise over the multitude of sounds and noises, another even wilder and wider jungle: sounds of nature, sounds of machines and technology. Civilization announces its progress by a lot of noise, and the more it progresses the noisier it gets. The dividing line between the two—voice and noise as well as nature and culture—is often elusive and uncertain. We have already seen in the Introduction that the voice can be produced by machines, so that there opens a zone of undecidability, of a between-the-two, an intermediacy, which will be, as we shall see, one of the paramount features of the voice.

Another dividing line separates voice from silence. The absence of voices and sounds is hard to endure; complete silence is immediately uncanny, it is like death, while the voice is the first sign of life. And that division as well, the one between the voice and silence, is perhaps more elusive than it seems—not all voices are heard, and perhaps the most intrusive and compelling are the unheard voices, and the most deafening thing can be silence. In isolation, in solitude, in complete loneliness, away from the madding crowd, we are not simply free of the voice—it can be that this is when another kind of voice appears, more intrusive and compelling than the usual mumbo-jumbo: the internal voice, a voice which cannot be silenced. As if the voice were the very epitome of a society that we carry with us and cannot get away from. We are social beings by the voice and through the voice; it seems that the voice stands at the axis of our social bonds, and that voices are the very texture of the social, as well as the intimate kernel of subjectivity.

THE VOICE AND THE SIGNIFIER

Let us start by considering the voice as it appears in this most common use and in its most quotidian presence: the voice which functions as the bearer of an utterance, the support of a word, a sentence, a discourse, any kind of linguistic expression. So let us first approach our object through the linguistics of the voice—if such a thing exists.

The moment we start looking at it more closely, we can see that even this most commonplace and ordinary use is full of pitfalls and paradoxes. What singles out the voice against the vast ocean of sounds and noises, what defines the voice as special among the infinite array of acoustic phenomena, is its inner relationship with meaning. The voice is something which points toward meaning, it is as if there is an arrow in it which raises the expectation of meaning, the voice is an opening toward meaning. No doubt we can ascribe meaning to all kinds of sounds, yet they seem to be deprived of it "in themselves," independent of our ascription, while the voice has an intimate connection with meaning, it is a sound which appears to be endowed in itself with the will to "say something," with an inner intentionality. We can make various other sounds with the intention of signifying something, but there the intention is external to those sounds themselves, or they function as a stand-in, a metaphoric substitute for the voice. Only the voice implies a subjectivity which "expresses itself and itself inhabits the means of expression.[2] But if the voice is thus the quasi-natural bearer of the production of meaning, it also proves to be strangely recalcitrant to it. If we speak in order to "make sense," to signify, to convey something, then the voice is the material support of bringing about meaning, yet it does not contribute to it itself. It is, rather, something like the vanishing mediator (to use the term made famous by Fredric Jameson for a different purpose)—it makes the utterance possible, but it disappears in it, it goes up in smoke in the meaning being produced. Even on the most banal level of daily experience, when we listen to someone speak, we may at first be very much aware of his or her voice and its particular qualities, its color and accent, but soon we accommodate to it and concentrate only on the meaning that is conveyed. The voice itself is like the Wittgensteinian ladder to be discarded when we have successfully climbed to the top— that is, when we have made our ascent to the peak of meaning. The voice is the instrument, the vehicle, the medium, and the meaning is the goal. This gives rise to a spontaneous opposition where voice appears as materiality opposed to the ideality of meaning. The ideality of meaning can emerge only through the materiality of the means, but the means does not seem to contribute to meaning.

Hence we can put forward a provisional definition of the voice (in its linguistic aspect): it is *what does not contribute to making sense.*[3] It is the material element recalcitrant to meaning, and if we speak in order to say something, then the voice is precisely that which cannot be said. It is there, in the very act of saying, but it eludes any pinning down, to the point where we could maintain that it is the non-linguistic, the extralinguistic element which enables speech phenomena, but cannot itself be discerned by linguistics.

If there is an implicit teleology of the voice, then this teleology seems to conceal the dwarf of theology in its bosom, as in Benjamin's parable. There is a rather astounding theological interpretation of this in Saint Augustine. In one of his famous sermons (no. 288), he makes the following claim: John the Baptist is the voice and Christ is the word, *logos*. Indeed, this seems to follow textually from the beginning of St. John's Gospel: in the beginning was the Word, but in order for the Word to manifest itself, there has to be a mediator, a precursor in the shape of John the Baptist, who identifies himself precisely as *vox clamantis in deserto*,[4] the voice crying in the desert, while Christ, in this paradigmatic opposition, is identified with the Word, *verbum*, *logos*.

> The voice precedes the Word and it makes possible its understanding. . . . What is the voice, what is the word? Examine what happens in you and form your own questions and answers. This voice which merely resonates and offers no sense, this sound which comes from the mouth of someone screaming, not speaking, we call it the voice, not the word. . . . But the word, if it is to earn its name, has to be endowed with sense and by offering the sound to the ear it offers at the same time something else to the intellect. . . . Now look closely at the meaning of this sentence: "He has to increase, I have to diminish". [John 3, 30]. How, for what reason, with what intent, why could the voice, i.e. John the Baptist, say, given the difference that we just established, "He has to increase, I have to diminish"? Why? Because the voices are being effaced as the Word grows. The voice gradually loses its function as the soul progresses to Christ. So Christ has to increase and John the Baptist has to be obliterated. (Augustine, quoted by Poizat 2001, p. 130)[5]

Thus the progression from the voice to meaning is the progression from a mere—albeit necessary—mediator to the true Word: there is only a small step from linguistics to theology. So if we are to isolate the voice as an object, an entity on its own, then we have to disentangle it from this spontaneous teleology, which goes hand in hand with a certain theology of the voice as the condition of revelation of the Word.[6] We have to make our way in the opposite direction, as it were: to make a descent from the height of meaning back to what appeared to be mere means; to catch the voice as a blind spot of making sense, or as a cast-off of sense. We have to establish another framework than that which spontaneously imposes itself with the link between a certain understanding of linguistics, teleology, and theology.

If voice is what does not contribute to meaning, a crucial antinomy follows, *a dichotomy of the voice and the signifier*. The signifier possesses a logic, it can be dissected, it can be pinned down and fixed—fixed in view of its repetition, for every signifier is a signifier by virtue of being repeatable, in view of its own iterability. The signifier is a creature that can exist only insofar as it can be cloned, but its genome cannot be fixed by any positive units, it can be fixed only by a web of differences, through differential oppositions, which enable it to produce meaning. It is a strange entity that possesses no identity of its own, for it is merely a bundle, a crossing of differences in relation to other signifiers, and *nothing else*. Its material support and its particular qualities are irrelevant—all that is needed is that it is different from other signifiers (following the famous Saussurean dictum that in language there are only differences without any positive terms, and another no less famous one that language is form and not substance).[7] The signifier is not endowed with any positivity, any quality definable on its own; its only existence is a negative one (that of being "different from other signifiers"), yet its mechanisms can be disentangled and explained in that very negativity, which produces positive effects of signification.

If we take Saussure as a provisional starting point—although this doxa of our times that "in the beginning was Saussure" (a very particular kind of Word) is rather dubious—then it is easy to see that the Saussurean turn has a lot to do with the voice. If we are to take seriously the negative nature of the linguistic sign, its purely differential and oppositive value, then the voice—as the supposedly natural soil of speech, its seemingly positive substance—has to be put into question. It has to be carefully discarded as the source of an imaginary blinding that has hitherto prevented linguistics from discovering the structural determinations which enable the tricky transubstantiation of voices into linguistic signs. The voice is the impeding element that we have to be rid of in order to initiate a new science of language. Beyond the sounds of language that traditional phonetics has painstakingly described—spending a great deal of time over the technology of their production, helplessly ensnared by their physical and physiological properties—lies a very different entity that the new linguistics has to unearth: *the phoneme*. Beyond the voice "with flesh and bones" (as Jakobson will say some decades later) lies the fleshless and boneless entity defined purely by its function—*the silent sound, the soundless voice*.

The new object demands a new science: instead of traditional phonetics, high hopes are now vested in phonology. The question of how different sounds are produced is seen as obsolete; what counts are the differential oppositions of phonemes, their purely relational nature, their reduction to distinctive features. They are isolated by their ability to distinguish the units of signification, but in such a way that the specific signifying distinctions are irrelevant, their only importance being that they take place, not what they might be. Phonemes lack substance, they are completely reducible to form, and they lack any signification of their own. They are just senseless quasi-algebraic elements in a formal matrix of combinations.

It is true that Saussure's *Course* has caused some confusion, since it is not in the part explicitly dealing with phonology that his novelty is to be found. We have to look elsewhere:

> In any case, it is impossible that sound, as the material element, should in itself be part of the language. Sound is merely something ancillary, a material that language uses. . . . Linguistic signals [signifiers] are not in essence phonetic. They are not physical in any way. They are constituted solely by differences which distinguish one such sound pattern from another. . . . What characterizes [the phonemes] is not, as might be thought, the specific positive properties of each; but simply the fact that they cannot be mistaken for one another. Speech sounds are first and foremost entities which are contrastive, relative and negative. (Saussure 1998, pp. 116–117)

If we take Saussure's definition in all its stringency, it turns out that it ultimately fully applies only to phonemes (such will be Jakobson's later criticism of Saussure): they are the only stratum of language which is made entirely of purely negative quantities; their identity is "a pure alterity" (Jakobson 1963, pp. 111, 116). They are the senseless atoms that, in combination, "make sense."

Phonology, defined in such a way, was destined to take a preeminent place in structural linguistics, soon turning into its showcase, the paramount demonstration of its abilities and explanatory strength. Some decades had to elapse for it to reach its fully developed form in Troubetzkoy's *Grundzüge der Phonologie* (1939) and in Jakobson's *Fundamentals of Language* (1956). Some criticism had to be made of the Saussurean presuppositions (for example, Jakobson's critique of Saussure's dogma about the linear nature of the signifier), some respect had to be duly paid to its other predecessors (Baudouin de Courtenay, Henry Sweet, and others), but its course was secure. All the sounds of a language could be described in a purely logical way; they could be placed into a logical table based simply on the presence or absence of minimal distinctive features, ruled entirely by one elementary key, the binary code. In this way, most of the oppositions of traditional phonetics could eventually be reproduced (voiced/voiceless, nasal/oral, compact/diffuse, grave/acute, labial/dental, and so on), but all those were now re-created as functions of logical oppositions, the conceptual deduction of the empirical, not as an empirical description of sounds found. As the ultimate exhibit, one could present the phonological triangle (Jakobson 1963, p. 138) as the simple deductive matrix of all phonemes and their "elementary structures of kinship," a device that would achieve some notoriety in the heyday of structuralism. Having dismantled the sounds into mere bundles of differential oppositions, phonology could then also account for the surplus that is necessarily added to purely phonemic distinctive features—the prosody, the intonation and the accent, the melody, the redundant elements, the variations, and so forth. Bones, flesh, and blood of the voice were diluted without remainder into a web of structural traits, a checklist of presences and absences.

The inaugural gesture of phonology was thus the total reduction of the voice as the substance of language. Phonology, true to its apocryphal etymology, was after killing the voice—its name is, of course, derived from the Greek *phone*, voice, but in it one can also quite appropriately hear *phonos*, murder. Phonology stabs the voice with the signifying dagger; it does away with its living presence, with its flesh and blood. This leads us to a provisional *facit*: there is no linguistics of the voice. There is only phonology, the paradigm of the linguistics of the signifier.

The phoneme is the way in which the signifier has seized and molded the voice. To be sure, its logic is pretty tricky and itself full of pitfalls and traps, it can never quite be tamed into the simple transparent matrix of differential oppositions that Saussure (and Lévi-Strauss and many others) dreamed about—that was the paramount dream of the early structuralist generation. Yet it is a logic whose mechanisms can be explored and laid down, it is a logic with which we can make sense, or, more modestly, with which we can make do in making sense (or at least nonsense). In order to speak, one has to produce the sounds of a language in such a way as to satisfy its differential matrix; the phoneme is the voice caught in the matrix, which behaves quite a bit like the Matrix from the movie. The signifier needs the voice as its support, just as the Matrix needs the poor subjects and their fantasies, but it has no materiality in itself, it just uses the voice to constitute our common "virtual reality." But the problem is that this operation always produces a remainder which cannot be made a signifier or disappear in meaning; the remainder that doesn't make sense, a leftover, a cast-off—shall we say an excrement of the signifier? The matrix silences the voice, but not quite.

How can we pursue this dimension of the voice? Let us first look at three different modes in which, in the most common experience, we stumble on the voice which is seemingly recalcitrant to the signifier: the accent, the intonation, and the timbre. We can have some inkling of the voice if we listen to someone with an accent.[8] Accent—*ad cantum*—is something which brings the voice into the vicinity of singing, and a heavy accent suddenly makes us aware of the material support of the voice which we tend immediately to discard. It appears as a distraction, or even an obstacle, to the smooth flow of signifiers and to the hermeneutics of understanding. Still, the regional accent can easily be dealt with, it can be described and codified. After all, it is a norm which differs from the ruling norm—this is what makes it an accent, and this is what makes it obtrusive, what makes it sing—and it can be described in the same way as the ruling norm. The ruling norm is but an accent which has been declared a non-accent in a gesture which always carries heavy social and political connotations. The official language is deeply wrought by the class division; there is a constant "linguistic class struggle" which underlies its constitution, and we need only remember Shaw's *Pygmalion* for an egregious demonstration.

Intonation is another way in which we can be aware of the voice, for the particular tone of the voice, its particular melody and modulation, its cadence and inflection, can decide the meaning. Intonation can turn the meaning of a sentence upside down; it can transform it into its opposite. A slight note of irony, and a serious meaning comes tumbling down; a note of distress, and the joke will backfire. Linguistic competence crucially includes not only phonology, but also the ability to cope with intonation and its multiple uses. Still, intonation is not as elusive as it may seem; it can be linguistically described and empirically verified. Jakobson tells the following story:

> A former actor of Stanislavskij's Moscow Theatre told me how at his audition he was asked by the famous director to make forty different messages from the phrase *Segodnja večerom*, "This evening," by diversifying its expressive tint. He made a list of some forty emotional situations, then emitted the given phrase in accordance with each of these situations, which his audience had to recognize only from the changes in the sound shape of the same two words. For our research work in the description and analysis of contemporary Standard Russian (under the auspices of the Rockefeller Foundation) this actor was asked to repeat Stanislavskij's test. He wrote down some fifty situations framing the same elliptic sentence and made of it fifty corresponding messages for a tape recorder. Most of the messages were correctly and circumstantially decoded by Moscovite listeners. May I add that all such emotive cues easily undergo linguistic analysis. (Jakobson 1960, pp. 354–355)

So all the shades of intonation which critically contribute to meaning, far from being an ineffable abyss, present no great problem to linguistic analysis; intonation can be submitted to the same treatment as all other linguistic phenomena. It requires some additional notation, but this is just the mark of a more complex and ramified code, an extension of phonological analysis. It can be empirically tested—with the help of Rockefeller (I love this detail)—that is to say, objectively and impartially.[9] It is no coincidence that the "subject" of this experiment was an actor, since theater is the ultimate practical laboratory of endowing the same text with the shades of intonation and thereby bringing it to life, empirically testing this every evening with the audience.

Another way to be aware of the voice is through its individuality. We can almost unfailingly identify a person by the voice, the particular individual timbre, resonance, pitch, cadence, melody, the peculiar way of pronouncing certain sounds. The voice is like a fingerprint, instantly recognizable and identifiable. This fingerprint quality of the voice is something that does not contribute to meaning, nor can it be linguistically described, for its features are as a rule not linguistically relevant, they are the slight fluctuations and variations which do not violate the norm—rather, the norm itself cannot be implemented without some "personal touch," the slight trespassing which is the mark of individuality. The impersonal voice, the mechanically produced voice (answering machines, computer voices, and so on) always has a touch of the uncanny, like the voice of the mechanical creature Olympia in Hoffmann's "The Sandman," this prototype of the uncanny, whose singing was just a bit too exact.[10] Or remember the immortal Hal 2000 meeting its death in Kubrick's 2001: *A Space Odyssey*, that archetypal scene of a machine pleading for its life and regressing to childhood in a completely mechanical way. The mechanical voice reproduces the pure norm without any side effects; therefore it seems that it actually subverts the norm by giving it raw. The voice without side-effects ceases to be a "normal" voice, it is deprived of the human touch that the voice adds to the arid machinery of the signifier, threatening that humanity itself will merge with the mechanical iterability, and thus lose its footing. But if those side-effects cannot be linguistically described, they are nevertheless susceptible to physical description: we can measure their frequency and amplitude, we can take their sonogram, while on the practical level they can easily enter the realm of recognition and identification, and become the matter of (dis)liking. Paradoxically, it is the mechanical voice which confronts us with the object voice, its disturbing and uncanny nature, whereas the human touch helps us keep it at bay. The obstacle it appears to present actually enhances the sense-making effect; the seeming distraction contributes to the better fulfillment of the goal.

But if the voice does not coincide with any material modality of its presence in speech, then we could perhaps come closer to our goal if we conceived of it as coinciding with the very process of enunciation: it epitomizes something that cannot be found anywhere in the statement, in the spoken speech and its string of signifiers, nor can it be identified with their material support. In this sense the voice as the agent of enunciation sustains the signifiers and constitutes the string, as it were, that holds them together, although it is invisible because of the beads concealing it. If signifiers form a chain, then the voice may well be what fastens them into a signifying chain. And if the process of enunciation points at the locus of subjectivity in language, then voice also sustains an intimate link with the very notion of the subject. But what is the texture of this voice, this immaterial string, and what is the nature of the subject implied in it? We will come back to that.

THE LINGUISTICS OF THE NON-VOICE

After accent, intonation, and timbre, qualities that pertain to the voice in speech, we can briefly consider, on our way to the object voice, manifestations of the voice outside speech. In a somewhat academic manner, we could classify them into "prelinguistic" and "postlinguistic" phenomena, the voices beneath and beyond the signifier (following, for example, Parret 2002, p. 28). Presignifying voices comprise the physiological manifestations such as coughing and hiccups, which appear to tie the human voice to an animal nature. Thus we can read in Aristotle:

> Voice then is the impact of the inbreathed air against the "windpipe," and the agent that produces the impact is the soul resident in these parts of the body. Not every sound, as we said, made by an animal is voice (even with the tongue we may merely make a sound which is not voice, or without the tongue as in coughing); what produces the impact must have soul in it and must be accompanied by an act of imagination, for voice is a sound *with a meaning*, and is not *merely* the result of any impact of the breath as in coughing; in voice the breath in the windpipe is used as an instrument to knock with against the walls of the windpipe. (Aristotle 2001, *De anima*, 420b 28–37)

If voice is a sound "of what has soul in it" (420b 6), then coughing is a soulless voice which ceases to be voice proper. Both coughing and hiccups emerge without the intention of the utterer and against his or her will, they represent a break in speech, a disruption of the ascent toward meaning, an intrusion of physiology into structure. But an intriguing reversal takes place here: those voices, somatic and unattractive as they may be, are hardly ever simply external to the structure—quite the opposite, they may well enter into its core or become its double. We can easily see that there is a whole "semiotics of coughing": one coughs while preparing to speak, one uses coughing as Jakobson's phatic communication, establishing a channel for communication proper; one can use coughing as bidding for time for reflection, or as an ironic commentary which jeopardizes the sense of the utterance; as a notification of one's presence; as an interruption of a difficult silence; as part of the pragmatics of telephone communication (see Parret 2002, p. 32). There may be no linguistic features, no binary oppositions, no distinctive traits, except for the overriding one: the non-articulate itself becomes a mode of the articulate; the presymbolic acquires its value only through opposition to the symbolic, and is thus itself laden with signification precisely by virtue of being non-signifying. Physiological and inarticulate as it may be, it cannot escape the structure. It can, by its very inarticulate nature, even become the embodiment of the highest sense.

One example will suffice as the most spectacular proof: the most famous hiccups in the history of philosophy, namely those by which Aristophanes is suddenly seized in Plato's *Symposium* at the very moment when it was his turn to deliver a speech in praise of love:

> When Pausanias finally came to a pause (I've learned this sort of fine figure from our clever rhetoreticians),[11] it was Aristophanes' turn, according to Aristodemus. But he had such a bad case of the hiccups—he'd probably stuffed himself again, although, of course, it could have been anything—that making a speech was totally out of the question. So he turned to the doctor, Eryximachus, who was next in line, and said to him: "Eryximachus, it's up to you—as well it should be. Cure me or take my turn." "As a matter of fact," Eryximachus replied, "I

shall do both. I shall take your turn—you can speak in my place as soon as you feel better—and I shall also cure you. While I am giving my speech, you should hold your breath for as long as you possibly can. This may well eliminate your hiccups. If it fails, the best remedy is a thorough gargle. And if even this has no effect, then tickle your nose with a feather. A sneeze or two will cure even the most persistent case. (Plato 1997, 185c–e)

The hiccups were so persistent that Aristophanes had to employ all Eryximachus' advices, and the talented Doctor Eryximachus came into history as what his name indicates: the fighter against hiccups.

What do Aristophanes' hiccups mean? This unintentional intrusion of an uncontrolled voice, which changed the order of speakers in the highly structured dramaturgy of the dialogue? Can hiccups be a philosophical statement? What does it mean that Aristophanes' speech, the most famous of all Plato's texts, the Freudian parable of the missing halves, is shifted because of the hiccups? Interpreters have been scratching their heads for more than two thousand years; some thought it was just Plato's realistic depiction of the gastronomic-philosophical feast (an instance of Pantagruelism, as Taylor put it); some thought it was a comical intermezzo introducing the comical poet by his trademark; but mostly they surmised that it cannot be so innocent, and must possess some hidden meaning. Lacan undertook a detailed reading of *Symposium* in the course of his seminar on transference (1960/61), and at some critical point he decided to consult his philosophical mentor, Alexandre Kojève. At the end of their exchange, as he was leaving, Kojève gave him this advice for further reflection: "'You will certainly not be able to interpret *Symposium* if you don't know why Aristophanes has hiccups'" (Lacan 1991, p. 78). Kojève himself did not divulge the secret; he left Lacan rather perplexed, but he spoke in such a way that ultimately the entire interpretation depends on understanding this unintelligible voice, for which one can only propose the formula: *it means that it means.* This involuntary voice rising from the body's entrails can be read as Plato's version of mana: the condensation of a senseless sound and the elusive highest meaning, something which can ultimately decide the sense of the whole. This precultural, non-cultural voice can be seen as the zero-point of signification, the incidence of meaning, itself not meaning anything, the point around which other—meaningful—voices can be ordered, as if the hiccups stood at the very focus of the structure. The voice presents a short circuit between nature and culture, between physiology and structure; its vulgar nature is mysteriously transubstantiated into meaning *tout court*.[12]

By definition, the presymbolic use of the voice is epitomized by the infant's babbling. This term, in its technical meaning, covers all the modalities of children's experimenting with their voice before they learn to use it in the standard and codified way. This is the voice which pertains to the infant by its very name—*in-fans*, the one who can't speak. Many linguists and child psychologists (most famously Piaget) have scrutinized this at some length, since what is at stake is the linguistically most crucial step linking the voice and the signifier, and the developmentally most delicate transition between the infant and the speaking being. They have seen in it "the unintentional egocentric soliloquy of the child," "a biologically conditioned 'linguistic delirium,'" and so on (see Jakobson 1968, pp. 24 ff. for a good overview), a chaotic voice-production which gradually becomes guided by a will to communicate and a disciplinatory assumption of the code. But if we think that here we will catch the voice prior to speech in its solipsistic and quasi-biological form, then we are prey to an illusion. Lacan stops to consider it for a moment in *Seminar XI*:

> The Piagetic error—for those who might think that this is a neologism, I would stress that I am referring to Mr. Piaget—is an error that lies in the notion of what is called the *egocentric* discourse of the child, defined as the stage at which he lacks . . . reciprocity. . . . The child, in this discourse, which may be tape-recorded, does not speak for himself, as one says. No doubt, he does not address the other, if one uses here the theoretical distinction derived from the function of the I and the *you*. But there must be others there . . . —they don't speak to a particular person, they just speak, if you'll pardon the expression, *à la*

cantonade. This egocentric discourse is a case of *hail to the good listener!* (Lacan 1979, p. 208)

Infants do not babble just like that. They do not address a definite interlocutor at hand, but their solipsism is nevertheless caught into the structure of address; they address someone behind the scenes, *à la cantonade*, as French theater lingo has it; they speak *à la cantonade*—in short, *à Lacan*, to someone who can hear them, to the good listener to whom they can send a greeting (*à bon entendeur salut*). So this voice, although it does not say anything discernible, is already captured in a discourse, it displays the structure of address—Jakobson himself talks about sound gestures (1968, p. 25), meaningless sounds as gestures of address, and of "dummy dialogue," where no information is transmitted and where children most often do not imitate adults—rather the opposite: adults imitate children, they resort to babbling in what is no doubt a more successful dialogue than most. So here again, on a different level (ontogeny, if such a thing exists), we see that the voice is already caught in the structural web, that there is no voice without the other.

If we follow this logic to the end—that is, to the beginning—then we find at its source the most salient inarticulate presymbolic manifestation of the voice, which is the scream. Is the scream, notoriously the first sign of life, a form of speech? Is the infant's first scream already a greeting to the good listener? Lacan discusses this in the context of what he calls "the transformation of the scream into an appeal."[13] There might be something like the mythical primal scream, which stirred some spirits for some time,[14] but, on this account, the moment it emerges it is immediately seized by the other. The first scream may be caused by pain, by the need for food, by frustration and anxiety, but the moment the other hears it, the moment it assumes the place of its addressee, the moment the other is provoked and interpellated by it, the moment it responds to it, scream retroactively turns into appeal, it is interpreted, endowed with meaning, it is transformed into a speech addressed to the other, it assumes the first function of speech: to address the other and elicit an answer.[15] The scream becomes an appeal to the other; it needs an interpretation and an answer, it demands satisfaction. There is a French pun that Lacan is fond of: cri pur, a pure scream, is turned into a cri pour, a scream for someone. If the elusive mythical scream was at the outset caused by a need, then it retroactively turns into a demand surpassing the need: it does not aim just at the satisfaction of a need, it is a call for attention, for a reaction, it is directed toward a point in the other which is beyond satisfaction of a need, it disentangles itself from the need, and ultimately desire is nothing but the surplus of demand over need.[16] So the voice is transformed into an appeal, a speech act, in the same moment as need is transformed into desire; it is caught in a drama of appeal, eliciting an answer, provocation, demand, love. The scream, unaffected as it is by phonological constraints, is nevertheless speech in its minimal function: an address and an enunciation. It is the bearer of an enunciation to which no discernible statement can be ascribed, it represents the pure process of enunciation before the infant is capable of any statement.

But the drama of the voice is twofold here: it is not only that the other is compelled to interpret infant's wishes and demands, it is also that the voice itself, the scream, is already an attempt at interpretation: the other can respond to the appeal or not, its answer depends on its whim, and the voice is something which tries to reach the other, provoke it, seduce it, plead with it; it makes assumptions about the other's desire, it tries to influence it, sway it, elicit its love. The voice is carried by an interpretation of the unfathomable other with which it tries to cope; it tries to present itself as an object of its desire, tame its inscrutability and whim. So there is a double movement in this initial drama, interpretation of the scream and scream as interpretation of the other, and both movements would thus find their intersection in Lacan's basic tenet that desire is the desire of the other.

The presymbolic uses of the voice have a feature in common: with physiological voices, with babbling and with the scream, it appears that we are dealing with a voice external to structure, yet this apparent exteriority hits the core of the structure: it epitomizes the signifying gesture precisely by not signifying anything in particular, it presents the speech in its minimal traits, which may later get obscured by articulation. The non-structured voice miraculously starts to represent the structure as such, the signifier in general. For the signifier in general, as such, is possible only as a non-signifier.

On the "postlinguistic" side there is the realm of the voice beyond language, the voice which requires a more sophisticated cultural conditioning than the acquisition of language. This is most spectacularly illustrated by singing, but first we must briefly consider another voice manifestation which is paradoxical: laughter. Its paradox lies in the fact that it is a physiological reaction which seems close to coughing and hiccups, or even more animal-like sounds (there is a whole array, from a mild smile to uncontrollable laughter), but on the other hand laughter is a cultural trait of which only humankind is capable. Indeed, there is an ancient proposal to define the human being as "the laughing animal" (on a par with "the speaking animal"?), to see in laughter the specificity of humankind, separating it from animality. There is again the amalgamation of the highest and the lowest, culture and physiology; the inarticulate quasi-animal sounds coincide with quintessential humanity—and, after all, can culture offer anything better than laughter? This is all the more enigmatic since laughter as a specifically cultural reaction often bursts out uncontrollably, against the will and intention of the hapless subject; it seizes him or her with an unstoppable force as a series of cramps and convulsions which irrepressibly shake the body and elicit inchoate cries which cannot be consciously contained. Laughter is different from the other phenomena considered above because it seems to exceed language in both directions at the same time, as both presymbolic and beyond symbolic; it is not merely a precultural voice seized by the structure, but at the same time a highly cultural product which looks like a regression to animality. Several philosophers have stopped to ponder on this paradox, and since I cannot deal with it any further here, I can only give two classical references: Descartes, *The Passions of the Soul*, paragraphs CXXIV–CXXVI; and Kant, *The Critique of Judgment*, paragraph 54.

Singing represents a different stage: it brings the voice energetically to the forefront, on purpose, at the expense of meaning. Indeed, singing is bad communication; it prevents a clear understanding of the text (we need supertitles at the opera, which dispel the idea of an initiated elite and put the opera on the level of the cinema). The fact that singing blurs the word and makes it difficult to understand—in polyphony to the point of incomprehensibility—has served as the basis for a philosophical distrust for this flourishing of the voice at the expense of the text: for instance, for the constant efforts to regulate sacred music, all of which tried to secure an anchorage in the word, and banish fascination with the voice. Singing takes the distraction of the voice seriously, and turns the tables on the signifier; it reverses the hierarchy—let the voice take the upper hand, let the voice be the bearer of what cannot be expressed by words. *Wovon man nicht sprechen kann darüber kann man singen:* expression versus meaning, expression beyond meaning, expression which is more than meaning, yet expression which functions only in tension with meaning—it needs a signifier as the limit to transcend and to reveal its beyond. The voice appears as the surplus-meaning. The birth of the opera was accompanied by the dilemma of *prima la musica, e poi le parole*, or the other way round; the dramatic tension between the word and the voice was put into its cradle, and their impossible and problematic relationship presented its driving force. The entire history of opera, from Monteverdi to Strauss (*Capriccio*), can be written through the spyglass of this dilemma.[17]

Singing, by its massive concentration on the voice, introduces codes and standards of its own—more elusive than the linguistic ones, but nevertheless highly structured. Expression beyond language is another highly sophisticated language; its acquisition demands a long technical training, reserved for the happy few, although it has the power to affect everyone universally. Yet singing, by focusing on the voice, actually runs the risk of losing the very thing it tries to worship and revere: it turns it into a fetish object—we could say the highest rampart, the most formidable wall against the voice. The object voice that we are after cannot be dealt with by being turned into an object of immediate intense attention and of aesthetic pleasure. To put it in a formula: "If we make music and listen to it, . . . it is in order to silence what deserves to be called the voice as the object *a*" (Miller 1989, p. 184). So the fetish object is the very opposite of the voice as object *a*; but, I should hasten to add, this gesture is always ambivalent: music evokes the object voice and obfuscates it; it fetishizes it, but also opens the gap that cannot be filled. I will come back to this.

Bringing the voice from the background to the forefront entails a reversal, or a structural illusion: the voice appears to be the locus of true expression, the place where what cannot be said can nevertheless be conveyed. The voice is endowed with profundity: by not meaning anything, it appears to mean more than mere words, it becomes the bearer of some unfathomable originary meaning which, supposedly, got lost with language. It seems still to maintain the link with nature, on the one hand—the nature of a paradise lost—and on the other hand to transcend language, the cultural and symbolic barriers, in the opposite direction, as it were: it promises an ascent to divinity, an elevation above the empirical, the mediated, the limited, worldly human concerns. This illusion of transcendence accompanied the long history of the voice as the agent of the sacred, and the highly acclaimed role of music was based on its ambiguous link with both nature and divinity. When Orpheus, the emblematic and archetypal singer, sings, it is in order to tame wild beasts and bend gods; his true audience consists not of men, but of creatures beneath and above culture. Of course this promise of a state of some primordial fusion to which the voice should bear witness is always a retroactive construction. It should be stated clearly: it is only through language, via language, by the symbolic, that there is voice, and music exists only for a speaking being (see Baas 1998, p. 196). The voice as the bearer of a deeper sense, of some profound message, is a structural illusion, the core of a fantasy that the singing voice might cure the wound inflicted by culture, restore the loss that we suffered by the assumption of the symbolic order. This deceptive promise disavows the fact that the voice owes its fascination to this wound, and that its allegedly miraculous force stems from its being situated in this gap. If the psychoanalytic name for this gap is castration, then we can remember that

Freud's theory of fetishism is based precisely on the fetish materializing the disavowal of castration.[18]

If there is no linguistics of the voice, only the linguistics of the signifier, then the very notion of a linguistics of the non-voice would seem preposterous. Obviously all the non-voices, from coughing and hiccups to babbling, screaming, laughing, and singing, are not linguistic voices; they are not phonemes, yet they are not simply outside the linguistic structure: it is as if, by their very absence of articulation (or surplus-articulation in the case of singing), they were particularly apt to embody the structure as such, the structure at its minimal; or meaning as such, beyond the discernible meaning. If they are not submitted to phonology, they nevertheless embody its zero-point: the voice aiming at meaning, although neither the one nor the other can be articulated. So the paradoxical fact would be that there may be no linguistics of the voice, yet the non-voice which represents the voice untamed by structure is not external to linguistics. Neither is the object voice which we are pursuing.

CHAPTER 2

THE METAPHYSICS OF THE VOICE

Let us now make a somewhat abrupt jump to Lacan. In the famous graph of desire we find, somewhat surprisingly, a line that runs from the signifier on the left to the voice on the right (Lacan 1989, p. 306):

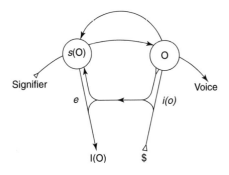

There is the signifying chain, reduced to its minimal features, which yields, as a result or as a leftover, the voice. It looks as though there is a reversal: the voice is not taken as a hypothetical or mythical origin that the analysis would have to break down into distinctive traits, not as a diffuse substance to be reduced to structure, a raw material to be tamed into phonemes, but, rather, the opposite—it stands at the outcome of the structural operation. We can put aside, for our particular purpose, the specific nature of the operation that Lacan tries to demonstrate—the retroactive production of meaning, the "quilting point," the nature of the subject involved in it, the more convoluted versions of this graph (pp. 313, 315), and so on. So why is there the voice as the outcome? Why does the signifier run out into voice as its result? And which voice do we find there—the one that phonology has killed? If it was successfully murdered, why does it recur? Does it not know that it is dead?

Maybe we can sum up this recurrence into a Lacanian thesis: the reduction of the voice that phonology has attempted—phonology as the paradigmatic showcase of structural analysis—has left a remainder. Not as any positive feature that could not be entirely dissolved into its binary logical web, not as some seductive imaginary quality that would escape this operation, but precisely as the object in the Lacanian sense. It is only the reduction of the voice—in all its positivity, lock, stock, and barrel—that produces the voice as the object.

VOICE AND PRESENCE

This dimension of the voice cannot be broken down into differential oppositions, since it was this dissolution that produced it in the first place; there is no meaning that could be assigned to it, since meaning springs only from those oppositions. It is a non-signifying remainder resistant to the signifying operations, a leftover heterogeneous to structural logic, but precisely as such it seems to present a sort of counterweight to differentiality; the differential logic always refers to absence, while the voice seems to embody a presence, a background for differential traits, a positive basis for their inherent negativity. To be sure, its positivity is extremely elusive—just the vibrations of air which vanish as soon as they are produced, a pure passing, not something that could be fixed or something that one could hold on to, since one can only fix the differences, as phonology has exhaustively done. In a more specific Lacanian sense, in the context of the graph, we could say that it presents the counterweight, not just to differentiality but also, and in the first place, to the subject. For the graph was, among other things, constructed to demonstrate that the minimal signifying operation necessarily yields the subject as a purely negative entity produced in the retroactive vector, an entity gliding along the chain without possessing a signifier of its own—the subject is always only represented by a signifier for another signifier, as the famous dictum goes (Lacan 1989, p. 316). In itself it is without foundation and without a substance, an empty space necessarily implied by the nature of the signifier—such was for Lacan the nature of the subject that can be assigned to structure. So the voice seems to endow this empty and negative entity with a counterpart, its "missing half," so to speak, a "supplement" which would enable this negative being to acquire some hold in positivity, a "substance," a relationship to presence.

So is the voice as the residue, the remnant of the phonological operation, to be related to presence? Does it offer a privileged—albeit admittedly elusive—evocation of the present, thus counteracting the purely negative differential features, the Saussurean determination in *absentia* which ultimately always gets the upper hand over presence as soon as we use language? Does the voice essentially relate to presence after the symbolic has done away with all its positive features? Is pure presence, then, the remaining residue? Does the object voice, as the necessary implication of the structural intervention, run into the notorious "metaphysics of presence" as its most recent and most insidious variation?

Obviously, the entire phonological enterprise was heavily biased, as Derrida has convincingly shown. There was a prejudice at its core—a prejudice that was not specific to phonology, but something it shared with the bulk of metaphysical tradition from which it has unwittingly inherited it, and maybe that prejudice defined that tradition as metaphysical in the first place, that is to say, as "phonocentric." It consisted in the simple and seemingly self-evident assumption that the voice is the basic element of language, its natural embodiment and consubstantial with it, whereas writing presents its derivative, auxiliary, and parasitic supplement (it merely fixes the spoken word), which is simultaneously secondary and dangerous (the dead letter threatens to kill the spirit). Or so the story goes.

On this account, the remainder is not to be looked for on the side of the voice at all—quite the contrary. If the entire metaphysical tradition "spontaneously" and consistently espoused the priority of the voice, it was because the voice always presented the privileged point of auto-affection, self-transparency, the hold in the presence. The voice offered the illusion that one could get immediate access to an unalloyed presence, an origin not tarnished by externality, a firm rock against the elusive interplay of signs which are anyway surrogates by their very nature, and always point to an absence. So if there is indeed a remainder, it has to be sought on the side of writing, that dead letter which disrupts the living voice, the supplement which usurps its subsidiary place to tarnish presence. And ultimately, it is not writing in its positive and empirical appearance that is at stake, but more fundamentally the trace, the trace of alterity which has "always-already" dislocated the origin.

Saussure himself was torn between two opposing tendencies: the one that prolonged the traditional stance and made him condemn writing as secondary to voice, but threatening to "usurp the principal role" (Saussure 1998, p. 25), and on the other hand his insight that "the essence of a language . . . has nothing to do with the phonic nature of the linguistic sign" (p. 7). The subsequent fate of phonology was thus caught between the two as well: between, on the one hand, its unquestionable prejudice that the voice was the natural material of language, and thus the evident place to start; and, on the other, its operations which dismantled the living presence of the voice into the lifeless differential matrix (that is, in the web of traces)—except for the residue which Lacan has taken to be the paradoxical object voice.

The Derridean turn has thus, by a very different route, turned the voice into a preeminent object of philosophical inquiry, demonstrating its complicity with the principal metaphysical preoccupations. If metaphysics, in this rather generalized view, is carried by the propensity to disavow the part of alterity, the trace of the other, to hold on to some ultimate signified against the disruptive play of differences, to maintain the purity of the origin against supplementarity, then it can do so only by clinging to the privilege of the voice as a source of an originary self-presence. The divide between the interior and the exterior, the model of all other metaphysical divides, derives from here:

> The voice is *heard* (understood)—that undoubtedly is what is called consciousness[1]—closest to the self as the absolute effacement of the signifier: pure auto-affection that necessarily has the form of time which doesn't borrow from outside of itself, in the world or in "reality," any accessory signifier, any substance of expression foreign to its own spontaneity. It is the unique experience of the signified producing itself spontaneously from within the self. . . . (Derrida 1976, p. 20; 1967a, p. 33)

This illusion—the illusion *par excellence*—is thus constitutive of interiority and ultimately of consciousness, the self and autonomy. The double sense of the French *entendre*, which means "to hear" as well as "to understand," points to the direct link between hearing the voice and the origin of conceptuality, between vocality and ideality. *S'entendre parler*—to hear oneself speak—would thus be the minimal definition of consciousness. I will not dwell on the numerous well-known, ramified and rather spectacular consequences that Derrida has drawn from this.

To hear oneself speak—or, simply, just to hear oneself—can be seen as an elementary formula of narcissism that is needed to produce the minimal form of a self. In his younger days, Lacan spent a great deal of time meditating over another elementary narcissistic device, the mirror. The mirror was to fulfill the same function: to provide the minimal support needed to produce self-recognition, the imaginary completion offered to the multiple body, along with the imaginary blinding it entails, the recognition which is intrinsically a miscognition, the constitution of an "I" which in the same gesture offers a matrix of relationships to one's equals, the ambivalent source of love and aggression—all the well-known panoply of the notorious mirror stage. Lacan was later to isolate the gaze and the voice as the two paramount embodiments of *objet petit a,* but his early theory has given an unquestionable privilege to the gaze as the paradigmatic instance of the Imaginary, elevating it into a model. Yet the voice can be seen as in some sense even more striking and more elementary: if the voice is the first manifestation of life, is not hearing oneself, and recognizing one's own voice, thus an experience that precedes self-recognition in a mirror? And is not the mother's voice the first problematic connection to the other, the immaterial tie that comes to replace the umbilical cord, and shapes much of the fate of the earliest stages of life? Does not the recognition of its own voice produce the same jubilatory effects in the infant as those accompanying self-recognition in a mirror?

There is a rudimentary form of narcissism attached to the voice which is difficult to delineate, since it seems to lack any outside support. It is the first "self-referring" or "self-reflective" move which appears as a pure auto-affection, at the closest to oneself, an auto-affection which is not re-flection, since it appears to lack a screen that would return the voice, a pure immediacy where one is both the sender and the receiver without leaving one's pure interiority. In a deceptive self-transparency, one coincides in both roles without a gap and with no need of any exterior mediation. We could call this an acoustic mirror, as it were (this is the title of Kaja Silverman's admirable book [1988]), without any external mirroring support. There is no need for recognition in one's external image, and one could see there the kernel of consciousness prior to any reflection. Re-flection demands bouncing back from an external surface, and it seems that the voice does not need this. The moment there is a surface which returns the voice, the voice acquires an autonomy of its own and enters the dimension of the other; it becomes a deferred voice, and narcissism crumbles. The best witness is, after all, Narcissus himself, whose story, maybe not surprisingly, involves both the gaze and the voice. But his curious "affair" with the nymph Echo, who could only echo his words, and could not initiate speech herself, is a story of a failed love and a failed narcissism. The voice returned was not his own voice, although it merely sent his own words back to him. It was his voice turned into the other, and he would rather die than abandon himself to the other ("'Ante,' ait, 'emoriar, quam sit tibi copia nostri,'" says Ovid—"I'd rather die than fall prey to you"). And when the nymph died, only her voice was left; it continues to echo our own voice, the voice without a body, the remainder, the trace of the object.[2]

Inside that narcissistic and auto-affective dimension of the voice, however, there is something that threatens to disrupt it: a voice that affects us most intimately, but we cannot master it and have no power or control over it. Where the voice presented itself as a problem for psychoanalysis, it was always as the intractable voice of the other that imposed itself upon the subject. In its most spectacular and obvious form, there is the widespread experience of psychosis based on "hearing voices," the vast field of auditory hallucinations which impose themselves as more real than any other voices. In a more common form, there is the voice of conscience, reminding us to do our duty, which was soon related by Freud to the voice of the superego—not just an internalization of the law, but the law endowed with a surplus of the voice. At the origin of psychoanalysis, there was the problem of the hypnotic voice which demanded submission, and its mechanism—the repetition of some formula which lost all meaning by being repeated—was based precisely on the attempt to isolate the object voice from meaning. If psychoanalysis was to establish itself by sharply opposing hypnosis and its suggestive powers, it had to take into account and analyze the ominous authority of that strange object. There was aphonia, a frequent hysterical symptom, a sudden inability to use one's voice, an enforced silence which makes the object voice appear all the more, maybe in its pure form. At the bottom of it was the problem of the mother's voice, the first representation of the dimension of the other, endowed with an array of retroactive fantasies of a primary fusion prior to the imposition of a signifier and a lack (compare, for example, the Kristevan *chora*), and also ambiguously giving rise to paranoiac fantasies of "entrapment": the voice which was both the first nest and the first cage (see Silverman 1988, pp. 72 ff., 101 ff.).

This is a rather quick and cursory list—we will have to come back to its items later—but it can serve as a somewhat overloaded reminder of a simple point: for psychoanalysis, the auto-affective voice of self-presence and self-mastery was constantly opposed by its reverse side, the intractable voice of the other, the voice one could not control. If we try to bring the two together, we could tentatively say that at the very core of narcissism lies an alien kernel which narcissistic satisfaction may well attempt to disguise, but which continually threatens to undermine it from the inside. At the time when Lacan, impelled by his initial insight, wrote the famous pages about the mirror stage, he still had no theory of the object, and he later had to add several lengthy postscripts to his early sketches—most notably in *Seminar XI* (Lacan 1979, pp. 67–119), where one section bears the title "The split between the eye and the gaze." The gaze as the object, cleft from the eye, is precisely what is dissimulated by the image in which one recognizes oneself; it is not something that could be present in the field of vision, yet it haunts it from the inside.[3] If it appears as part of the image—as it does, for example, in the experience of the double which spawned a whole library of Romantic literature—it immediately disrupts the established reality, and leads to catastrophe. By analogy, there is a schism between the voice and the ear (see Miller 1989, pp. 177–178). The same inner disruption of narcissism has to be introduced here, and the same inherent ambiguity of the seemingly self-transparent auto-affection.

As soon as the object, both as the gaze and as the voice, appears as the pivotal point of narcissistic self-apprehension, it introduces a rupture at the core of self-presence. It is something that cannot itself be present, although the whole notion of presence is constructed around it and can be established only by its elision. So the subject, far from being constituted by self-apprehension in the clarity of its presence to itself, emerges only in an impossible relation to that bit that cannot be present. Only insofar as there is a Real (the Lacanian name for that bit) as an impossibility of presence is there a subject. The voice may well be the key to the presence of the present and to an unalloyed interiority, but it conceals in its bosom that inaudible object voice which disrupts both. So if, for Derrida, the essence of the voice lies in auto-affection and self-transparency, as opposed to the trace, the rest, the alterity, and so on, for Lacan this is where the problem starts. The deconstructive turn tends to deprive the voice of its ineradicable ambiguity by reducing it to the ground of (self-)presence, while the Lacanian account tries to disentangle from its core the object as an interior obstacle to (self-)presence. This object embodies the very impossibility of attaining auto-affection; it introduces a scission, a rupture in the middle of the full presence, and refers it to a void—but a void which is not simply a lack, an empty space; it is a void in which the voice comes to resonate.

A BRIEF COURSE IN THE HISTORY OF METAPHYSICS

The most convincing part of Derrida's extensive analyses is his ability to demonstrate how a seemingly marginal theme—that of the primacy of voice over writing, the phonocentric bias—consistently recurs throughout the whole history of metaphysics, and how it is inherently and necessarily linked with all major metaphysical preoccupations. This one very limited angle seems to be sufficient to produce a history of metaphysics in all its vast ramifications. The sheer extent of evidence is overwhelming, its coherence compelling. Yet the phonocentric bias may not be the whole story of the metaphysical treatment of the voice. There exists a different metaphysical history of voice, where the voice, far from being the safeguard of presence, was considered to be dangerous, threatening, and possibly ruinous. There is a history of the voice receiving a metaphysical vote of no confidence. Not just writing, but also the voice can appear as a menace to metaphysical consistency, and can be seen as disruptive of presence and sense. Lacan did not have to invent the ambiguity of the voice and its perilous reverse side; metaphysics has been well aware of it all along. We can see this particularly in philosophical treatments of music—again a rather limited perspective, to be sure, but it casts long shadows.

So let us attempt a very brief survey of some paradigmatic cases. In one of the oldest (albeit rather questionable and mythical) texts about music, the Chinese emperor Chun (c. 2200 BC) offers the following simple precept: "Let the music follow the sense of the words. Keep it simple and ingenuous. One must condemn pretentious music which is devoid of sense and effeminate" (quoted by Poizat 1991, pp. 197–198). Despite the simplicity of this piece of advice (and coming from an emperor, it is more than advice, it immediately raises intricate issues of the relationship between music and power), the main concerns, which will recur throughout history with astonishing obstinacy, are already there in a nutshell: music, and in particular the voice, should not stray away from words which endow it with sense; as soon as it departs from its textual anchorage, the voice becomes senseless and threatening—all the more so because of its seductive and intoxicating powers. Furthermore, the voice beyond sense is self-evidently equated with femininity, whereas the text, the instance of signification, is in this simple paradigmatic opposition on the side of masculinity. (Some four thousand years later, Wagner will write in a famous letter to Liszt: "*Die Musik ist ein Weib*," music is a woman.) The voice beyond words is a senseless play of sensuality, it possesses a dangerous attractive force, although in itself it is empty and frivolous. The dichotomy of voice and *logos* is already in place.

A couple of millennia or so later, it is still firmly in place with Plato:

A change to a new type of music is something to beware of as a hazard of all our fortunes. For the modes of music are never disturbed

Music

without unsettling of the most fundamental political and social conventions. . . . It is here, then, I said, that our guardians must build their guardhouse and post of watch.

It is certain, he said, that this is the kind of lawlessness that easily insinuates itself unobserved.

Yes, said I, because it is supposed to be only a form of play and to work no harm.

Nor does it work any, he said, except that by gradual infiltration it softly overflows upon the characters and pursuits of men and from these issues forth grown greater to attack their business dealings, and from these relations it proceeds against the laws and the constitution with wanton license, Socrates, till finally it overthrows all things public and private. (Plato 1978, *Republic* IV, 424c–e)

Music is no laughing matter, to say the least. It cannot be taken lightly, but has to be treated with the greatest philosophical concern and the utmost vigilance. It is a texture so fundamental that any license inevitably produces general decadence; it undermines the social fabric, its laws and mores, and threatens the very ontological order. For we must assign an ontological status to music: it holds the key to a harmony between "nature" and "culture," the natural and the man-made law.[4] Should we interfere with that sphere, everything is put into question and the foundations are undermined. Decadence starts with musical decadence: in the beginning, in the great times of origin, music was regulated by law and was one with it, but things quickly got out of hand:

Afterward, in course of time, an unmusical license set in with the appearance of poets who were men of native genius, but ignorant of what is right and legitimate in the realm of the Muses. Possessed by a frantic and unhallowed lust for pleasure, they . . . created a universal confusion of forms. Thus their folly led them unintentionally to slander their profession by the assumption that in music there is no such thing as a right and a wrong, the right standard of judgment being the pleasure given to the hearer, be he high or low. (Plato 1978, *Laws* III, 700d–e)

Once one blasphemously gives way to pleasure as the standard ("It is commonly said that the standard of rightness in music is its pleasure-giving effect. That, however, is an intolerable sentiment; in fact, 'tis a piece of flat blasphemy": Plato 1978, *Laws* II, 655d), once one has re-fused to comply with the law in music, there is no end to the insidi-ous consequences—impudence, moral disintegration, the collapse of all social bonds.

> So the next stage of the journey toward liberty will be refusal to sub-mit to the magistrates, and on this will follow emancipation from the authority and correction of parents and elders; then, as the goal of the race is approached, comes the effort to escape obedience to the law, and, when that goal is all but reached, contempt for oaths, for the plighted word, and all religion. The spectacle of the Titanic nature of which our old legends speak is re-enacted; man returns to the old con-dition of a hell of unending misery. (Plato 1978, *Laws* III, 701 b–c)

In order to forestall this truly apocalyptic vision—the end of civ-ilization, a return to chaos initiated by innocuous-looking changes in musical forms—one has to impose a firm regimentation of musical matters. The first rule, the prime antidote for combating the monster, is already known: "The music and the rhythm must follow the speech" (Plato 1978, *Republic* III, 398d, 400d). For the core of the danger is the voice that sets itself loose from the word, the voice beyond logos, the lawless voice.

Other prescriptions follow. One must proscribe the modes that mollify the soul or induce laxity—the "dirgelike" mixed Lydian, the higher Lydian ("for they are useless even to women who are to make the best of themselves, let alone to men": Plato 1978, *Republic* 398e), as well as the Ionian. One must retain those that are fit for men, both for warriors and for manly modesty and moderation—the Dorian and the Phrygian.[5] Again, the sexual division is seen to run through mu-sic (and this will continue to our day with the sexual connotations of major and minor tonalities, *durus* and *mollis*).[6] Consequently, one has to ban the polyharmonic instruments that permit free transitions among the modes, the "modulations," and in particular the flute, "the most many-stringed of instruments" (ibid., 399d). There is in fact an ad-ditional, simpler and more compelling reason for this: one cannot utter words while playing the flute. The wind instruments have the vicious property that they emancipate themselves from the text, they act as substitutes for the voice, they isolate the voice beyond words. No wonder Dionysus chose the flute as his preferred instrument (remember also Pan's pipes, not to mention the mythical connections of the flute with the Gorgon, and so on), while Apollo decided on the lyre. "We are not innovating, my friend, in preferring Apollo and the instruments of Apollo to Marsyas and his instruments" (ibid., 399e). And no wonder the flute is fit for women:

> I would like to make a further motion: let us dispense with the flute-girl who just made her entrance; let her play for herself or, if she prefers, for the women in the house. Let us instead spend our evening in conversation. (Plato 1978, *Symposium* 176e)

The flute is played by a girl, and her proper audience are women (and it seems there is but a quick slide which leads from flute to questionable virtue), while men will engage in philosophy.

This view of the flute will also be endorsed by Aristotle:

> And there is a further objection [to the flute]: the impediment which the flute presents to the use of the voice detracts from its educational value. The ancients therefore were right in forbidding the flute to youths and freemen, although they had once allowed it. (Aristotle 2001, *Politics* VIII, 1341a 23–27)

> Bacchic frenzy and all similar emotions are most suitably expressed by the flute. . . . (ibid., 1342b 5–6)

But back to Plato. It seems that there lies in music both the best remedy and the ultimate danger, the cure and the poison. It is curious how Derrida's famous analysis of *pharmakon* (see "Plato's Pharmacy" in Derrida 1972), the remedy and the ruin, as applied to writing, can also apply to the voice.

> Education in music is most sovereign, because more than anything else rhythm and harmony find their way to the inmost soul and take strongest hold upon it, bringing with them and imparting grace, if one is rightly trained, and otherwise the contrary. . . . (Plato 1978, *Republic* III, 401 d–e)

So the crucial question is how to strike a balance between its beneficial and dangerous effects, where to draw a line between redemption and catastrophe:

> Now when a man abandons himself to music, to play upon him and pour into his soul as it were through the funnel of his ears those sweet, soft, and dirgelike airs . . . and gives his entire time to the warblings and blandishments of song, the first result is that the principle of high spirit, if he had it, is softened like iron and is made useful instead of useless and brittle. But when he continues the practice without remission and is spellbound, the effect begins to be that he melts and liquefies till he completely dissolves away his spirit, cuts out as it were the very sinews of his soul and makes of himself a "feeble warrior."
> (Plato 1978, *Republic* III, 411a–b)[7]

How, then, can one hope to achieve the right measure with this dangerous sort of enjoyment? Up to a point, music is sublime and elevates the spirit; beyond a certain limit, however, it brings about decay, the decline of all spiritual faculties, their disintegration in enjoyment. Where should one stop? Can the philosopher set a limit to this unbounded, limitless enjoyment? Can he keep the cure without introducing the fatal poison?

Let us again jump another millennium—or almost—and open Saint Augustine's *Confessions*, book X, 33. There we read the following striking meditation about "sinning by the ear":

> Now, in those melodies [*sonis*] which Thy words breathe soul into, when sung with a sweet and attuned voice, I do a little repose. . . . But with the words which are their life and whereby they find admission into me, themselves [sc. melodies, *soni*] seek in my affections a place of some estimation, and I can scarcely assign them one suitable. For at one time I seem to myself to give them more honor than is seemly [*decet*], feeling our minds to be more holily and fervently raised unto a flame of devotion, by the holy words themselves when thus sung, than when not; and that the several affections of our spirit, by a sweet variety, have their own proper measures in the voice and singing, by some hidden correspondence wherewith they are stirred up. But this

contentment of the flesh, to which the soul must not be given over to be enervated, doth oft beguile me, the sense not so waiting upon reason, as patiently to follow her; but having been admitted merely for her sake, it strives even to run before her, and lead her. (Augustine 1992)

By now we cannot be surprised to find again the voice as the paramount source of danger and decay. The remedy, too, is familiar: stick to the Word, the Word of God, make sure the Word maintains the upper hand, and thus be rid of the voice beyond the Word, the unbounded voice. So Athanasius acted most wisely when he prescribed that the Psalms should be sung "with so slight inflection of voice that it was nearer speaking than singing." Should not singing, rather, be banned to avoid the ambiguity?

> When I remember the tears I shed at the Psalmody of Thy Church, in the beginning of my recovered faith; and how at this time, I am moved, not with the singing, but with the things sung, when they are sung with a clear voice and modulation most suitable [*cum liquida voce et convenientissima modulatione*], I acknowledge the great use of this institution. Thus I fluctuate between peril of pleasure, and approved wholesomeness; . . . by the delight of the ears, the weaker minds may rise to the feeling of devotion. Yet when it befalls me to be more moved with the voice than the words sung, I confess to have sinned penally, and then had rather not hear music. (ibid.)

Again, it is a question of the limit, the impossible good measure, for music is both what elevates the soul to divinity and a sin, *delectatio carnis*. It presents carnality at its most insidious, since in music it seems liberated from materiality; the voice is both the subtlest and the most perfidious form of the flesh.

Saint Augustine's oscillation adumbrates very well the bulk of what was to happen in the next thousand years and more in the troubled and intricate relationship between the Church and music.[8] The main problem that kept emerging, with uncanny perseverance, was that of regimentation and codification of sacred music, which ultimately always took the form of confining the voice to the letter, to Holy Scripture. But whatever the attempted regulations, there was always a crack, a loophole, a remainder that kept recurring, a remnant of a highly ambiguous enjoyment. It could, for instance, take the form of *iubilus*, the space allotted to Alleluia, where the general principle of one syllable to one note was omitted, and the mere voice could take over in its own jubilation, the melisma without a support. In a curious development, the notes without words were later underpinned with new words and whole sequences (in the technical sense of the term), thus threatening heretical intrusions into the Text. But is not *iubilus*, although perilous, at the same time also the most appropriate way to praise God? Saint Augustine himself says so: the jubilation expresses what cannot be expressed by words, the singers are so overwhelmed with joy that they abandon words and give way to their heart. "*Et quem decet ista iubilatio, nisi ineffabilem deum?*" ("And to whom does this jubilation pertain, if not to the ineffable God?")[9] So it is only the pure voice beyond words that matches the ineffability of God. But then again, can we ever be sure that it is really God whom we are praising?

We can follow the same predicament with the enormous problems posed by the introduction of polyphony, since when several voices sing at the same time, and follow their own melodic lines, the text becomes unintelligible. We see it again in the battle against chromatics, since the semitones threaten to undermine the harmonic structure and introduce the mollification of the spirit, the proscribed enjoyment. Each new musical invention had devastating effects and was immediately seen, in a very Platonic manner, as a road to moral ruin. Pope John XXII had to issue a curious decree concerning music, *Docta sanctorum Patrum*, in 1324, as an effort to put things in order, but to no avail. In the sixteenth century the Council of Trent had to wrestle with the same problem, and commended the same antidote of intelligibility versus voice: *in tono intelligibili, intelligibili voce, voce clara, cantu intelligibili* . . . (see Poizat 1991, pp. 144–145). All the documents seem to have been written by the same hand and guided by the same single obsession: to pin down the voice to the letter, to limit its disruptive force, to dissipate its inherent ambiguity.

Yet not everything fitted within this monotonous picture. Some mystical currents proposed an astonishing reversal of this common

Medieval Mystics

paradigm: music is the only appropriate way to God, since it is aiming precisely at the God beyond the word. It is a way to a limitless and ineffable being, a quality of which Saint Augustine was already aware. What is at stake is an enjoyment beyond the signifier, something that opens the perspective of the Lacanian problem of feminine enjoyment (which Lacan himself also tackled precisely through the women mystics). But if God is the musical principle *par excellence*, and the divine Word attains its true dimension only in the singing voice, then the radical consequence could follow that the mere word belongs to the Devil. This extreme conclusion was indeed drawn by Hildegard of Bingen, the famous twelfth-century abbess, who—beside her philosophical preoccupations and conferring with some of the most illustrious men of her time—largely devoted her time to composing. In *Ordo virtutum*, a musical morality play, we have the story of a soul being tempted by the Devil and rescued by the virtues—virtues personified and, of course, singing. In a most curious *tour de force*, the Devil is the only masculine and the only speaking role, being confined just to words, to mere *logos*. An inherently non-musical creature, the Devil is the Devil because he cannot sing. (One could add: no wonder his temptations didn't amount to much.) Of course the Church was bound to be doubtful and worried—the synod in Trier, in 1147, almost condemned Hildegard as a heretic, asking whether her visions were to be assigned to the Devil rather than to God. Is the voice that she hears and writes down really the voice of God? Is there a way to tell? It took the authority of Bernard of Clairvaux to rescue Hildegard.[10]

The question that was raised finally boiled down to this: does music come from God or from the Devil? For what is beyond the word announces both the supreme elevation and the vilest damnation. What raises our souls to God makes God ambiguous; beyond the Word, we cannot tell God from the Devil. Music may well be the element of spiritual elevation beyond worldliness and representation, but it also introduces, for that very reason, an indomitable and senseless enjoyment beyond the more tractable sensual pleasures. There is no assurance or transparency to be found in the voice—quite the contrary, the voice undermines any certainty and any establishment of a firm sense. The voice is boundless, warrantless, and—no coincidence—on the side of woman. But if it introduces this fatal ambivalence, then the only consistent course would be to ban church music altogether—and indeed, this radical conclusion in the opposite extreme was drawn by the Puritans: for fifteen years, from 1645 to 1660, the time of Cromwell, music was banned from the Anglican Church, music books and sheets were burned and organs demolished as "the Devil's pipes" (see Poizat 1991, p. 44). God was restored to the Word, and to silence.

Let me finish this "brief history of metaphysics" with the French Revolution, although many more detours should be taken into account and many more authors examined. At the height of the victorious Revolution, somebody had the brilliant idea of creating, in 1793, the *Institut national de la musique,* an institution through which the state would now take care of music in the best interest of the people.[11] François-Joseph Gossec, who was in charge of the project, has duly written in a programmatic text that its goal should be to promote music "which would support and animate the energy of the defenders of equality and to prohibit music which mollifies the French soul by its effeminate sounds in the salons and in the temples consecrated to imposture" (quoted by Attali 1977, p. 111). Music has to be drawn out of the courts, churches, and concert halls; it has to be performed in the open air, accessible to everyone; the melodies should be such that the people can sing along, not pompous and pretentious artifices which serve only the degenerate. Gossec himself entered music history as the initiator of mass choral singing, and one of the first composers for brass orchestras. Musicians should become state employees, not dependent on the generosity of the rich, and the whole musical enterprise should be well planned and organized from above.[12]

So the tables could be reversed and the same weapons could be turned against the Church, now seen as the major agent of the voice against sense. But the defenders of reason were for once unwittingly in perfect accord with their enemies: the senseless and effeminate voice was equally dangerous to both. It is highly indicative that one of the first decrees of the Revolution was the prohibition of public singing by castrati, who became the emblematic and monstrous figureheads of the perversity and corruption of the *ancien régime*, the embodiments of its degenerate *jouissance* epitomized by the voice.[13] They were not only the heroes of the baroque and classical opera (up to and including Mozart), but also the figureheads of Catholic music; their cradle and sanctuary was the Sistine Chapel, the core of perversity at the very heart of the Church.

From this brief and necessarily schematic survey we can draw the tentative conclusion that the history of "logocentrism" does not quite go hand in hand with "phonocentrism," that there is a dimension of the voice which runs counter to self-transparency, sense, and presence: the voice against *logos*, the voice as the other of *logos*, its radical alterity. "Metaphysics" has always been very well aware of that, as we have seen, compulsively clinging to a simple exorcizing formula, repeating it over and over again, compelled by the same invisible hand throughout millennia. Maybe what defined it as metaphysics was not just the demotion of writing, but also the banishment of the voice. The "phonocentric" voice was just one part of the story. It presented the voice as the illusory pledge of presence, reduced its inherent ambivalence, and disavowed its part of alterity. The presence of the present in the voice becomes doubtful the moment sense is eluded, and this dissociation is at the core of the Lacanian operation. By this simple division, however, we have not yet reached the proper dimension of the object voice. It is only here that the Lacanian problem really starts.

SHOFAR

In the simple paradigm I have tried to draw up, *logos*—in the widest sense of "what makes sense"—was opposed by the voice as an intrusion of otherness, enjoyment, and femininity. But this division is not exhaustive, and we can see that, rather obviously, there is also another kind of voice: the voice of the Father, the voice that inherently sticks to *logos* itself, the voice that commands and binds, the voice of God. If there is to be a founding law, a covenant, the voice has to play a crucial part in it. This is the problem Lacan raises in his seminar on anxiety ("Yahweh's voice," May 22, 1963; Lacan 2004, pp. 281f.), taking his inspiration in the striking analysis that Theodor Reik has made of *shofar*, a primitive form of horn used in Jewish religious rituals, one of the most ancient wind instruments.

Where does the astounding force of shofar come from? It is, for instance, blown four times at the closure of Yom Kippur, in very long continuous sounds which are reputed to fill the soul with an irresistible profound emotion.[14] There is no melody, just the prolonged sounds reminiscent of a bull roaring. Reik sees the key to its secret in the Freudian myth of *Totem and Taboo*:

> The specially anxious, groaning, blaring and long-sounding tone of shofar becomes understandable by the reminiscence of a roaring bull; it obtains its fateful significance by presenting, to the unconscious psychic life of the listener, the anxiety and the ultimate death struggle of the divine father—one could say his "swan song," if the comparison wasn't so utterly out of place here. . . . When the image of the father was rediscovered in the totemic animal and worshipped as divine, those who recognized it imitated its voice by onomatopoetic sounds. The imitation of the animal's cry signified both the presence of God among the believers and their identification with him. The horn, the most characteristic trait of the totemic God, gave birth in the course of centuries to an instrument which was now used as the means of acoustic imitation. (Reik 1928, pp. 235–236)

So we have to recognize, in the sound of shofar, the voice of the Father, the cry of the dying primal father of the primitive horde, the leftover which comes both to haunt and to seal the foundation of his law. By hearing this voice, the community of believers establishes its covenant, its alliance with God; they assert their submission and obedience to the law. The law itself, in its pure form, before commanding anything specific, is epitomized by the voice, the voice that commands total compliance, although it is senseless in itself. The letter of the law can acquire its authority by the remnant of the dead father, that part of him which is not quite dead, what remained after his death and continues to testify to his presence—his voice—but also to his absence: it is *a stand-in for an impossible presence*, enveloping a central void. It functions as the ritual repetition of his sacrifice and the reminder of the impossible origin of the law, covering up its lack of origin. But this gesture is highly ambiguous, for who is it that has to be reminded? Who is ultimately the addressee of that voice? In Lacan's words: "To put it bluntly, is not the one whose memory has to be awoken, whom one has to remind, is it not God himself?" (Lacan 2004, p. 290). For the function of that voice, apart from representing God, is also to remind God that he is dead, in case he has forgotten.

The sound of shofar has textual support in the Bible, and Reik carefully lists all its numerous occurrences. Each of them is remarkable; they all take place at dramatic moments, most often when a covenant has to be established or reasserted; but no doubt the most significant among them is the moment of the foundation of the Law, when Moses receives the Tablets of the Law on Mount Sinai. It was the sound of shofar which, at that foundational instance, testified to the presence of God for the people, for they could hear only this terrible and commanding sound; only Moses could speak to God and make out what he said. Shofar, conventionally translated as trumpet, was the element of the voice in the midst of thunder as the natural noise:

> On the morning of the third day there were peals of thunder and lightning, and a heavy cloud over the mountain, and a very loud trumpet blast, so that all the people in the camp trembled. (Exodus 19: 16)

> When the people witnessed the thunder and lightning, the trumpet blast and the mountain smoking, they all feared and trembled. So they took up a position much farther away and said to Moses, "You speak to us, and we will listen; but let not God speak to us, or we shall die." (Exodus 20: 18)

So shofar, whose sound is louder than all the thunder, is there as the voice without content that sticks to the Law, the support of the Law, underpinning its letter. There is, in this inaugural moment, a division between the voice heard by the people, as a terrible commanding presence, and the Law of which only Moses could "make sense." But *there is no law without the voice.*[15] It seems that the voice, as a senseless remainder of the letter, is what endows the letter with authority, making it not just a signifier, but an act. It is, as Lacan says, "that something which completes the relation of the subject to the signifier in what might be called, in a first approach, its *passage à l'acte*" (Lacan 2004, p. 288).[16] Those "primordial signifiers" are inherently "acts," "namely something that happens when the signifier is not just articulated, which supposes only its relation, its coherence with the others in a chain, but when it is uttered and vocalized" (ibid.). The voice seems to possess the power to turn words into acts; the mere vocalization endows words with a ritual efficacy, the passage from articulation to vocalization is like a *passage à l'acte*, a passage to action and an exertion of authority; it is as if the mere addition of the voice could represent the originary form of performativity—we will come back to that. But what is at stake here is neither the notion of act nor that of vocalization, but the status of the object which is at the bottom of both, and "has to be detached from phonematization." The voice, as opposed to distinctive oppositions in phonematization, appears as "a new dimension, isolated as such, a dimension apart, the properly vocal dimension" (ibid.)—shofar is the voice independent of the vocalization of the signifier. In this isolation it bears witness to that remainder of a presupposed and terrible Father's *jouissance* which could not be absorbed by the Law, that reverse side of the Father that Lacan calls *le-père-la-jouissance*, his ultimate deadly cry that accompanies the instituted law. It is the part which can never be simply present, but is not simply absent either: the object voice is the pivotal point precisely at the intersection of presence and absence. It discloses the presence and gives ground to its imaginary recognition—recognizing oneself as the addressee of the voice of the Other – but at the same time it is what inherently lacks and disrupts any notion of a full presence, it makes it a truncated presence built around a lack—the lack epitomized by the surplus of the voice.

The metaphysical picture I have drawn in broad outline is therefore misleading. If the Law, the Word, *logos*, had to constantly fight the voice as its other, as the senseless bearer of enjoyment, feminine decadence, it could do so only by implicitly relying on that other voice, the voice of the Father accompanying the Law. So that ultimately, we have not the battle of *logos* against the voice, but that of *the voice against the voice*. Yet is that inaudible voice pertaining to *logos* entirely different from the anathematized voice bringing unbounded enjoyment and decay? Is the enjoyment that the law persecutes as its radical alterity anything other than the aspect of enjoyment pertaining to law itself? Is the voice of the Father of an altogether different species from the feminine voice? Does the voice of the persecutor differ sharply from the persecuted voice? The secret may be that they are both the same; that there are not two voices, but only the object voice which cleaves and bars the other in an ineradicable "extimacy."

> And why not interpret one face of the Other, the God face, as supported by feminine *jouissance*? . . . And since it is there too that the function of the father is inscribed in so far as this is the function to which castration refers, one can see that while this may not make for two Gods, nor does it make for one alone. (Lacan in Mitchell and Rose 1982, p. 147)[17]

For what endows the Law with authority is also what irretrievably bars it, and attempts to banish the other voice, the voice beyond *logos*, are ultimately based on the impossibility of coming to terms with the Law's inherent alterity, placed at the point of its inherent lack which voice comes to cover. This structural point is what Lacan, in his algebra, has designated by $S(\bcancel{A})$, the point of the always-missing ultimate signifier which would totalize the Other, the point of the absent foundation of the Law, and also the point which has an intrinsic relation with femininity and the nonexistence of The Woman.[18] It is at this point of alterity in the Other that the object is situated. Masculine and feminine positions would then be two ways of tackling the same impossibility; they arise from the same predicament as two internally linked versions of dealing with the same object which retains an ineradicable ambiguity.

CHAPTER 3

THE "PHYSICS" OF THE VOICE

Let us now pursue another thread. We have seen that from the point of view of signifying structure, of signifiers as mere bundles of differential oppositions, materiality seems to be irrelevant; the signifier functions by putting it in brackets. But it is by no means irrelevant to the voice. Indeed, the voice appears as the link which ties the signifier to the body. It indicates that the signifier, however purely logical and differential, must have a point of origin and emission in the body. There must be a body to support it and assume it, its disembodied network must be pinned to a material source, the bodily emission must provide the material to embody the signifier, the disembodied signifying mechanics must be attached to bodily mechanics, if only in its most intangible and "sublimated" form, the mere oscillation of air which keeps vanishing the moment it is produced, materiality at its most intangible and hence in its most tenacious form. The first obvious quality of the voice is that it fades away the moment it is produced. *Verba volant, scripta manent*: Lacan reversed this classical proverb, since it is only the voice which remains there, on the spot where it was emitted and which it cannot leave, where it is born and where it dies at the same moment—at least until the emergence of the good-hundred-year-old technology of sound reproduction, which blurred many lines—while the letters fly around and, by flying, form the whirlwind of history.

Alain Badiou begins his latest great book, his *opus magnum, Logiques des mondes*, with an assertion which exemplifies the basic tenet of what he calls "democratic materialism": "There are only bodies and languages." This is indeed a doxa which can be seen as a modern—postmodern—avatar of more illustrious predecessors: let us say, of Descartes's division into *res extensa* and *res cogitans*, where both parts have undergone considerable change: the body has evolved since the Cartesian machines, covered by clothes and hats, to a virtual body, a body of multiple enjoyment, a multiply sexed body, a cyber body, a body without organs, a body as life-force and production, a nomadic body, and so on; and thought has evolved from the soul and ideas to the multiplicity of signs and languages, reduced to many versions of semiotics; instead of body and soul, multiple pleasures and signs. Nevertheless, both parts remain as the firm evidence, the dual substance, of what there is. But in this double world—this is Badiou's whole point— there are also truths, which are neither bodies nor languages nor mixtures of the two, nor are they somewhere else either, in some special Platonic spot. They are "incorporeal bodies, languages deprived of sense, generic infinities, unconditioned supplements. They become and they are suspended, like the poet's conscience, 'between nothing and the pure event.'"[1] So the truths, which emerge as consequences of events, present a break in the world of what exists, a rupture in the continuities of bodies and languages.

Now the voice as the object, the paradoxical creature that we are after, is also a break. Of course it has an inherent link to presence, to what there is, to the point of endorsing the very notion of presence, yet at the same time, as we have seen, it presents a break, it is not to be simply counted among existing things, its topology dislocates it in relation to presence. And—most important in this context—it is *precisely the voice that holds bodies and languages together.* It is like their missing link, what they have in common. The language is attached to the body through the voice, as if the voice were to fulfill the function of the pineal gland in a new Cartesian division of substances. And I suppose we can reach what Badiou is after by another path: the emergence of event and truth through the break presented by the object voice.

The body implied by the voice, disembodied as it may seem, is enough to be cumbersome and embarrassing; in all its living presence it is also like the corpse one cannot dispose of (as in Hitchcock's *The Trouble with Harry,* 1955). There is no voice without a body, but yet again this relation is full of pitfalls: it seems that the voice pertains to the wrong body, or doesn't fit the body at all, or disjoints the body from which it emanates. Hence all the troubles with what Michel Chion (1982) has called the *acousmatic voice.*

THE ACOUSMATICS OF THE VOICE

The acousmatic voice is simply a voice whose source one cannot see, a voice whose origin cannot be identified, a voice one cannot place. It is a voice in search of an origin, in search of a body, but even when it finds its body, it turns out that this doesn't quite work, the voice doesn't stick to the body, it is an excrescence which doesn't match the body—if you want a quick but vivid example of this, think of Hitchcock's *Psycho,* which revolves entirely around the question "Where does the mother's voice come from? To which body can it be assigned?" We can immediately see that the voice without a body is inherently uncanny, and that the body to which it is assigned does not dissipate its haunting effect.

Chion borrowed the word "acousmatic" from Pierre Schaeffer and his famous *Traité des objets musicaux* (published in 1966, the same year as Lacan's *Écrits*). The word has a precise technical meaning: according to Larousse, "acousmatic" describes "the noise which we hear without seeing what is causing it." And it gives its philosophical origin: "The Acousmatics were Pythagoras' disciples who, concealed by a curtain, followed his teaching for five years without being able to see him." Larousse follows Diogenes Laertius (VIII, 10): "[His pupils] were silent for the period of five years and only listened to the speeches without seeing Pythagoras, until they proved themselves worthy of it."[2] The Teacher, the Master behind a curtain, proffering his teaching from there without being seen: no doubt a stroke of genius which stands at the very origin of philosophy—Pythagoras was allegedly the first to describe himself as a "philosopher," and also the first to found a philosophical school. The advantage of this mechanism was obvious: the students, the followers, were confined to "their Master's voice," not distracted by his looks or quirks of behavior, by visual forms, the spectacle of presentation, the theatrical effects which always pertain to lecturing; they had to concentrate merely on the voice and the meaning emanating from it. It appears that at its origin philosophy depends on a theatrical *coup de force:* there is the simple minimal device which defines the theater, the curtain which serves as a screen, but a curtain not to be raised, not for many years—philosophy appears as the art of an actor behind the curtain.[3]

The point of this device was ultimately to separate the spirit from the body. It was not only that the disciples could follow the meaning better with no visual distractions, it was the voice itself which acquired authority and surplus-meaning by virtue of the fact that its source was concealed; it seemed to become omnipresent and omnipotent. The beauty of it is that this mechanism is the simplest possible, and purely formal—it works automatically: the Master, "by the very cunning of the scene" (*Hamlet*, II/2.586), as it were, turns into a spirit without a body. The body distracts the spirit, it is a cumbersome impediment, so it has to be reduced to the spectrality of mere voice, and entrusted to its disembodied body. The separation thus depends entirely on the spirit acquiring a new kind of body; the spirit is all in the voice, the voice suddenly endowed with aura and authority. Pythagoras became the object of a cult in his lifetime; he was revered as a divinity (Diogenes Laertius, VIII, 11), and no doubt this was not unrelated to that device.

This simple mechanism has indeed been used in various religious rituals, and we can immediately recall the very relevant fact that in the Old Testament God regularly appears as an acousmatic voice—but this is a trait he shares with many other deities, as if there were a direct hidden link between the acousmatic voice and divinization. The voice whose source cannot be seen, because it cannot be located, seems to emanate from anywhere, everywhere; it gains omnipotence. Could we go so far as to say that the hidden voice structurally produces "divine effects"?

But the uses of this device are multiple. To give a light-hearted example from popular culture, think of *The Wizard of Oz*, that very Freudian tale about the nature of transference. (Lyman Frank Baum was, by the way, born in May 1856, just like Freud, and his *Wizard of Oz* was published in 1900, just like *The Interpretation of Dreams*. There is perhaps a story to be written: *Freud avec Baum*.) At the center of the story is precisely the acousmatic voice in which all the wizardry of the wizard consists. Dorothy and her companions make their way to the Emerald City in the hope of obtaining help from the wizard, who will deliver them, but the wizard can be the wizard only as long as his is a voice whose source is hidden,[4] and once the veil is lifted, once the screen is overturned, he necessarily turns into a ludicrous and powerless old man who is no source of rescue, but is himself in great need of help. A more sinister example is *The Testament of Doctor Mabuse* (Fritz Lang,

1933), another great cinematic display of the same mechanism, where again the evil master is merely the voice behind the screen, but it turns out that the effect of authority could be brought about by a mere gramophone, that is, by another screen disguising the origin.

Radio, gramophone, tape-recorder, telephone: with the advent of the new media the acousmatic property of the voice became universal, and hence trivial. They all share their acousmatic nature, and in the early days of their introduction there was no shortage of stories about their uncanny effects, but these gradually waned as they became common, and hence banal. It is true that we cannot see the source of voices there, all we see is some technical appliance from which voices emanate, and in a *quid pro quo* the gadget then takes the place of the invisible source itself. The invisible absent source is substituted by the gadget which disguises it and starts to act as its unproblematic stand-in. The curious remainder of wonderment is the dog intently inspecting the cylinder of a phonograph, and we will come back to that.

We have a grand literary testimony from the early days, a great author seeing with incisive clarity what was at stake. In *The Guermantes Way*, the third volume of Proust's *In Search of Lost Time*, the narrator finds himself in Doncières, a small provincial town, seeing his friends, and receives a telephone call from his grandmother. "The telephone was not yet at that date as commonly in use as it is today," says Proust (2001, p. 418), lines written during the First World War and published in 1920. The narrator has to rush to the post office to take the call, and to partake of the magic whereby "the absent rise up at our side, without our being permitted to set eyes on them" (ibid.). But they rise at our side in a presence which is more acute, more real than the "real" presence, and at the same time the token of separation, the mark of an impossible presence, a phantom of presence, invoking death at its heart.

A real presence, perhaps, that voice that seemed so near—in actual separation! But a premonition also of an eternal separation! Many are the times, as I listened thus without seeing her who spoke to me from so far away, when it has seemed to me that the voice was crying to me from the depths out of which one does not rise again, and I have felt the anxiety that was one day to wring my heart when a voice would thus return (alone and attached no longer to a body which I was never to see again), to murmur in my ear words I longed to kiss as they issued from lips for ever turned to dust. (ibid., p. 419)

The voice, separated from its body, evokes the voice of the dead. It is the first time the narrator has spoken to his grandmother over the telephone, and he is overwhelmed by a sudden new experience.

After a few seconds of silence, suddenly I heard that voice which I mistakenly thought I knew so well; for always until then, every time that my grandmother had talked to me, I had been accustomed to follow what she said on the open score of her face, in which the eyes figured so largely; but her voice itself I was hearing this afternoon for the first time. . . . Fragile by reason of its delicacy, it seemed constantly on the verge of breaking, of expiring in a pure flow of tears; then, too, having it alone beside me, seen without the mask of her face, I noticed in it for the first time the sorrows that had cracked it in the course of a lifetime. (ibid., pp. 419–420)

Suddenly hearing that voice as he has never heard it before, at its closest and yet unreachable, he is seized by mortal anguish:

"Granny!" I cried to her, "Granny!" and I longed to kiss her, but I had beside me only the voice, a phantom as impalpable as the one that would perhaps come back to visit me when my grandmother was dead. (ibid., pp. 420–421)

And at the same time he is seized by an immediate and irresistible desire to rejoin her, that very minute, as soon as possible. So he takes the train back to Paris the next day and rushes to her apartment, longing to free himself "at the first possible moment, in her arms, from the phantom, hitherto unsuspected and suddenly called into being by her voice" (ibid., p. 424). But too late, too late—a gap has come into existence which is now impossible to bridge.

I found her reading. I was in the room, or rather I was not yet in the room since she was not aware of my presence. . . . Of myself—thanks to that privilege which does not last but which gives one, during the brief moment of return, the faculty of being suddenly the spectator of one's own absence—there was present only the witness, the observer, in travelling-coat and hat, the stranger who does not belong to the house. . . . (ibid., p. 425)

It is as if the presence has been broken, the acousmatic voice has invoked a presence both more real and irretrievably divided, and finding its missing half, the grandmother in flesh and blood, can only make the divide palpable; the impalpable ghost does not vanish but invades the living, he himself a stranger in the presence of a strange woman.

> I who had never seen her save in my own soul, always in the same place in the past, through the transparency of contiguous and overlapping memories, suddenly in our drawing-room which formed part of a new world, that of Time, . . . for the first time and for a moment only, since she vanished very quickly, I saw, sitting on the sofa beneath the lamp, red-faced, heavy and vulgar, sick, day-dreaming, letting her slightly crazed eyes wander over a book, an overburdened old woman whom I did not know. (ibid., p. 426)

The voice filled him with yearning to rush back and to embrace the body from which it emanated, but all he could find in its place was an old woman he did not know.

Among the new media it is, perhaps surprisingly, the cinema which has opened a whole new realm of experiencing the uncanny nature of the acousmatic voice. Surprisingly, because the cinema is based on fitting sight to sound, bringing together both halves, re-creating the seamless flow of the visible and the audible, but in the very endeavor to make them tally it appears that, at immutable margins, they do not fit. Michel Chion's insightful book *La voix au cinéma* (1982) has made us acutely aware of this. The acousmatic voice in cinema is not simply the voice whose source is outside the field of vision, like the "objective" commentator's voice or the "subjective" narrator's voice—those two function rather as directions for watching, guidelines for the gaze, an interpretation of what we see. They are never as innocent as they may seem; they can cheat and delude us, they can be subjected to a number of sophisticated uses, but this is a different problem. The acousmatic voice proper is the one which we cannot locate, and its paradigm is the mother's voice in *Psycho*. It is paradigmatic, for "the mother of all acousmatic voices" is precisely the mother's voice, by definition the acousmatic voice *par excellence*, the voice whose source the infant cannot see—his tie with the world, his umbilical cord, his prison, his light. Which body does it emanate from? *Psycho* offers a drastic and unsettling answer, but its gruesome extreme (a far cry from Proust's delicacy) points to a crack, and gives us an inkling that the acousmatic voice can never be simply pinned down to this particular woman.

Some cinematic examples use the acousmatic power of the telephone. Think of *When a Stranger Calls* (Fred Walton, 1979), where an anonymous threatening phone call can suddenly change the entire familiar domestic set-up, and populate it with hidden forces. The source of the voice can be anywhere—indeed, "when a stranger calls," as the title most economically indicates, everything changes immediately and radically, the home is seized by *Unheimlichkeit*, and as in this film, the stranger, of course, always calls from inside the house: the invisible source is closest, and the home cannot be a home until the source of the voice is disclosed.

The screen which conceals the voice disturbs our peace of mind, it forces us mentally to step onto the other side. "Pythagoras' curtain doesn't suffice to divert our curiosity, which is instinctively, almost unstoppably occupied by what lies behind" (Schaeffer 1966, p. 184). The situation seems to repeat the famous Hegelian parable about the curtain which conceals the interiority of appearances and behind which we must step—not only in order to see what lies behind, but in order for something to be seen there, namely ourselves stepping behind the curtain.[5] So with the acousmatic voice we have "always-already" stepped behind the screen and encircled the enigmatic object with fantasy. The voice behind the screen not only fuels our curiosity, but also implies a certain disavowal epitomized by the formula "I know very well, but nevertheless. . . ."[6] "I know very well that the voice must have some natural and explicable cause, but neverthe-less I believe it is endowed with mystery and secret power." It taunts and troubles us, against our better judgment. It presents a puzzling causality, as an effect without a proper cause. "The acousmatic situa-tion . . . entails that the idea of the cause seizes us and haunts us" (Chion 1998, p. 201). And we could argue that the efficacy of the acousmatic mechanism pertains precisely to the basic quality of the voice we have encountered from the outset: it always displays some-thing of an effect emancipated from its cause. There is a gap between its source and its auditory result, which can never be quite bridged.[7] This is also the point which should serve as a reminder that the methodological isolation of the voice in which we engage for partic-ular purposes is always a simplification: the object voice emerges in counterpoint with the visible and the visual, it cannot be disentangled from the gaze which offers its framework, so that both the gaze and the voice appear as objects in the gaps as a result of which they never quite match.

The real problem with the acousmatic voice is: can we actually ever pin it down to a source? This is the process that Chion calls dis-acousmatization, the process of dissipating the mystery. When the voice gets attached to the body, it loses its omnipotent charismatic character—it turns out to be banal, as in The Wizard of Oz. The aura crumbles, the voice, once located, loses its fascination and power, it has something like castrating effects on its bearer, who could wield and brandish his or her phonic phallus as long as its attachment to a body remained hidden. We may well wonder what kind of effect Pythagoras' appearance in the flesh could have had on the hapless dis-ciples who had spent five years in awe of his voice behind the curtain. We can well surmise that it was not unlike the scene in The Wizard of Oz:

> Toto . . . tipped over the screen that stood in a corner. As it fell with a crash they looked that way, and the next moment all of them were filled with wonder. For they saw, standing in just the spot the screen had hidden, a little old man, with a bald head and a wrinkled face, who seemed to be as much surprised as they were. The Tin Woodman, raising his axe, rushed towards the little man and cried out, "Who are

you?" "I am Oz, the Great and Terrible," said the little man in a trembling voice, "but don't strike me—please don't—and I'll do anything you want me to." (Baum 1995, p. 111)

It may well be that, once the lifted screen uncovered a pitiable old man, the disciples' main concern was to maintain the illusion, so that the disillusionment which they must have experienced did not affect the big Other. Another screen had to be raised to prevent the big Other from seeing what they saw, and this second veil entailed a dividing line between the initiated and the uninitiated. Perhaps it is no coincidence that the Pythagorean school was the first to institute the division into esoteric and exoteric knowledge, the esoteric being reserved for those who had seen the Master, and the exoteric for those who knew his teachings merely by his voice, so that the line concerned not the doctrine itself, only its form. Does not the term esoteric imply maintaining the veil after the veil has been lifted?

On another level, the terrorizing murderous stranger in *When a Stranger Calls* turns out to be a trivial, broken and desperate creature the moment he ceases to be the threatening presence surmised on the other end of the line, and we see words coming out of his mouth. Just like, I suppose, any anonymous poison-tongue caller when he or she is found out.

Chion compares the disacousmatization to striptease: it can be a process of several stages, the veils can be lifted one after another; one can, for example, see the bearer of the voice first from a distance, or from the back, or in a number of ambiguous situations; there can be hiatuses and red herrings (for instance, magisterially in *Psycho*, where several times we almost believe we have seen the elusive source of the voice). The ultimate stage is finally reached when one actually sees the orifice, the bodily aperture, from which the voice is coming, the mouth. That is: when one sees the gap, the crack, the hole, the cavity, the void, the very absence of phallus, just as in Freud's famous scenario. This is how Freud accounted for fetishism: one stops at the last-but-one stage, just before the void becomes apparent, thus turning this penultimate stage into a fetish, erecting it as a dam against castration, a rampart against the void.[8] In this light we can grasp the whole problem of the fetishism of the voice, which fixes the object at the penultimate stage, just before confronting the impossible fissure from which it is supposed to emanate, the slit from which it allegedly originates, before being engulfed by it. The voice as a fetish object consolidates on the verge of the void.

One of the emblematic images of modernism is Munch's *The Scream* (1893). It has been subjected to many illustrious analyses, and I can only add a footnote here: we see the void, the orifice, the abyss, but with no fetish to protect us or to hold on to. Many interpreters (including Munch himself) have seen the distorted landscape in the background as the effect of the scream spreading through nature, but we could also read it in the opposite direction: as the landscape which eddies into the black hole of the mouth, as if the scream would suck the background into the orifice, contract it instead of expanding through it. The painted scream is by definition mute, stuck in the throat; the black opening is without the voice which would mollify it, fill it, endow it with sense, hence its resonance is all the greater. Not only are we unable to hear the scream, it is also the homunculus, the strange screaming creature, the alien, who cannot hear us; he/she/it has no ears, he/she/it cannot reach anybody by the scream, nor can he/she/it be reached. If disacousmatization posed the problem of pinning down the voice whose source is hidden, here we have the opposite problem: a source of voice to which no voice can be assigned, but which for that very reason represents the voice all the more. Munch's picture should perhaps be related to Schönberg's opera *Erwartung* (1908)—perhaps we can hear the creature scream in the cry of the hysterical woman in the middle of the night, in that antivoice, in Schönberg's attempt to deprive the voice of its fetish aura.[9] From the one and the other, from the hidden link between the two, there follows the whole program of modernism: it hinges on the tenet that *there must be an object other than the fetish*. We can recall that one of the modernist manifestos was Adorno's famous paper "Über den Fetischcharacter in der Musik und die Regression des Hörens" (1938, later included in *Dissonanzen*, 1956): "On the fetish character in music and the regression of hearing."

Voice as doodle

From all this we must draw a paradoxical conclusion: ultimately, *there is no such thing as disacousmatization*. The source of the voice can never be seen, it stems from an undisclosed and structurally concealed interior, it cannot possibly match what we can see. This conclusion may seem extraordinary, but it can be related even to banal everyday experience: there is always something totally incongruous in the relation between the appearance, the aspect, of a person and his or her voice, before we adapt to it. It is absurd, this voice cannot possibly stem from this body, it doesn't sound like this person at all, or this person doesn't look at all like his or her voice. Every emission of the voice is by its very essence *ventriloquism*. Ventriloquism pertains to voice as such, to its inherently acousmatic character: the voice comes from inside the body, the belly, the stomach—from something incompatible with and irreducible to the activity of the mouth. The fact that we see the aperture does not demystify the voice; on the contrary, it enhances the enigma.

> An unbridgeable gap separates forever a human body from "its" voice. The voice displays a spectral autonomy, it never quite belongs to the body we see, so that even when we see a living person talking, there is always a minimum of ventriloquism at work: it is as if the speaker's own voice hollows him out and in a sense speaks "by itself," through him. (Žižek 2001b, p. 58)

Ventriloquists usually display their art by holding a puppet, a doll, a dummy, which is supposed to be the origin of the voice (remember Michael Redgrave in *Dead of Night?*). They offer a dummy location for the voice which cannot be located, a hold for disacousmatization. But suppose that we are ourselves the dummy (the Turkish puppet?), while the voice is the dwarf, the hunchback hidden in our entrails?

So the voice as the object appears precisely with the impossibility of disacousmatization. It is not the haunting voice impossible to pin down to a source; rather, it appears in the void from which it is supposed to stem but which it does not fit, an effect without a proper cause.[10] In a curious bodily topology, it is like a bodily missile which separates itself from the body and spreads around, but on the other hand it points to a bodily interior, an intimate partition of the body which cannot be disclosed—as if the voice were the very principle of division into interior and exterior. The voice, by being so ephemeral, transient, incorporeal, ethereal, presents for that very reason the body at its quintessential, the hidden bodily treasure beyond the visible envelope, the interior "real" body, unique and intimate, and at the same time it seems to present more than the mere body—in many languages there is an etymological link between spirit and breath (breath being the "voiceless voice," the zero point of vocal emission); the voice carried by breath points to the soul irreducible to the body. One could use a French pun, and say that the voice is *plus-de-corps*: both the surplus of the body, a bodily excess, and the no-more-body, the end of the corporeal, the spirituality of the corporeal, so that it embodies the very coincidence of the quintessential corporeality and the soul. The voice is the flesh of the soul, its ineradicable materiality, by which the soul can never be rid of the body; it depends on this inner object which is but the ineffaceable trace of externality and heterogeneity, but by virtue of which the body can also never quite simply be the body, it is a truncated body, a body cloven by the impossible rift between an interior and an exterior. The voice embodies the very impossibility of this division, and acts as its operator.

THE VOICE AND THE DRIVE

How can we relate the bodily topology of the voice to our initial thread, the antinomy of meaning and the voice as the antinomy between the signifier and the object? It is here that we must make use of the "classical" psychoanalytic divide between desire and drive, and attempt to treat the voice as the object of the drive. It is as if, in one and the same place, we had two mechanisms: one which strives toward meaning and understanding, and on the way obfuscates the voice (that which is not the matter of understanding), and on the other hand a mechanism which has nothing to do with meaning but, rather, with enjoyment. Meaning versus enjoyment. It is an enjoyment normally streamlined by meaning, steered by meaning, framed by meaning, and only when it becomes divorced from meaning can it appear as the pivotal object of drive.

To put it schematically, in every utterance there is on the one hand the dimension of signification, which in the last instance concurs with the dimension of desire. It is true, of course, that desire exceeds meaning, it is like a negative force which cannot be stabilized in any fixed meaning. This is where Freud, in *The Interpretation of Dreams,* pinpointed the dream as the paramount wish-fulfillment, *Wunscherfüllung,* the satisfaction of desire precisely in what apparently runs counter to signification, but actually accomplishes its course; where the "nonsense" of dreams lays bare the signifying mechanism. The solution of the riddle of dreams is the satisfaction of desire tied to the signifier. On the other hand there is the dimension of the drive which does not follow the signifying logic but, rather, turns around the object, the object voice, as something evasive and not conducive to signification. So that in every spoken utterance one could see a miniature drama, a contest, a diminished model of what psychoanalysis has tried to conceive as the rival dimensions of desire and drive.

In desire, we have the fireworks of what Lacan has notoriously called "the unconscious structured like a language"; but the drive, Freud dixit, is silent—insofar as it turns around the object voice, it is a voice that does not speak, and it *is not at all structured like a language.* Desire is what drives the scream to articulation, it emerges in its function of appeal to the other, it is another name for the dialectic between the subject and the other—and Lacan entitled one of his most famous écrits "The subversion of the subject and the dialectic of desire." The negativity of desire is the lever of transubstantiation of the voice into the signifier, the principle which propels the meaning which is, by definition, addressed to the other, but desire itself, being the driving force, can never itself be exhausted by any meaning. The object voice, on the other hand, is the by-product of this operation, its side-result that the drive gets hold of, circling around it, coming back to the same place in a movement of repetition. If the subject, the desire, and the other are intertwined in a dialectical movement, then the voice is their "non-dialectical" moment.

The voice ties language to the body, but the nature of this tie is paradoxical: *the voice does not belong to either.* It is not part of linguistics, which follows from my initial argument (after all, Saussure himself spoke of the non-phonic nature of the signifier; Derrida will insist on this at great length in *Grammatology*), but it is not part of the body either— not only does it detach itself from the body and leave it behind, it does not fit the body either, it cannot be situated in it, "disacousmatized." It floats, and the floating voice is a much more immediately striking phenomenon than the floating signifier, *le signifiant flottant*, which has caused so much ink to flow. It is a bodily missile which has detached itself from its source, emancipated itself, yet remains corporeal. This is the property which it shares with all the objects of the drive: they are all situated in a realm which exceeds the body, they prolong the body like an excrescence, but they are not simply outside the body either. So the voice stands at a paradoxical and ambiguous topological spot, at the intersection of language and the body, but this intersection belongs to neither. *What language and the body have in common is the voice, but the voice is part neither of language nor of the body.* The voice stems from the body, but is not its part, and it upholds language without belonging to it, yet, in this paradoxical topology, this is the only point they share—and this is the topology of *objet petit a*. This is where we could put Lacan's pet scheme of the intersection of two circles to use in a new application: the circle of language and the circle of the body, their intersection being extimate to both.

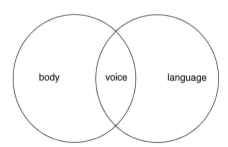

In order to conceive the voice as the object of the drive, we must divorce it from the empirical voices that can be heard. Inside the heard voices is an unheard voice, an aphonic voice, as it were. For what

Lacan called *objet petit a*—to put it simply—does not coincide with any existing thing, although it is always evoked only by bits of materiality, attached to them as an invisible, inaudible appendage, yet not amalgamated with them: it is both evoked and covered, enveloped by them, for "in itself" it is just a void. So sonority both evokes and conceals the voice; the voice is not somewhere else, but it does not coincide with voices that are heard.

We could use the distinction between *aim* and *goal* that Lacan introduces to explain the mechanism of the drive: the drive reaches its aim without attaining its goal, its arrow comes back from the target like a boomerang. The drive is satisfied through being thwarted, without attaining its end; it is "inhibited in its goal," *zielgehemmt*, says Freud (PFL 11, p. 119); nevertheless it does not miss its aim; its path to the goal is curved onto itself, it encircles its object—the aim is merely the path taken, and the drive is entirely "on the way."[11] So if the goal of the utterance is the production of meaning, then the voice, the mere instrument, is the aim attained on the way, the by-product of the way to the goal, the object around which the drive turns; the side-satisfaction, but one which suffices to fuel all the machinery.[12]

HIS MASTER'S VOICE, HIS MASTER'S EAR

Let us consider the HMV label, one of the most successful logos in the history of advertising, the logo which has stuck in the collective memory as one of the emblematic labels of the past century, instantly recognizable by everyone. Its creation is surrounded by a saga:[13] Nipper, the dog in the picture, was born in 1884 and so named because of his tendency to nip the backs of visitors' legs. When his first master, Mark Barraud, died destitute in Bristol in 1887, Nipper was taken to Liverpool by Mark's younger brother Francis, a painter. Liverpool was the place where the most important event in this dog's life happened: he discovered the recently invented phonograph, and Francis Barraud "often noticed how puzzled he was to make out where the voice came from." Three years after Nipper died (in 1895, the year of Freud's and Breuer's *Studies on Hysteria*), he committed this scene to canvas. Barraud completed the painting in 1898 and registered it in 1899, first as "Dog Looking at and Listening to a Phonograph"; he then decided to rename it "His Master's Voice," and tried to exhibit it at the Royal Academy, but was turned down. He had no better luck with magazines— "No one would know what the dog was doing," was given as the reason. Next he tried the Edison Bell Company, the leading manufacturer of the cylinder phonograph, but again without success. "Dogs don't listen to phonographs," the company said. He finally struck luck with the newly formed Gramophone and Typewriter Company, which showed interest on condition that he replace the Edison phonograph in the picture with one of their own products. The deal was finally agreed in September 1899, and the painting made its first public appearance on the Gramophone and Typewriter Company's advertising literature in January 1900 (coinciding with the publication of *The Interpretation of Dreams*, both inaugurating the new century). The painting and title were finally registered as a trademark in 1910.

Francis Barraud was a man of one picture, like Thomas Aquinas's man of one book, *homo unius libri*. He spent much of the rest of his working life painting twenty-four replicas of his original. He died in 1924, the impoverished artist succeeding with a vengeance. Throughout the century, the "His Master's Voice" label has enjoyed a unique reputation with both the music business and the public. Over the years a large market developed in collecting the vast array of items produced in its image, so that *A Collectors' Guide*, published in 1984 and updated in 1997, is a bulky volume. It is now used only by EMI as the marketing identity for HMV shops in Europe, and the original is displayed in the EMI headquarters in Grosvenor Square, London.

Why is this image of interest to us? What lessons can be drawn from it?

First of all, the dog exhibits the emblematic posture of listening; he is placed in an exemplary attitude of dog-like obedience which pertains to the very act of listening. Listening entails obeying; there is a strong etymological link between the two in many languages: to obey, obedience, stems from French *obéir*, which in turn stems from Latin *ob-audire*, derivative of *audire*, to hear; in German *gehorchen*, *Gehorsam* stem 'from *hören*; in many Slav languages *slušati* can mean both to listen and to obey; the same goes apparently for Arabic, and so on. Etymology offers a hint of an inherent tie: listening is "always-already" incipient obedience; the moment one listens one has already started to obey, in an embryonic way one always listens to one's master's voice, no matter how much one opposes it afterward. There is something in the very nature of the voice which endows it with master-like authority (which lends itself perfectly to many political uses; we will come back to that). And the dog, in the phantasmatics of our culture, is the ideal embodiment of listening and obedience.

The picture's problem is how to paint the voice, and it solves it brilliantly with a montage. It leaves out the level of using the voice for "intersubjective communication"; it makes the voice appear in its object-like quality by assembling together the animal and the machine, short-circuiting humanity. It could be seen as a peculiar counterpoint to Munch's *The Scream* (painted five years earlier—should one write "*Munch avec Barraud*"?): Munch's picture focuses on the human voice, but in its impossibility of communication, of reaching the other; while Barraud's picture presents a "successful communication," with the caveat that it pertains to the communion of animals and machines. Human communication may not be possible any longer, according to the vulgate of the reception of Munch's picture, but the other one works, at least in one way: the message is triumphantly transmitted to the hapless dog. The object emerges in the very disparity of technology and animality, in the juxtaposition, the montage of the two. And this is precisely how Lacan describes the drive—as a montage, something contrived, not grounded in some natural order or instinct; a montage without finality, seeming to have neither head nor tail, like a surrealist collage.

> If we bring together the paradoxes that we just defined at the level of *Drang*, at that of the object, at that of the aim of the drive, I think that the resulting image would show the working of a dynamo connected up to a gas-tap, a peacock's feather emerges, and tickles the belly of a pretty woman, who is just lying there looking beautiful. (Lacan 1979, p. 169)

The montage of the dog and the phonograph with its absurd cylinder (is there an invisible peacock's feather protruding from it and tickling the dog's ears?) could be seen as the embodiment of such a montage. The drive always functions as this absurd alliance between animality and machinality: they don't fit, but it works nevertheless.

What is the purpose of the painting, its striking advertising value? It demonstrates rather forcefully that this new wonder, the gramophone, works—even the dog is deceived. The sound is so realistic that even animals are taken in. The high fidelity of the sound finds its perfect match in the high fidelity of the dog. The dog doesn't see the source of the voice, he is puzzled and staring into the mysterious orifice, but he believes—he believes all the more for not seeing the source; the acousmatic master is more of a master than his banal visible versions.

So there is the question of deception that exactly matches Lacan's use of the parable of the contest between the two painters:

> In the classical tale of Zeuxis and Parrhasios, Zeuxis has the advantage of having made grapes that attracted the birds. The stress is placed not on the fact that these grapes were in any way perfect grapes, but on the fact that even the eye of the birds was taken in by them. This is proved by the fact that his friend Parrhasios triumphs over him for having painted on the wall a veil, a veil so lifelike that Zeuxis, turning toward him, said, *Well, and now show us what you have painted behind* it. By this he showed that what was at issue was certainly deceiving the eye [*tromper l'œil*]. A triumph of the gaze over the eye. (Lacan 1979, p. 103)[14]

There are two opposed strategies of deception: the birds are duped by looks, the animals are deceived by the appearance of reality; while the humans are deceived by the veil which does not merely imitate reality, but conceals it. The properly human way of deception is the lure; the deception lies in the fact that the gaze has been enticed to penetrate behind the veil of appearance—in a paramount Hegelian moment, for there is nothing behind the curtain except the subject himself who has been lured behind. The gaze has already pierced the veil and entered what cannot be seen; it was duped by taking a step behind the appearances. And we have already seen that the acousmatic

Voice / Gaze

Voice (Sure?)

voice has an analogous structure—one is duped by the voice behind the screen by not seeing its source, one is troubled by the enigma of its cause. The acousmatic voice combines the two levels, the voice and the gaze, for the voice, as opposed to the gaze, does not conceal, it is given in a seeming immediacy and immediately penetrates interiority, it cannot be quite held at bay. Thus the deception lies in the inability to find its match in the visible, in the gap which always persists between the two, in the impossibility of their coordination, so that *the visible as such can start to function as the veil of the voice.*

The gramophone in our picture—is it the grapes or the veil? It deceives the dog by being the "authentic reproduction," the genuine appearance of the voice; the dog obeys as the birds pick the grapes. But at the same time, the gramophone is the veil, it hides the source of the voice, and the dog is taken in by the reproduction all the more since its source is disguised. All his senses try to figure out what is behind the screen, so he starts on the animal level and is humanized, as it were, by the deception; he has to learn the lesson that the voice is an acousmatic creature (irretrievably acousmatic, not just of a not-yet-discovered origin). The picture presents a sort of intersection, an overlapping of the two levels, or the necessary crossing of the one into the other. *Trompe-l'oreille*—one has always-already started to listen behind the veil, the nature of the voice is that of being veiled by the visible. We could see, in this montage, a sort of parable of the drive: the dog starts on the animal level, in the realm of the need aiming directly at reality as the place of satisfaction, but he stumbles on a paradox, a veiling or redoubling of reality itself, and finds unexpected satisfaction in an ersatz object irreducible to the veil of reality.

The HMV label presents one side of the voice, the voice as authority, in an emblematic image. This power of the voice stems from the fact that it is so hard to keep it at bay—it hits us from the inside, it pours *water* directly into the interior, without protection. The ears have no lids, as Lacan never tires of repeating; they cannot be closed, one is constantly exposed, no distance from sound can be maintained. There is a stark

opposition between the visible and the audible: the visible world
presents relative stability, permanence, distinctiveness, and a location
at a distance; the audible presents fluidity, passing, a certain inchoate,
amorphous character, and a lack of distance. The voice is elusive, always changing, becoming, elapsing, with unclear contours, as opposed to the relative permanence, solidity, durability of the seen. One
could say it is by its nature on the side of the event, not of being, in
Badiou's parlance. It deprives us of distance and autonomy. If we want
to localize it, to establish a safety distance from it, we need to use the
visible as the reference. The visible can establish the distance, the nature, and the source of the voice, and thus neutralize it. The acousmatic voice is so powerful because it cannot be neutralized with the
framework of the visible, and it makes the visible itself redoubled and
enigmatic. This immediate connection between the exterior and the
interior in the voice is the source of all the mythical stories of the
magic force of enthralling voices (Sirens), something that makes us
lose reason and easily leads to disaster, to a lethal enjoyment. And this
is also where the mechanism of psychosis, "hearing voices," uses,
takes on, only the hallucinatory trait which pertains to the voice itself.
Voices may be all in the head, without an external source, because we
always hear the voice inside the head, and the nature of its external
source is always uncertain the moment we close our eyes.

I must briefly add that if the logic of vision seems opposed to the
logic of audition, if the visible appears to be on the side of distance
and stability, then Lacan's theory of the gaze as an object aims precisely at dissipating this spontaneous illusion, at collapsing this distance of the eye from what is seen, this exception of the spectator
from the picture. "The scission of the eye and the gaze," as the section
dealing with the gaze is called in *Seminar XI*, means precisely that the
gaze is the point where the distance crumbles, where the gaze is itself
inscribed into the picture, as the point where the image "regards" us,
looks back at us (Lacan 1979, pp. 95 f.). The illusion of distance has to
be unmasked as an illusion, while with the voice the problem tends
to be the opposite: how to establish a distance at all, to draw the dividing line between "the interior" and the external world. Where

does the voice come from? Where do we hear it? How do we tell the external voice from the voice in the head? This is the first ontological decision, the first epistemological break, the source of all subsequent ontology and epistemology.

But all this is one side of the ambivalence; the voice as authority is one part of the story. On the other hand it is also true that the sender of the voice, the bearer of vocal emission, is someone who exposes himself, and thus becomes exposed to the effects of power which not only lie in the privilege of emitting the voice, but pertain to the listener. The subject is exposed to the power of the other by giving his or her own voice, so that the power, domination, can take not only the form of the commanding voice, but that of the ear. The voice comes from some unfathomable invisible interior and brings it out, lays it bare, discloses, uncovers, reveals that interior. By so doing it produces an effect which has both an obscene side (disclosing something hidden, intimate, revealing too much, structurally too much) and an uncanny side—this is how Freud, following Schelling, described the uncanny: something that "ought to have remained . . . secret and hidden but has come to light" (PFL 14, p. 345). One could indeed say that there is an effect—or, rather, an affect—of shame that accompanies voice: one is ashamed of using one's voice because it exposes some hidden intimacy to the Other, there is a shame which pertains not to psychology, but to structure.[15] What is exposed, of course, is not some interior nature, an interior treasure too precious to be disclosed, or some true self, or a primordial inner life; rather, it is an interior which is itself the result of the signifying cut, its product, its cumbersome remainder, an interior created by the intervention of the structure. So by using one's voice one is also "always-already" yielding power to the Other; the silent listener has the power to decide over the fate of the voice and its sender; the listener can rule over its meaning, or turn a deaf ear. The trembling voice is a plea for mercy, for sympathy, for understanding, and it is in the power of the listener to grant it or not.

The voice cuts both ways: as an authority over the Other and as an exposure to the Other, an appeal, a plea, an attempt to bend the Other.[16] It cuts directly into the interior, so much so that the very status of the exterior becomes uncertain, and it directly discloses the interior, so much so that the very supposition of an interior depends on the voice. So both hearing and emitting a voice present an excess, a surplus of authority on the one hand and a surplus of exposure on the other. There is a too-much of the voice in the exterior because of the direct transition into the interior, without defenses; and there is a too-much of the voice stemming from the inside—it brings out more, and other things, than one would intend. *One is too exposed to the voice and the voice exposes too much*, one incorporates and one expels too much.

There is a constitutive asymmetry in the voice, an asymmetry between the voice stemming from the Other and one's own voice. Incorporating the voice of the Other is essential if one is to learn to speak; for the acquisition of language depends not simply on emulating the signifiers, but crucially consists in incorporating the voice. The voice is the excess of the signifier, initially displayed as the excess of the demand of the Other, the demand beyond any particular demands, demand as such, and at the same time the demand put to the Other, the two encompassing the asymmetry of emission and exposure.[17] So the voice presents at its clearest the mechanism of the object of the drive, its topology, its topological paradox. All the objects of the drive function precisely through the mechanism of—excessive—incorporation and expulsion (hence the opposition between the breast and the feces) and are thus, first, extra-corporeal, non-corporeal "supplements" of the body (hence Lacan's myth of the lamella: 1979, pp. 197 f.), and, second, they are the very operators of the division into an exterior and an interior, while in themselves they do not belong to either, they are placed in the zone of overlapping, the crossing, the extimate.

CHAPTER 4

THE ETHICS OF THE VOICE

A long tradition of reflections on ethics has taken as its guideline *the voice of conscience*. If the first spontaneous understanding of voice as the medium of speech is omnipresent and trivial, then this second one is not uncommon either. There is a widespread figure of speech (but is there anything else in speech but figures?), a metaphor (*idem*), which associates voice and conscience. We should pause at the extraordinary fact that ethics has so often been associated with the voice, that the voice has been the guiding trope of reflections on moral questions, both in popular reasoning and in the grand philosophical tradition. Is this internal voice of a moral injunction, the voice which issues warnings, commands, admonishments, the voice which cannot be silenced if one has acted wrongly, simply a metaphor? Is it the voice that one actually hears, or is the internal voice still a voice, or is a voice that has no empirical manifestation perhaps the voice in the proper sense, closer to the voice than the sounds one can physically hear? And why the voice? Its metaphoricity has uncertain edges. Is the external voice literal and the internal one metaphorical? But perhaps this is *the* metaphor which constitutes internality and consciousness, so that the very notion of the literal/external depends on taking this metaphor literally. What is the tenuous and tenacious connection between voice and conscience? Is ethics about hearing voices? Given the link between conscience and consciousness (both are modes of *con-scio*), is consciousness about hearing voices? If I have boldly attempted a brief history of metaphysics through the spyglass of the voice, let me add insult to injury and attempt a brief history of ethics in the same vein.[1]

THE VOICE OF THE DAEMON

At the origin of this history is the best-known of all internal voices, the Socratic voice, the daemon which accompanies Socrates throughout his life. In a very famous passage from *Apology*, Socrates says in his defense in front of the tribunal:

> I have a divine or spiritual sign which Meletus has ridiculed in his deposition. This began when I was a child. It is a voice, and whenever it speaks it turns me away from something I am about to do, but it never

encourages me to do anything. This is what has prevented me from taking part in public affairs, and I think it was quite right to prevent me. (Plato 1997, *Apology*, 31d)

The voice, this daemon, is like Socrates' shadow, or his guardian angel (and it seems that the very figure of the guardian angel in Christianity stems from Saint Augustine's reading of Socrates). The quote is short, yet in it we can discern five points that serve our purpose:

1. The origin of this voice is supposed to be divine and supernatural, it comes from beyond, yet it dwells in the innermost realms of Socrates' consciousness, the most intimate and simultaneously the most transcendent. It is an "atopical voice," the intersection of the inner and the outer.

2. It is not a prescriptive voice, not a voice telling Socrates what to do; he has to decide that for himself. It merely dissuades him from certain actions, preventing him from doing wrong, but not advising him how to do good. The voice has a negative, apotreptic function, and for this reason it has a close connection to the Socratic stance in philosophy: this is precisely the stance which Socrates adopts in relation to his many interlocutors; he relates to them, at least in principle, in the same way that the daemon relates to him. He does not proffer advice or positive theories, he only dissuades them from bad ways of thinking, from received opinion, not thrusting his own views upon them; he does not offer ready-made answers (although this basic attitude tends to get blurred the moment it is put into practice). His own function in relation to others is apotreptic; he simply wants to open the ways of philosophy to others, just as the daemon has done for him, and in order to achieve this he adopts the posture of his daemon and emulates its strategy. He turns into the champion of the voice which was given him beyond his will or intention; his role is to become its agent.[2]

3. It is a voice with which one cannot argue; it is not a matter of weighing the pros and cons. The voice is always right, but not on the basis of logical argument—ultimately, it is not a matter of *logos* at all.

4. The daemon is not a universal function which would pertain to all, to humanity as such; it belongs to Socrates as the mark of his dis-

tinction, it is his special link to divinity, but one which defines his mission in philosophy: to make it universally available, to turn it into an appeal, a call for philosophy, an opening to universalization.

5. In what follows our quote, it transpires that this voice actually dissuaded Socrates from taking part in active political life: the voice pertains to the moral law as opposed to the positive written laws of the community; the voice is sustained by "the unwritten law." (This divide is vividly enacted in *Antigone*, with the division between the divine unwritten laws and the human laws of the *polis*.) We could also see here in a nutshell what Kant will call, a couple of millennia later, the opposition between morality and legality. This division hinges on a certain understanding of the divide between the voice and the letter, where morality is conceived as a matter of the voice and legality as a matter of the letter.

Socrates is a creature of the voice. It is not only that he comitted nothing to writing, so that his revolution in thought was supported merely by the voice, the voice which vanished without trace, as voices do, but keeps reverberating through the history of philosophy, his act of thought being sustained merely by the voice divorced from the letter; it is also that this support in the voice itself takes support from his inner voice, his daemon, of which he was merely the agent.

This Socratic theme will be taken up by a whole tradition, although often in ways that differ greatly from the source: the voice of concience started to function as the firm guide in ethical matters, the bearer of moral injunctions and commands, the imperative inner voice, inescapable and compelling in its immediacy and overwhelming presence, a voice one cannot silence or deny—should one do so, a disaster is certain to follow. It is a voice which circumvents all discursive argument and offers firm ground for moral judgment beyond discursivity, beyond the intricacies of deductions, justifications, and deliberations. Its allegedly infallible authority stems from beyond *logos*.

We can see this mechanism, perhaps at its purest, in that part of *Émile* that Rousseau has entitled "La profession de foi du Vicaire savoyard,"

"The profession of faith of the Savoy vicar" (Rousseau 1969, pp. 565–606), which embodies for him the sound, firm, and astute basis of morality. In the Savoy vicar Rousseau found his own private Socrates, a man of no written work, supported by mere voice and following his own inner voice. The core of true nature in this supposed embodiment of natural reason is nothing but "the immortal and celestial voice," "the sacred voice of nature," "the interior voice" which is "infallible" (ibid., pp. 598 ff.):

> Conscience! Conscience! Divine instinct, immortal and celestial voice; firm guide of an ignorant and limited being, but one which is also intelligent and free; the infallible judge of good and evil, it is you that make man similar to God; it is you that make out the excellence of his nature and the morality of his actions; without you I do not sense anything in myself which would elevate me above the beasts, just the sad privilege to stray from error to error with the help of an intelligence [*entendement*] without a rule and a reason without a principle. (Rousseau 1969, pp. 600–601)[3]

Human dignity cannot be defined by reason and understanding alone, for they merely lead us from error to error if they are not anchored in the voice as their guide and principle, the touch of the divine in the human being. The voice is the link with God, while reason and understanding on their own are deprived of the divine spark, they are simply the deplorable side of our privilege over animals. Other voices can try to tamper with this divine voice, "the shrill voice" of prejudice (ibid., p. 601), "the voice of the body" ("conscience is the voice of the soul, passions are the voice of the body," ibid., p. 594). It seems that human consciousness is a vocal affair, it is a struggle between voices (perhaps we could conceive it as an opera, something that was very dear to Rousseau), yet in this struggle the divine voice ultimately imposes itself, it gains the upper hand, the true voice against the false voices.[4] This voice is necessarily endowed with an immediate moral authority: however much we calculate and argue about morality, all this is groundless without a firm footing in the voice, its immediate intuition and the sentiment it carries.

Rousseau's position may seem terribly naive and simple, but it was deeply embedded on the one hand in the struggle which opposed the Enlightenment generation to the Church and the bearers of traditional authority, and on the other in the struggle at the heart of the Enlightenment itself, where Rousseau figured rather as an exception. He starkly opposed the more radical materialism and atheism, in particular Helvétius and his *De l'esprit* (1758), a book which was burned in February 1759 by a parliamentary decree because of its undiluted materialism and attack on Christianity (thus representing one of the emblematic ties between the spirit and fire that Derrida speaks about in his own *De l'esprit*, whose title is taken from Helvétius). Rousseau took the opposite stance of vigorously defending religion—for him there could be no virtue without religion, but of course the "natural religion," which in its turn entailed an equally vigorous criticism of the Church as an institution, its dogmas and its practices. But no matter how hard he tried, a few years later, in 1762, *Émile* would end up in flames as well, and Rousseau could escape arrest only by fleeing to Geneva.

The natural religion was an inner oracle, a pure spring of internal truth, while the Church was based on the idea of original sin, of man as a sinful being who needs constant surveillance and protection, constantly subject to suspicion—original sin was the tenet of Christianity which gave the Church license for permanent terror. Rousseau's religion, professed by the Savoy vicar, was belief in the God within, his unalloyed intimate presence epitomized by the voice. But from this follows a paradox which permeates *Émile*: in order for this inner voice to come to light, one has to be rid of all the sediment of corrupt social voices, of bad habits inherited from bad history. Émile, who was an orphan, had to be educated by the Teacher, and the main function of the Teacher was an apotreptic one: to protect poor Émile from all evil influences, to dissuade him from ingrained bad habits so that he could discover the inner voice for himself. So belief in the pure inner voice gave the Teacher an unmitigated mandate to terrorize the hapless child in a manner far worse than what the Church did, so that original purity and original sin entailed the same effect. The poor child is constantly exposed to surveillance and inspection, at the mercy of the Teacher. Émile should thus be led to the point where he would be able to authorize himself, independently of any outer authority, on the basis of his true inner nature, but the Teacher alone can decide what this true nature is, he is the only one who, in the clamor of voices, can tell the good ones from the innumerable host of false pretenders. The pure inner voice thus becomes inherently tied up with the overpowering presence of the Other.

THE VOICE OF REASON

It may seem strange, and rather symptomatic, that we can find this line of the voice in Kant also. Strange, because Kant, albeit a great admirer of his contemporary Rousseau, was at the opposite end of the spectrum in matters of ethics: firm ground can be provided only by the moral law, which, in its universality—or, rather, in its injunction to universalization—is purely formal. Every moral action should be submitted to the test of universality, and there seems to be no room for voices or moral feelings (indeed, Kant harshly criticized all attempts to ground morals on moral feelings). Ethics should be grounded in reason alone. We can contrast Rousseau's invocation of conscience quoted above with the Kant's invocation of duty:

> Duty! Thou sublime and mighty name that dost embrace nothing charming or insinuating but requirest submission and yet seekest not to move the will by threatening aught that would arouse natural aversion or terror, but only holdest forth a law which of itself finds entrance into the mind . . . : what origin is worthy of thee, and where is the root of thy noble descent which proudly rejects all kinship with the inclinations and from which to be descended is the indispensable condition of the only worth which men alone can give themselves? (Kant 1993, p. 90)

The rhetoric of invocation is the same, but its purpose is the opposite: duty as the moral law is the direct opposite of feeling, it is an injunction to cut all ties with the natural, inclinations, sentiments, the affections, the inner oracle:

But the concept of duty cannot be derived from [the moral sense], for we would have to presuppose a feeling for law as such and regard as an object of sensation what can only be thought by reason. . . . The moral law is, in fact, a law of causality through freedom and thus a law of the possibility of a supersensuous nature. . . . (ibid., pp. 40, 49)

And, last but not least, it entails cutting all ties to the divine—moral law pertains to reason alone and cannot have any other source, natural or supernatural. Yet a few pages earlier, we are surprised to find that even reason is endowed with a voice. While debating what appears to him as the monstrous proposal to promote one's own happiness as the supreme moral goal, Kant says that this principle would entirely destroy morality:

> were the voice of reason with respect to the will not so distinct, so irrepressible, and so clearly audible even for the commonest man [*die Stimme der Vernunft in Beziehung auf den Willen . . . so deutlich, so unüberschreibar* (literally "unovercryable"), *selbst für den gemeinsten Menschen so vernehmlich*], it would drive morality to ruin. (Kant 1993, p. 36)

The proponents of false morals can continue their confused speculations only if they plug their ears against that "heavenly voice [*himmlische Stimme*]" (ibid.).

So after the voice of the heart, the voice of nature, the divine voice, there is also the voice of reason, which, while silent, is nevertheless so loud that no matter how loudly we cry, we can never cover or silence it. Reason itself is endowed with the divine voice, it coincides with it—does Kant nevertheless follow Rousseau? Does he just "innocently" use a common metaphor inherited from tradition, or does he name a specific instance crucial to the functioning of reason? Crucial, although it should not be there in the first place? Is this the blind spot of Kantian reason? (Its unhearable cry?) In any case, with Kant the voice acquires a different form: for Socrates, the voice merely dissuaded him from doing wrong (and was reserved for Socrates' ears only); for Rousseau, the divine and natural (same thing) voice was the guide telling every human being how to act, a compass in every situation, provided one lent it an ear; while the Kantian voice does not command or prevent anything, it neither advises nor deters. It is merely a voice which demands, inexorably imposes, one thing alone: submission of the will to the rationality and formality of the moral law, the categorical imperative. The voice of reason is merely the injunction to submit to reason, it has no other content. It is a purely formal voice, the form of a voice, imposing pure formality, submission to form. Reason itself is powerless—something that Kant will develop at some length in *The Contest of Faculties* (1794),[5] where the whole argument will hinge on the postulate that the faculty of philosophy should be divorced from any lever of power, yet precisely as deprived of any ties to power it can rely on the power of reason, which will ultimately prevail. The advantage of the faculty of philosophy (as opposed to theology, law, and medicine) is that it autonomously pursues only the ends of knowledge and truth, and because it does not mingle with power, its power is overpowering: only the voice which is completely silent can "overcry" all other voices. The voice of reason, silent as it may be, is the power of the powerless, the mysterious force which compels us to follow reason. It is the power which emerges at the point of reduction of all other power. *The voice is the power of reason.*

The Kantian voice of reason is closely linked to the enigma of the subject of enunciation of the moral law—and here we rejoin the line of the voice as pure enunciation. Who is it that addresses us in the second person and admonishes us: "So act that the maxim of your will could always hold at the same time as the principle giving universal law" (Kant 1993, p. 30)? Who is the subject enunciating the categorical imperative? Which authority addresses everybody as "you" in an appeal which is both intimate and universal? The source of this demand obviously cannot reside in the subject; it speaks to us from a place that is unattainable for the subject, although it is the very locus of the subject's autonomy. Here we can argue that the subject of enunciation structurally coincides with the voice of reason, the voice whose origin cannot be determined. The innermost realm of consciousness stems from a place beyond consciousness, it is an atopical voice addressing us from inside, the interior *atopos*. Kant gives way to a long tradition by qualifying this voice as divine, since any evocation of divinity directly opposes his central ambition to pose a principle independent from any divine authority, and to cut all ties between ethics and theology.

A century and a half later, Freud, in a famous passage from *The Future of an Illusion* (1927), used the very same metaphor, and in a very Kantian context:

> We may insist as often as we like that man's intellect is powerless in comparison with his instinctual life [*Triebleben*], and we may be right in this. Nevertheless, there is something peculiar about this weakness. The voice of the intellect is a soft one, but it does not rest till it has gained a hearing. [*Die Stimme des Intellekts ist leise, aber sie ruht nicht, ehe sie sich Gehör geschafft hat.*] Finally, after a countless succession of rebuffs, it succeeds. This is one of the few points on which one may be optimistic about the future of mankind, but it is in itself a point of no small importance. And from it one can derive yet other hopes. The primacy of the intellect lies, it is true, in a distant, distant future, but probably not in an infinitely distant one. (PFL 12, p. 238)

So hopes for the future of mankind are again vested in the voice of reason, which, soft and quiet as it may be, will nevertheless gain the upper hand, and will ultimately get heard. The power of reason resides, again, in its voice, whose origin escapes us. In *The New Introductory Lectures* (1933), Freud does not shy away from an even more categorical and extreme formulation: "Our best hope for the future is that intellect—the scientific spirit, reason—may in process of time establish a dictatorship in the mental life of man [*die Diktatur im menschlichen Seelenleben*]" (PFL 2, p. 208).[6] So that soft powerless voice which one can barely hear emerges as the most improbable candidate for a dictatorship; its barely perceptible sound has all the makings of a future dictator. Democracy in psychic life seems to bode ill for the future of mankind and, rather, looms as detrimental.

Freud pits reason against the life of the drives (*Triebleben*) and opposes the two in a permanent conflict. The power of the drives seems to require no explanation; it appears to be self-evident, since drives are by definition forces exerting pressure. But where does the power of reason come from? On what force can reason rely in the battle against this most powerful of opponents, the indomitable and almighty power of the interplay of drives which always find a way, including the most unlikely and strenuous ways, to ensure their satisfaction? What force can we employ against the inexorable compulsion to repetition which drives the drives? Here Freud clearly bets on the underdog which, in the face of this formidable adversary, is endowed only with the tiny trickle of the voice. And a very soft and weak voice at that—not the blaring voice of the superego, which has no problems making itself heard. The voice of reason is not the voice of the superego, despite Freud's misleading assumption about the concurrence of the two, and it is not the voice of the subject (and his ego) either—but it is perhaps not unrelated to the unconscious. Indeed, Lacan is quick to make the connection:

> The voice of reason is low, Freud says somewhere, but it always says the same thing. The parallel hasn't been drawn to the effect that Freud says exactly the same thing about unconscious desire. Its voice, too, is low, but its insistence is indestructible. Perhaps there is a relation between the two. (Lacan 1979, p. 255; translation modified)

So the strange fate of Freudian reason would have to be linked to the unconscious. Reason is ambiguously described not simply in terms of the agency of repression, despite its purported dictatorial role, but rather in terms of the repressed: as that which will always make itself heard, however much we try to suppress it—it will get heard under the harshest of censorships, just like unconscious desire. Reason would be powerless if it did not have an ally in the unconscious, and its voice seems to be precisely the pivotal point which links the formality of intellect to the powers of the id, and welds them together. Can we not read an indication of this already in the very motto of *The Interpretation of Dreams*, taken from Virgil: *Flectere si nequeo superos, Acheronta movebo*?[7] Could we not bend its meaning in the sense that reason has to employ the infernal regions in order to get heard and to prevail? And that its tenuous link with hell is its voice?

So Freud, a century and a half later, continues Kant: the same faith in reason and its ultimate prevalence and the same reliance on its voice appear to be alive and well, even seemingly with increased self-confidence after a century and a half of steep and spectacular scientific progress and the general trust it inspired—but the quote about the dictatorship of reason is, ominously, from 1933, on the very brink of another kind of dictatorship,[8] and Freud's appeal to reason has rather the resonance of a desperate plea at a time when reason was spectacularly failing to prevail.

We must, of course, hasten to add that Freud uses the term *reason* in a definitely non-Kantian way, in a much wider and less precise sense: he includes it in a broader perspective of scientific progress and intellect as such, he uses it in the habitual common sense, whereas Kantian reason is beyond science—science is a matter for *Verstand*, understanding, not *Vernunft*, reason. Science is an affair of progress in knowledge, but reason is not, and practical reason, with its moral law, is situated in a realm beyond the possible reach of science—it concerns the non-sensual, the non-empirical. Still, both Kant and Freud share the common assumption of the voice of reason, along with its mysterious power of ultimately imposing itself and gaining a hearing against all odds. This enigmatic force has nothing to do with divinity, but it does have a paradoxical link with unconscious desire. Lacan, in another famous passage, even drew the radical conclusion that the two coincide: the Kantian categorical imperative, he says, is simply desire in its pure form.[9] Indeed, the nature of desire, as defined by psychoanalysis, is endowed with the unconditional character usually reserved for the law: it turns the unconditional of the demand into an "absolute condition" (Lacan 1989, p. 287); it introduces "an incommensurable measure, an infinite measure" (Lacan 1992, p. 316), the measure by which any object falls short and is deemed "pathological" in the Kantian sense of the word. Desire cannot bear compromise with any particular object, which is always experienced as "this is not it," in a process where desire runs into a permanent dissatisfaction. The ethics, as promulgated by Lacan in *The Ethics of Psychoanalysis*, is the ethics of insistence on desire, of desire as an uncompromising insistence. Hence the notorious maxim of this ethics: not to give way on one's desire: *ne pas céder sur son désir*.[10] If human psychic life has not quite yet reached the stage of the dictatorship of reason, it is not because subjects are swayed by desire instead of listening to reason— quite the contrary, they are swayed to yield on this maxim, they give way on their desire, they give up on reason because they do not persevere in their desire.

But if we follow this radical suggestion, then "reason according to Freud" would have to be divorced from simple reliance on human intellectual resources, scientific progress, and so on, and taken again in its circumscribed and restricted Kantian sense, where it would now appear in a new light: not as reason destined to tame the wild forces of the unconscious, but the reason of the unconscious desire itself. The locus of delusions and illusions (those that have a promising future, ideally held in check by the voice of reason, for Freud), as well as the locus of swaying, yielding, and compromises, would have to be situated in the ego, that is, in the authority usually held to be the site of reason; whereas reason tied to the unconscious—should we say "unconscious reason"?—could serve as an antidote to them.

So is the voice of reason, in this view, the voice of unconscious desire? Does desire have a voice, soft or loud? We will come back to that, but for the moment we could venture the following: the voice of (unconscious) reason in its persistence is perhaps not what would protect us from the irrationality of the drives but, quite the contrary, the lever which impels desire to the drive. We must remember that the "heroism of desire" (the heroism of the adage "not to give way on one's desire") is not Lacan's last word on ethical matters. Curiously, he never returned to it after the seminar on ethics (1959/60), and we find in his subsequent work a tendency to a demotion of desire: it is not to be found among "the four fundamental concepts of psychoanalysis," and we can read later in *Écrits*: "For desire is a defense, a prohibition against going beyond a certain limit in *jouissance*" (1989, p. 322). The heroism of desire would have to be abandoned for another principle, tentatively "from desire to drive." Schematically, the ethics of desire drives the subject to reject any compromise of finding satisfaction in any particular object; no object can measure up to desire and its negative force, every object has to be sacrificed in order to retain desire in its purity. But it is this very purity which functions as the defense and has to be sacrificed in its turn; the drive emerges when desire is driven to sacrifice not only its objects but its purity itself, and the voice is perhaps ultimately the operator which enables this transition.

Our brief history of the ethics of the voice finds its conclusion, its last and perhaps purest form, in Heidegger, with the voice which says nothing in particular but insists as a pure injunction. Very briefly: in the paragraphs of *Being and Time* (which, by the way, appeared the same year, 1927, as Freud's *The Future of an Illusion*) dealing with *Gewissen*, "The existential-ontological foundations of conscience" (## 55–60), we can find the whole phenomenology of the call (*der Ruf*) of conscience:

> *What* does the conscience call to him to whom it appeals? Taken strictly, nothing. The call asserts nothing, gives no information about the world-events, has nothing to tell. Least of all does it try to set going a "soliloquy" in the Self to which it has appealed. "Nothing" gets called to [zu-*gerufen*] this Self, but it has been *summoned* [*aufgerufen*] to itself—that is, to its ownmost potentiality-for-Being [*Seinkönnen*]. The tendency of the call is not such as to put up for "trial" the Self to which the appeal is made; but it calls Dasein forth (and "forward") [*vor*(-*nach*-"*vorne*"-)*rufen*] into its ownmost possibilities, as a summons to its ownmost *potentiality-for-Being-its-Self.* . . . *Conscience discourses solely and constantly in the mode of keeping silent.* (Heidegger 1973, p. 318)

So there is a pure call, which is not sonorous, not commanding anything, a mere convocation and provocation, the call to an opening to Being, to get out of the closure of one's self-presence. And the notion of responsibility—ethical, moral responsibility—is precisely a response to this call—it is impossible not to respond to this call; by evading it one evades one's fundamental responsibility, and one is always called upon. The very notion of responsibility has the voice at its core; it is a response to a voice.

Where does the voice come from? It comes from the innermost realm of our being, but at the same time it is something that transcends us, it is in ourselves more than ourselves, yet again, a beyond at our most intimate.

> Indeed the call is precisely something which *we ourselves* have neither planned nor prepared for nor voluntarily performed, nor have we ever done so. "It" calls ["*Es" ruft*], against our expectations and even against our will. . . . The call comes *from me* and yet *from beyond me*. (1973, p. 320)

The intimacy from which the call comes is described as *unheimlich*, uncanny ("The call points *forward to Dasein*'s potentiality-for-Being, and it does this as a call which comes *from* uncanniness [*Unheimlichkeit*]"; ibid., p. 325.) The call, the cry, the voice, the appeal—their proper location is *unheimlich*, with all the ambiguity that Freud has given this word: the internal externality, the expropriated intimacy, the *extimacy*—the excellent Lacanian word for the uncanny. So the call is the call to exposure, the opening to Being, which is opposed to a self-reflective monologue within oneself; it hinges on that which, within oneself, one cannot appropriate, and which starkly opposes *Dasein* to self-consciousness. The voice is pure alterity, it prevents self-reflexivity. In this role it even assumes a structural function closely akin to that of time, the central category of Heidegger's book. The analogy goes so far that some readers have proposed that instead of *Being and Time* we could rewrite (or rename) Heidegger's project as *Being and Voice*.[11]

And even more: if the voice is the opening toward Being, the opening which extracts us from submersion in the existing things and disrupts the closed circle of self-presence and self-reflection, does it not follow that the voice ultimately coincides with Being itself? Being is nothing but the opening "manifested" by the voice, and this consequence is condensed, in Heidegger's later work, in the "metaphor" of "the voice of Being," *die Stimme des Seins* (but again, where is the limit of metaphoricity?). Being is accessible only through the mute, aphonic voice, *die lautlose Stimme*:

The only one among all entities man experiences, in being called by the voice of Being, the miracle of all miracles: that the existent *is* [dass *Seindes* ist]. The one who is called in his essence to the truth of Being is thus constantly tuned [*gestimmt*] in an essential mode. . . . The originary thought is an echo of the inclination of being [*Widerhall der Gunst des Seins*], in which the Unique glimmers and lets itself happen [*lichtet und sich ereignen lässt*]: that the existent is. This echo is the human response to the Word of the mute voice of being. The response of thought is the origin of human speech [*Wortes*], which in the first place engenders language as the reverberation [*Verlautung*] of the Word in words. (Heidegger 1976, pp. 307, 310; my translation)

So speech is "always-already" a response, a response to this voice, and always bears the responsibility in relation to the voice of Being.

Thus we have passed from the "ethical" category of the voice of conscience to the "fundamental ontological" category of the voice of Being (Heidegger will eventually give up the very term ontology). All human thinking is a response to that mute voice, the voice without statement or content, the voice as the zero-point and origin of all sense, the meaning which is adulterated in language composed of words, but which at the same time persists as its guideline, organizing language as its echo, its reverberation, its preservation. Therein lies all the ambiguity of Heidegger's position: on the one hand voice is deprived not only of all articulation but of all phonic substance, it is a silent voice which escapes presence (that which constituted the essential foothold of the voice throughout the metaphysical tradition); on the other hand he nevertheless poses it as the point of the (impossible) origin, a call before language, a call to which language responds as an echo, the meaningless source of all meaning, more fundamental than language, where the origin, although purified of all metaphysical traits, nevertheless functions as a "pure origin," as if in a perspective illusion where the voice retroactively turns into the origin[12]—an illusion since, for us, it is but the consequence of the advent of language, its extimate surplus.

I cannot dwell any longer here on this question, which demands a much lengthier elaboration.

THE VOICE OF THE SUPEREGO

Let us now return to the red thread of the voice as an ethical figure. Through all these attempts which we have briefly considered, a certain opposition has persisted between the voice, its pure injunction, its imperative resonance, on the one hand, and on the other discursivity, argument, particular prescriptions or prohibitions or moral judgments, a wide variety of ethical theories.[13] In this opposition, although it recurred in very different settings, we strangely find again, in an altered form, our initial division into the voice—as the object—and the signifier. We could say that the figure of the voice of conscience implies a certain view of morality where the signifying chain cannot be sustained by itself; it needs a footing, an anchorage, a root in something which is not a signifier. Ethics requires a voice, but a voice which ultimately does not say anything, being by virtue of that all the louder, an absolute convocation which one cannot escape, a silence that cannot be silenced. The voice appears as the non-signifying, meaningless foundation of ethics. But what kind of foundation? If it is conceived as the divine voice—infallible because divine, and thus a firm guarantee—then it would turn into a positivity which would relegate the subject to a passive stance of carrying out orders—a pitfall one can avoid only if one conceives the voice as a pure call which commands nothing specific and offers no guarantee. In one and the same gesture it delivers us to the Other and to our own responsibility.

This ethical voice can be related to the voice of pure enunciation which we have already detected in linguistic utterances. But if in linguistics voice could represent enunciation beyond statement, enunciation as the invisible internal surplus of statement, then in the domain of ethics we have to confront *enunciation without a statement*.[14] This is the crucial point, the touchstone of morality: the voice is enunciation, and we have to supply the statement ourselves. The moral law is like a suspended sentence, a sentence left in suspense, confined to pure enunciation, but a sentence demanding a continuation, a sentence to be completed by the subject, by his or her moral decision, by the act. The enunciation is there, but the subject has to deliver the statement and thus assume the enunciation, respond to it and take it on his or her shoulders. The voice does not command or prohibit, but it nevertheless necessitates a continuation, it compels a sequel.

Yet this ethical voice is utterly ambiguous: if it is at the very core of the ethical, as the voice of the pure injunction without positive content, it is also at the core of straying away from the ethical, evading the call, albeit in the name of ethics itself. The psychoanalytic name for this deflection is the superego.

It can easily be seen that the superego stems from a voice and is endowed with a voice. Freud keeps coming back to this: "it is as impossible for the super-ego as for the ego to disclaim its origin from things heard [*seine Herkunft aus Gehörtem*]" (PFL 11, p. 394). If for Freud the vocality of the superego is just one of its features, then for Lacan it is the essential feature constitutive of the superego: "the superego in its intimate imperative . . . is above all a voice and very vocal, and with no other authority than that of being the fat voice [*sans plus d'autorité que d'être la grosse voix*]" (Lacan 1966, p. 684). From this we can deduce a succinct thesis: the difference between the ethical voice and the superego runs between the voice of pure enunciation and the fat voice. Moreover, the fat voice always comes up with directions, but these can be entrusted only to the voice. It is not a suspended sentence that we would have to resume but, rather, a moral agency in relation to which we are always deficient: however hard we try, we will always fall short, and the more we try to live up to it, the bigger the gap. It is a voice that always reduces the subject to guilt, and the guiltier we are the guiltier we will become, in a self-propelling process; we even relish our self-reproaches and our failures. That is the obscene side of the superego: its malevolent neutrality, its *Schadenfreude,* its malicious indifference to the subject's well-being. To put it in Kantian terms: the voice of the superego is not the voice of reason but, rather, the voice of reason run amok, reason berserk. The superego is not the moral law, despite Freud's declarations to the contrary,[15] but a way of eluding it.

The dividing line is very thin. We can see it in Kant: there is a slide from what Kant calls respect (*die Achtung*) for the moral law on the one side to what he calls awe (*die Ehrfurcht*) of it on the other, prostration in the face of it. Respect is the drive (*der Triebfeder*: Kant 1993, pp. 75 f.) of the moral law, the condition of its assumption by the subject, presenting the paradox of being an *a priori* feeling, the only non-pathological feeling in the Kantian edifice. Moral law can become effective only because we are driven by respect for it. But a few pages later Kant says:

> In the boundless esteem for the pure moral law . . . whose voice makes even the boldest sinner tremble and forces him to hide himself from its gaze, there is something so singular that we cannot wonder at finding this influence of a merely intellectual Idea on feeling to be inexplicable to speculative reason. . . . (Kant 1993, p. 83)

He describes the effect of moral law on the subject as essentially that of humiliation (ibid., p. 82). The purely formal moral law suddenly becomes endowed with a voice which makes us tremble, a gaze from which we cannot hide, the humiliation (*die Ehrfurcht*)[16] which is not just respect but above all fear, awe, dread: all the elements that can be connected, by a single stroke, under the heading of superego. The voice of enunciation circumscribed a certain locus of the moral law without giving it any positive substance or content, while the voice of the superego obfuscates this locus, fills it with its vocality, thus seemingly presenting the awsome figure of "the Other of the Other," the Other without a lack, the horrendous Other—not merely the Other of law, but at the same time the Other of its transgression. For the excess of the voice here functions precisely as transgression of the law, and the admonishments that this voice issues cannot be turned into "principles giving universal law" but, rather, diverge from universality.

This obscene ("non-universalizable") part of the superego is always entrusted to the voice: we can think of the secret rules and rituals which hold certain communities together—rules of initiation (including the harsh humiliation of newcomers), of belonging to an in-group, the dividing line between insiders and outsiders, and so on. Those rules could never be put down in writing, they have to be whispered, hinted at, and confined to the voice. The voice is ultimately what distinguishes the superego from the law: the law has to be underpinned by the letter, something that is publicly accessible, in principle available at all times, while in contravention and in supplement to the law there are rules entrusted to the voice, the superegoic rules which most often take the form of transgression of the law, but which actually and effectively hold communities together and constitute their invisible glue.

The fact that institutions rely on inherent transgressions of laws and written regulations is a matter of common experience and there is, of course, nothing subversive about it. Bakhtin described the long tradition of carnivals, to some extent still alive and well in some of the most patriarchal societies, based on a prescribed transgression of all social codes, but confined to specific times and spaces—the institutional transgressions function in this carnivalesque manner, upholding the "normal" functioning of the law, as an internal "perversion" which sustains its rule. Transgression operates in a mode which is not publicly utterable; its lure lies in offering a portion of enjoyment, of transgressive enjoyment, as if in compensation, as it were, for the hardship the law demands, but this apparent indulgence will only strengthen the law and endow it with "surplus-authority." The Other rules all the more through the transgressions of its rule which seemingly undermine it; we are caught all the more in its vicious circle.[17] The "ethical voice" of pure enunciation, on the other hand, implies a dimension of the Other which offers no guarantee and circumscribes its lack.

So if "the voice of reason" gains a positive existence—if it grows fat, as it were—then it turns into the superegoic perversion of reason. Lacan, in *Seminar I*, formulated another of his remarkable slogans: "The superego is at the same time the law and its destruction" (Lacan 1975, p. 119). In this underside of the law we can hear an echo of the primal father, the shadow which will always follow and haunt the law. If in Freud's scenario the law was instituted by the murder of the primal father, if it was the law of the dead father, that is, of his name, then the trouble is that the father was never quite dead—he survived as the voice (this was the function of shofar).[18] The voice appears as the part of the father which is not quite dead; it evokes the figure of enjoyment, and thus adumbrates the slide to destruction of the law based on his name. There is no law without the voice,[19] and the dividing line is tenuous, but crucial: if the superego is the supplement of the law, its shadow, its obscure and obscene double,[20] then we should add that the alternative, or disjunction, between the two is not exhaustive: the voice of the moral law, at the interstice of both, does not coincide with either.

To conclude our brief survey of the ethics of the voice: we can see that the voice plays a crucially pivotal role which places it in an ambiguous position. The voice which sustains the moral law has been called divine by the whole tradition from Socrates to Rousseau, and even by Kant, and this divine transcendent law was at the same time placed at the most intimate kernel of the subject. With Heidegger this voice has been brought to its minimum: an opening to a radical alterity, an opening to Being, a call eluding self-appropriation and self-reflection, something outside the existent and situated in the realm of the uncanny. What all this tradition has in common is that the voice comes from the Other, but this is the Other within. The ethical voice is not the subject's own, it is not for the subject to master or control it, although the subject's autonomy is entirely dependent on it. But it does not pertain simply to the Other either, although it stems from it: it would belong to the Other if it were reducible to positive commands, if it were not merely an opening and an enunciation. (In simplified Kantian terms, we could maintain that reason pertains to the Other, but its voice does not.) The voice comes from the Other without being part of it; rather, it indicates and evokes a void in the Other, circumscribing it, but not giving it a positive consistence. It has no properties, yet it cannot be circumvented.

So again we find the ambiguous ontology—or, rather, topology— of the status of the voice as "between the two," placed precisely at the curious intersection. The voice can be located at the juncture of the subject and the Other, just as it was before, in a different register, placed at the intersection of body and language, circumscribing a lack in both. The schema used above can now be put to new use:

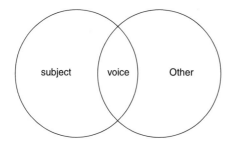

The voice is the element which ties the subject and the Other together, without belonging to either, just as it formed the tie between body and language without being part of them. We can say that the subject and the Other coincide in their common lack embodied by the voice, and that "pure enunciation" can be taken as the red thread which connects the linguistic and ethical aspects of the voice.

CHAPTER 5

THE POLITICS OF THE VOICE

The political dimension of the voice, its deep involvement in the constitution of the political, can perhaps best be approached at the origin, at the very beginning of political philosophy, on the first pages of Aristotle's *Politics*. There we can read this:

> Now, that man is more of a political animal than bees or any other gregarious animals is evident. Nature, as we often say, makes nothing in vain, and man is the only animal whom she has endowed with the gift of speech. And whereas mere voice [*phone*] is but an indication of pleasure or pain, and is therefore found in other animals (for their nature attains to the perception of pleasure and pain and the intimation of them to one another, and no further), the power of speech is intended to set forth the expedient and inexpedient, and therefore likewise the just and the unjust. And it is a characteristic of man that he alone has any sense of good and evil, of just and unjust, and the like, and an association of living beings who have this sense makes a family and a state. (Aristotle 2001, 1253a 7–18)

We might be rather surprised to learn that the very institution of the political depends on a certain division of the voice, a division within the voice, its partition. For in order to understand the political, we have to discern the mere voice on the one hand and speech, the intelligible voice, on the other. There is a huge divide between *phone* and *logos*, and everything appears to follow from there, despite the fact that *logos* itself is still wrapped in voice, that it is *phone semantike*, the meaningful voice which relegates the mere voice to prehistory. There is a crucial divide between the word and the voice, a new avatar of our initial divide between the signifier and the voice, which has immediate and dramatic political consequences.[1]

To follow Aristotle, mere voice is what animals and men have in common, it is the animal part of man. It can indicate only pleasure and pain, experiences shared by both animals and humans. But speech, *logos*, does not merely indicate, it expresses or, better still, it manifests: it manifests the advantageous (useful) and the harmful, and consequently the just and the unjust, the good and the evil. If one receives a blow, one may well scream, that is, emit a voice to vent one's pain, and that is what a horse or a dog would also do. But at the same time one can say: "I have been wronged" (harmed, ill-treated), and thereby the speech introduces the measure of right and wrong. It does not just give vent to feelings, it introduces a standard of judgment.

At the bottom of this is the opposition between two forms of life: *zoe* and *bios*. *Zoe* is naked life, bare life, life reduced to animality; *bios* is life in the community, in the *polis*, political life.

> The tie between the bare life and politics is the same as the tie that the metaphysical definition of man as "the living being endowed with language" is looking for in the articulation between *phone* and *logos*. . . . The question "How does the living being have language?" exactly corresponds to the question "How does the bare life inhabit *polis*?" The living being possesses *logos* by suppressing and retaining in it its own voice, just as it inhabits *polis* by letting its own bare life be ex-cepted by it. (Agamben 1997, pp. 15–16)

This dense passage by Agamben points exactly to the crucial juncture: the analogy, which is more than an analogy, between the articulation *phone–logos* and *zoe–bios*. Voice is like bare life, something that is supposedly exterior to the political, while *logos* is the counterpart of *polis*, of social life ruled by laws and the common good. But the whole point—the point of Agamben's book— is, of course, that there is no such simple externality: the basic structure, the topology of the political, is for Agamben that of an "inclusive exclusion" of naked life. This very exclusion places *zoe* in a central and paradoxical place; the exception falls into interiority. ("Let us call the *relation of exception* the extreme form of relation which includes something by its exclusion": ibid., p. 26.)[2] This then, yet again, puts the voice in a most peculiar and paradoxical position: the topology of *extimacy*, the simultaneous inclusion/exclusion, which retains the excluded at its core. For what presents a problem is not that *zoe* is simply presocial, the animality, the outside of the social, but that it persists, in its very exclusion/inclusion, at the heart of the social—just as the voice is not simply an element external to speech, but persists at its core, making it possible and constantly haunting it by the impossibility of symbolizing it. And even more: the voice is not some remnant of a previous precultural state, or of some happy primordial fusion when we were not yet plagued by language and its calamities; rather, it is the product of *logos* itself, sustaining and troubling it at the same time.

VIVA VOCE

If the voice is excluded, and thereby included, in the very constitution of the political and its underlying *logos*, this topology has some practical and empirically observable consequences. We can see that the voice, in its function as the internal exterior of *logos*, the apparent pre-*logos*, the extra-*logos*, is called upon and necessary in certain well-defined and crucial social situations. A more detailed phenomenology and analysis of these is called for, but here are just a few examples taken from very different levels. They all concern what Althusser called Ideological State Apparatuses—Church, court, university, elections—and they all circumscribe a particular highly codified and ritualized area within them, the strategic points where their ritual character is displayed and performed, and their symbolic impact is staged.

The voice is intimately linked with the dimension of the sacred and ritual in intricately structured social situations where using the voice makes it possible to perform a certain act. One cannot perform a religious ritual without resorting to the voice in that sense: one has, for example, to say prayers and sacred formulas *labialiter, viva voce,* in order to assume them and make them effective, although they are all written down in sacred texts and everybody (supposedly) knows them by heart. Those words, carefully stored on paper and in memory, can acquire performative strength only if they are relegated to the voice, and it is as if the use of the voice will ultimately endow those words with the character of sacredness and ensure their ritual efficacy, in spite of—or, rather, *because of*—the fact that the use of the voice does not add anything to their content. It appears that this use of the voice echoes the supposedly archaic voice, the voice not bound by *logos,* and recalls the use of shofar in Jewish religious rituals that, as we have seen, Lacan proposed as a model for the object voice. The three great "religions of the Book" all rely on Holy Scripture where the truth is manifested, yet the scripture, the holy letter, can become effective only if and when it is assumed by a living voice. It can function as a social tie, the link between the community of believers, only if and when a voice pronounces what has been written ever since the foundational moment of origin and stored by tradition, and what all believers keep in their memories anyway.

Secular examples follow the same pattern: court proceedings have very strict rules about the parts of the process and the depositions that have to be made by voice. A guide for jurors in French courts states:

> The orality of the debates is the fundamental rule of the court [*cour d'assises*]. This rule decrees that the court can form its conviction only on the basis of the elements orally and contradictorily debated in the court. This is why the court and the jurors cannot consult the files [*dossiers*] during sessions. . . . This is also why one cannot read the deposition of a witness who is going to testify before she or he has testified: the file is always secondary. (quoted in Poizat 2001, p. 75)

The fact that this is a French prescription has some significance. The same rule generally applies everywhere (for example, in the German civil code: "The parties debate the legal dispute in front of the applicable court orally [*mündlich*]"; quoted by Vissmann 2002, p. 142), but its birthplace is the French Revolution. The principle of orality, the use of the "living voice," and the principle of the public nature of court proceedings were the two main tenets pursued by the Enlightenment against various modes of corruption of legal practice in the *ancien régime*, and they were both implemented by decrees of the Revolution, such as the Law of 16–29 September 1791: "The interrogation of witnesses must always be carried out by the living voice [*de vive voix*] without writing down the testimonies" (quoted by Vissmann 2002, p. 141). This requirement was formally codified by the Napoleonic Code (1806). The degradation of the written record as secondary (to the point of its prohibition) was part of the democratization of court proceedings: the key role was assigned to the jury, and the juror could in principle be anyone (subject to certain regulations), but the difficulty was that the majority of potential jurors were illiterate. The living voice was the instrument by which the legal system could be extracted from the hands of specialists, their incomprehensible lingo and a host of anachronistic regulations.[3] The voice was the medium of democratization of justice, and it was supported by another element of "political fiction," namely that democracy is a matter of immediacy, that is, of the voice; the ideal democracy would be the one where everybody could hear everybody else's voice (hence Rousseau's model case of Geneva). The prohibition of writing was a revolutionary oddity, soon to be replaced by the requirement that every legally relevant word, uttered by the living voice, should be written down; its living presence must be fixed by a written protocol which alone can function as a legal *act*. Yet the written word has no power if it is not preceded by, and based in, the living voice. The authority of writing depends on its being the faithful copy of the voice. The second act, in the sense of a legal document, must follow the first one, the act of the voice, and the hierarchy of the two is the crucial legal fiction.

There are, to be sure, various exceptions to this rule, but the living presence of the voice is the element which defines the ritual nature of court proceedings. The most technical depositions by experts have to be read aloud by them, and only the voice transforms them from mere constative statements into performatives. The same statement acquires the value of a performative when read aloud in front of the court, while it remains the "dead letter" of a constative as long as it is just written down in the files. This is the point where even the President of the USA could not get away with a written deposition, but had to take the witness stand. So here again we have the scripture, the written law on the basis of which the court has to decide, yet for the law to become effective, for the law to be enacted, one has to have recourse to the voice, to orality. If the court is to decide whether the present case can be subsumed under the law, how the letter of the law applies to it, if the court is to determine the truth of the present case and relate it to the law, then it can do so only by the voice, *viva voce*. (We should note in passing the link between the voice and establishing the truth: there is a point where truth has to be vocal and where the written truth, although literally the same, will not do.)[4]

If the living voice is essential to justice as the implementation of laws, it also plays a key role in legislature. "Parliament," after all, stems from *parlare*, it is a place reserved for speech. But here the situation is reversed in relation to justice: there the living voice was obligatory for the implementation of the letter of the law, while here debating in the living voice, oral discussion with the possibility of objection, takes place in order to result in the letter of the law. The law is not the presupposition but the consequence of the vocal ritual; it cannot be passed, at least in principle, without passing through vocality. Both situations, in their inverted symmetry, mutually support each other and form two halves of the same fictitious entity.

If in this brief survey we make another leap and go from the juridical to the university, then we can see that within Anglo-American academia there is an institution actually called *viva voce*, or just viva: the defense of a dissertation, of a doctoral thesis, which has to be made "in the living voice." In most universities all examinations and tests are nowadays done by writing, so in theory one could actually survive the whole of academic life and get a degree without ever opening one's mouth. Until the viva: at this point, when undergoing the key initiatory ritual, one has to "give voice," one must not just display one's knowledge but perform one's knowledge. The corpus of a candidate's knowledge has been written down in the dissertation, which—supposedly and optimistically—the members of the committee have all carefully read, but this is not enough, it has to be enacted through the voice and only thus made effective. The general experience of those tedious occasions shows that they are indeed simply a question of vocal display; the supposed testing and questioning of the candidate's knowledge has very little to do with that knowledge itself, and has an entirely ritual and vocal character (supplemented by narcissistic struggles and departmental politics under the banner of promoting pure science).

But if the viva presents one extreme of the school system, its ritual exit, then the voice is also omnipresent in schooling from the outset, to the point of being imperceptible. The minimal mechanism of school (this dominant Ideological State Apparatus for Althusser) depends on the teacher's voice, which defines its ritual character and functions in a way somewhat analogous to justice. The teacher is the transmitter of Knowledge by his voice: Knowledge is all stored in books, but it can become effective only when relegated to the voice. Everything may well be written in the textbook, but this will never be enough until the teacher assumes it by his or her voice which enacts it, even if she or he merely reads aloud from the textbook. All Knowledge is accessible to everyone in the textbook, but the school as institution functions only by the voice. If with the viva we had a student who had to "give voice" in order to qualify for Knowledge, then from the outset Knowledge has to be staged by the teacher's voice.

The last example is slightly different and less straightforward: elections, in a great number of languages, have retained a connection with the voice—giving one's voice for a candidate, counting the voices. In English the link is weak—one counts the ballots; it is evident in German: *für jemanden stimmen, seine Stimme abgeben, Abstimmung, Stimmabgabe*; in French: *compter les voix, donner sa voix*; Swedish: *att rösta på*; in Slav languages: *glasovanje, glasanje*, and so on. Is this, yet again, a metaphor? How is it that the voice gives rise to so many metaphors with uncertain limits? Its historic origin is voting by the voice,[5] that is, by acclamation. Catholic bishops, for example, were elected that way were for a long time; more generally, an element of acclamation ritually accompanied every coronation of a monarch. Monarchs—God forbid—were never elected; nevertheless the people had to "give its voice" when the monarch assumed his role.[6] The coronation, the inauguration of a monarch, could not be properly accomplished without formal acclamation, relying on a certain understanding of the adage *vox populi, vox Dei*. In a paradoxical connection, God's will, manifesting itself in the choice of the monarch, could be implemented only by expressing itself through the voice of the people, who had no say.[7] The people had no power of decision, they merely possessed the voice to condone God's will, and the voice of God could manifest itself only through the voice of the people. The people were called upon, and could respond only by the call. The origin of the adage *vox populi, vox Dei* is elusive, but one can trace it back at least to the coronation of the "monarch of all monarchs," Charlemagne, Charles the Great; the first mention of it comes in a letter from Alcuin to Charles the Great (in 798). His coronation, in 800, posed formidable problems of ritual acclamation, for it was decided, in contravention of previous custom, that this acclamation should take place after the coronation and not precede it, thereby setting the model for the future.

Elections have retained an element of this ritualistic use of the voice. In our highly technically sophisticated society, one still has to give one's voice, or one has to ritually perform, as it were, the myth of a society organized and tied together by the voice, where the people are still called upon to give their voice in favor of the ruler. The underlying fantasy is that of a *Gemeinschaft* in which all members can hear each other, and the fundamental social tie is the vocal tie. But the electoral voice has to be a silent voice (a silenced voice?): it has to be given by writing (by crossing or encircling), and it has to be performed in a small cabin, a cell-like cubicle, in complete isolation (in French it is actually called l'*isoloir*), in complete silence. Furthermore, it has to be done one by one, so that the collective outburst of the acclamatory voice is broken down, nipped in the bud, seemingly deprived of its essential qualities and its spectacular effects. It is the voice measured and counted, the voice submitted to arithmetic, the voice entrusted to a written sign, a mute voice deprived of any sonority, but no matter how hard they try to smother and dismember it, it is still a voice. If the letter of the constitution is to be enacted, in democratic societies, it has yet again to be enacted by the voice.

THE ANTIPOLITICS OF THE VOICE

Those reemergences of the voice in the midst of social life, which in principle is based on "the letter of the law," those occurrences linked to quasi-sacred or ritualistic occasions, present some highly telling and symptomatic points where the element of the voice as such is called upon to perform a crucial social function. They point to the necessary appearance of the voice at certain ritualistic points of a society which is thoroughly governed and organized by written laws, rules, and prescriptions—it is the fiction of the universal accessibility of the letter and of its unchangeable nature which makes the law possible, as opposed to the fleeting nature of voices. When the voice is needed on those occasions, it is the voice properly circumscribed, tamed, pacified, yet the voice which is absolutely necessary to complement the letter, or to complete and accomplish the letter; it is like its lost half which enables its enactment. It is the voice which, ritually, ensures the proper authority of the letter.[8] This is also where the ritual use of the voice differs from its attachment to the superego: what is at stake in the ritual is the codification of the voice and its public presentation, it is used as the lever of social performativity, as a seal of community and the acknowledgment of its symbolic efficacy, the voice as the practice of the letter; while with the superego the main point is to escape publicity and to keep its code hidden—if it makes a public appearance, it always produces an effect of the obscene.

But this ritual use of the voice is not the only story or the whole story—far from it. All the cases which were briefly given here as examples rely on a structure of division of labor, as it were: there is a co-existence of the letter and the voice, and it is quite clear where and when the voice should intervene in order to enact the letter. The two functions are clearly delimited and circumscribed, and the intervention of the voice is called upon in specific and well-defined places and times. This division gives an impression of a peaceful coexistence, a complementarity, as if the letter would find in the use of the voice the missing half it has been seeking. The voice is used only in the place and at the time allotted to it, and everything depends on the boundary being maintained, although it can be blurred or problematic. The division of labor between the letter and the voice can no doubt acquire a variety of perverse forms, but it is nevertheless at the same time a remedy, a tool to oppose obnoxious effects of power and to limit its misuse, although its value and efficacy have to be carefully examined in particular cases.

In sharp contrast to this, there is another kind of voice, a very different use and function of voice which has the effect not of enacting, but of putting into question the letter itself and its authority. It is precisely the (appropriately called) authoritarian voice, voice as authoritarian, the voice as the source of authority against the letter, or the voice not supplementing but supplanting the letter. Most tellingly, all phenomena of totalitarianism tend to hinge overbearingly on the voice, which in a *quid pro quo* tends to replace the authority of the letter, or put its validity into question. The voice which appears limitless and unbound, that is, not bound by the letter, the voice as the source and immediate lever of violence.

To give a light-hearted and entertaining example of what is in itself rather sinister, we can think of Chaplin's rendition of "the great dictator." Indeed, the structural use of the voice in "totalitarianism" has never been depicted more convincingly. Several things have to be noted.[9]

1. What we hear in the famous opening speech by the Tomanian dictator Hynkel is a nonexistent language with all the makings of German (some ludicrous identifiable German words are mixed in). We don't understand a word (or literally just a word here and there, like sauerkraut); it is the voice and its theater which are isolated as the essential feature of the dictator, the voice beyond meaning. The whole speech is but a staging and a choreography of the voice.[10]

2. At the same time, we have an invisible English translator interpreting the speech, that is to say, providing the senseless voice with a meaning in a sort of consecutive translation. This mechanism is formidable and striking, and seems to be literally ubiquitous: the anthropologist Junzo Kawada, who has studied the (political) role of the voice in various societies, tells us that in the Mosi tribe in Burkina-Faso, for example, the chief (king) always speaks in an incomprehensible low voice and needs an interpreter who explains to the people what the chief really said.[11] But it is essential that the chief is there as the source of the voice; he has to emit the voice, pure voice without signification, and his vizier, as it were, some second-in-command, then takes care of the meaning. This device seems to have functioned in many societies—Salazar (1995) has scrutinized it in seventeenth-century France, a society very much ruled by "the cult of the voice," as the title of his book runs.[12] We can isolate it, as we have seen, on a completely different level, in the biblical "originary scene" where Moses has to interpret the voice of God heard on Mount Sinai for the people

who could hear only the thunder and the trumpet, in a clear division between the voice and the law. This same device is now enacted here in this caricature: the master as the source of funny voices, side by side with the invisible interpreter in charge of the meaning.

3. But the great appeal of the scene is that it is quite clear that what the interpreter is saying is not an accurate translation of the speech but, rather, its transformation into something that is "politically correct," fit for the ears of outsiders. It is clear that for insiders the dictator is saying something that can only be entrusted to the voice, and does not bear translation. We can surmise that he is promising them relief from the strict laws, the "license to kill"; there is an implied promise of spoils, loot, plunder, an orgy, a promise to suspend the law—something that could not be publicly put into words—while the interpreter is presenting the whole thing for the ears of the big Other, for the historic record, and consequently playing it down, providing it with a rationale, unsuccessfully struggling to put it into a good perspective. So the interpreter does not need to translate the funny voices for the public, who understand it only too well; he has to act as a mediator for the Other, which is different from the audience of insiders. The paradox of the scene is that we have two versions, the dictator's speech and its translation, but we don't understand the one, yet nevertheless know that the other is false. Still, we know perfectly well what is going on: the very discrepancy between the two versions provides the exact clue: it is in the mirroring of the two versions that "the object dictator" appears. Note that the whole thing is placed under the sign of the double cross, so we have been amply warned that this is a matter of "double-crossing."

4. The speech at the beginning—the speech of the dictator Hynkel—is then mirrored by the final speech, the speech made by the Jewish barber disguised as Hynkel, the barber who is the exact double of the dictator and, being mistaken for the dictator, has to address the masses in that role. His speech is the very opposite of the initial speech; it is presented in forceful words filled with humanism, an appeal to humanity and brotherhood. Yet, in a final irony, the response of the masses appears to be the same: there is the same enthusiasm,

despite the fact that the conveyed meaning is the very opposite. This is intriguing, since the masses don't know that this is not the real Hynkel but his Jewish double—are we to understand that the masses are infinitely gullible, susceptible to any manipulation? On top of that, the final scene is accompanied by music from *Lohengrin*, of all things, a gesture that can only heighten the final ambivalence. Can the final scene cancel, obliterate, retroactively undo, *aufheben*, the effects of the first one, of which it is a remake? Or does the voice resound beyond the alleged humanist message, irreducible to it, threateningly pointing to something else?

The totalitarian use of the voice is not at all in the same vein as instances of the division of labor. We should not read it as an invocation of the sacred and of ritual,[13] or rather: precisely because this is not the dimension of the sacred and of ritual, it has to make even more of a pretense of it, it has to mimic, to emulate, to ape the ritual as closely and spectacularly as it can. The voice, although put at the very core, has a very different function here: the Führer may well be Chancellor of the Third Reich, commander in chief of the army, and occupy many political functions, yet he is not the Führer by virtue of the political functions he happens to be charged with, not by election and also not on the basis of his abilities. It is the relationship of the voice which makes him the Führer, and the tie that links the subjects to him is enacted as a vocal tie; its other part is the answer to the voice by mass acclamation which is an essential feature of the speech. It is the voice that makes the law—*Führerworte haben Gesetzkraft*, as Eichmann will say in Jerusalem; his words supported by the mere voice make the law, the voice immediately turns them into law, that is, the voice suspends the law. This is what Carl Schmitt proclaimed in 1935: the "Führer's will and plan" are manifested in oral guidelines (*Leitsätze*), which are "in immediate and most intense way positive law" (quoted by Vissmann 2002, p. 139). Schmitt was a great legal theorist, and he could not have been more explicit.

In the person of the Führer, *zoe* and *bios* coincide.[14] He represents the unity of *Volk* and its aspirations, its biopolitical ambition and endeavor—and Foucault's term "biopolitics" aims precisely at the annihilation of the distinction between *zoe* and *bios*—that is, in our particular perspective, at the same time between voice and *logos*. The biopolitical swallows the sacred, the voice swallows the letter, the division collapses. The collapse of that distinction necessarily brings forth the emergence of the "bare life" on the other side: the life which anybody can kill with impunity, yet the life which cannot be sacrificed, that is, subjected to an economy of sacrifice, gift, atonement, expiation, in some gesture of exchange with the (divine) Other. Such is the life of Jews, the paramount *homines sacri* of our day.[15]

The use of the voice in Stalinism (usually seen as the other part of the spurious entity of "totalitarianism")[16] indicates a different kind of structure. It is immediately obvious that Stalinist rulers—starting with Stalin himself—were never good public speakers. The voice of the Stalinist ruler is the very opposite of the Führer's voice and its spectacular efficacy. When the Stalinist ruler makes a public speech, he reads in a monotonous voice, without proper intonation and rhetorical effects, as if he himself doesn't understand what he is saying. Party congresses were always staged as monotonous readings of an endless string of endless speeches, during which history was supposed to take place, but which had an irresistibly soporific effect—this was definitely history without any drama. The speech will be published anyway the next day in densely covered pages of the official newspaper, so nobody listens (nor does anybody read the paper). Yet the performance is essential and indispensable—not because of the delegates in the hall, nor the people supposedly gathered in crowds around radios and loudspeakers, but as a scene staged for the benefit of the big Other. The performance is meant for the ears of the big Other of history, and after all, Stalinist measures were always justified in terms of the realization of the great historical laws, in view of a future which would supposedly validate them.

If the main objective of the fascist ruler was to produce an Event here and now, if fascism put all its resources into the mechanisms of fascination and spectacle, if the voice was the ideal medium of producing such Events in establishing a direct link between the ruler and the masses, then the main concern of the Stalinist Party congresses was that nothing would happen, that everything would run according to the preestablished scenario. The written script is not to be disguised—on the contrary, the Stalinist ruler is but an agent, a functionary of the script, and the point of monotonous reading is to present as few diversions as possible. Not the authority of the voice, but the authority of the letter is the guideline—it is the letter which is the Event, the voice is but its appendage, a necessary appendage since speeches have to be read aloud to be effective; publication doesn't suffice; but the voice is to be reduced to the smallest possible quantity. The fact that the speaker appears not to understand what he is reading is thus structural, not a reflection of his intellectual capacities, although at times it was hard to tell the one from the other. This situation is almost the opposite to that of fascism: the Führer's words, supported by the immediate charismatic presence of the voice, were immediately legislative, as we have seen, while the Stalinist ruler endeavors to efface himself and his voice; he is merely the executor of the text, just as he is the mere tool of the laws of history, not their creator. He is not the legislator, but merely the secretary (albeit Secretary-General), carrying out the objective and scientifically established course of history, the humble soldier in the service of the Other. He acts not in his own name but in the name of the proletariat, progress, the world revolution, and so on, and in the big Other nothing is entrusted to the voice—it's all in the letter and its law.

If Stalinist rulers were bad speakers, then it is perhaps telling that those who opposed Stalinism were also great orators. Trotsky, the archenemy, was a brilliant orator; Tito, while not brilliant, was obviously ill at ease when reading and often relied on spontaneous asides in popular language, directly addressing the "simple people" of which he was, allegedly, part himself. The special case is that of Castro: hardly an opponent of Stalinism, but following a very different logic in his public appearances. He presents something like an impossible synthesis of two opposing elements: on the one hand he delivers his speeches as a rule without a written prop, in fiery style, relying infinitely on the inspiration of the moment, with baroque rhetoric and unwavering confidence in the immediacy of the voice; yet on the other hand his improvised monologues take hours and hours, become crushingly repetitive and spontaneously turn into orations by Party leaders with equally soporific effects, thus achieving their telos in spite of the opposite starting point.

If in Stalinism everything happens in the name of the big Other of history, then in fascism the Führer himself assumes the role of the Other. He has no need for objective laws; his justification is to embody the unity and the aspiration of the Nation, its "will to power," its need for life-space and for racial purification. Life, strength, power, blood, soil—and the voice in continuation of this series, the voice instead of, in place of, the law. In this light, all the legacy of the Enlightenment— human rights, democracy, and so on—could only appear as an obstacle to the biopolitical agenda. The catastrophe of Stalinism, on the contrary, was that it was heir to the Enlightenment, and represented its inner perversion. Its terror was the terror of the letter and the law in the name of the Other, but the very hiding of the voice behind the letter was the source of perversion: the Stalinist's voice was weak and monotonous, a mere appendage to the letter, yet this staging, this reduction of the voice to the minimum, its self-effacement, in order to exhibit the letter as all the more objective, independent of the subjectivity of its executor—this reduction was the source of the Stalinist's power. The smaller he showed himself to be, the greater his power, reduced to the hidden appendage, the tiny addition of the voice, but one which decides the validity of the letter.

THE VOICE AND THE LETTER

Agamben, in the first pages of *Homo sacer*, defines sovereignty, following Carl Schmitt, as a paradox:

> The sovereign is at the same time outside and inside the juridical order. . . . The sovereign, having the legal power to suspend the validity of the law, is legally situated outside the law. This means that the paradox can equally be formulated in this way: "The law is exterior to

itself," or rather: "I, the sovereign, who am outside the law, declare that there is no outside of the law." (Agamben 1997, p. 23)

So sovereignty is structurally based on exception. The sovereign is the one who can suspend the legal order and proclaim the state of emergency where the usual laws are no longer valid, and the exception becomes the rule. The state of emergency has the most intimate link with the dimension of "bare life": indeed, it is proclaimed when our bare lives are endangered (with natural catastrophes, wars, upheavals, September 11, . . .) and when one is obliged, in the name of bare life, to cancel the validity of the normal rule of law. But it is up to the sovereign to decide whether the danger is indeed such that it calls for this extreme measure, so the very rule of law depends on the decision and the judgment emanating from a point outside the law. And the very moment when it is declared that this is now a matter of our bare lives, survival and therefore a non-political matter, we are dealing with sovereignty and politics in their pure forms, with the showcase of the political.

We can see that this paradox largely coincides with the relationship between the voice and the letter that we have been examining. The letter of the law, in order to acquire authority, has to rely, at a certain point, on the tacitly presupposed voice; it is the structural element of the voice which ensures that the letter is not "the dead letter," but exerts power and can be enacted. This can take the form of a division of labor and a "peaceful coexistence," problematic as it may be, but the tension between the two permanently threatens something far more sinister: *the voice is structurally in the same position as sovereignty*, which means that it can suspend the validity of the law and inaugurate the state of emergency. The voice stands at the point of exception which threatens to become the rule, where it suddenly displays its profound complicity with the bare life, *zoe* as opposed to *bios*, that Aristotle was talking about. The emergency is the emergence of the voice in the commanding position, where its concealed existence suddenly becomes overwhelming and devastating. The voice is precisely at the unlocatable spot in the interior and the exterior of the law at the same time, and hence a permanent threat of a state of emergency.

A "politics of the voice" follows from there, displaying the voice as pivotal and ambivalent. The passage from voice to *logos* is an immediately political passage which, in the second step, entails the re-emergence of the voice in the midst of the political. If the relation voice/*logos* is analogous to the relation voice/letter, we can see that the voice, the object voice, is again placed at the intersection of both. There has to be a part of voice which endows the letter with authority, there is a point where the letter has to rely on a tacitly presupposed voice for its authority, and this inaudible part of the voice reemerges with quite a bit of glamor in the ritualistic use of the voice where the hidden voice appears in a positive sonority, as a stand-in for itself, as it were. The paradoxical topology of the voice as essentially between-the-two that we have been pursuing all along can be prolonged here to the relation between *phone* and *logos* as well as *zoe* and *bios*.

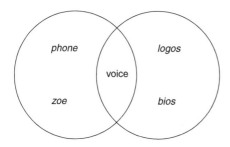

In all our cases the two entities overlap in an element which does not belong to either of them, yet holds them together. This location—the intersection, the void—turns the voice into something precarious and elusive, an entity which cannot be met in the full sonority of an unambiguous presence, but is not simply a lack either. The moment this voice is taken as something positive and compelling on its own, we enter the realm where obnoxious consequences are quick to follow. In politics it quickly turns into His Master's Voice, supplanting the law.

But in the realm of the "politics of the voice," we should also pursue the same operation as in the realm of ethics: the ritualistic social uses of the voice and its "authoritarian" perversion do not cover the whole field. It is also here that we have to disentangle, from the sonorous and shrill voices, the non-sonorous voice of pure enunciation, the enunciation without a statement: the enunciation to which one has to supply the statement, the political statement in response to that voice—not by listening/obeying, not by merely performing social rituals, but by engaging in a political stance. It is a voice tacitly implied not only in the law, but also in the wide social-symbolic texture, the symbolic fabric stored in tradition and mores, something we can never simply assume by compliance and submission, but something which demands an act, a political subjectification which can take many different forms. The symbolic efficacy depends on the excess of the voice it inaudibly hides in its entrails—if I started this section by invoking Althusser, I can conclude it by briefly touching upon his mechanism of interpellation, which is but another name for that voice, the call which sustains social injunctions and symbolic mandates. Althusser saw very clearly that the assumption of the symbolic implies a response to a call, and he provided it with an excellent name, but there is a divide, a precarious shifting line, in the interpellating voice: on the one hand there is the process of becoming a subject by recognizing oneself as the addressee of that call, which would then be a version of His Master's Voice issuing positive prescriptions; on the other there is at the same time a voice which interpellates without any positive content—something one would perhaps rather escape by obeying the sonorous voice of statements and commands; nevertheless this pure excess of the voice is compelling, although it does not tell us what to do and does not offer a handle for recognition and identification. If one wants to become a subject, recognition and obedience are never quite enough; in addition to and apart from these, one has to respond to the "mere voice" which is just an opening, a pure enunciation compelling a response, an act, a dislocation of the imposing voices of domination. If in the first case one turns into a subject precisely by assuming the form of the autonomous "I," disavowing its heteronomic origin, so that ideological domination and autonomous subjectivity work hand in hand, as Althusser has forcefully shown, then in the second case one becomes a subject only by fidelity to the "foreign kernel" of the voice which cannot be appropriated by the self, thus by following precisely the heteronomic break in which one cannot recognize oneself. The ideological interpellation can never quite silence this other voice, and the distance between the two voices opens the space of the political.[17]

In a famous quote in "Analysis Terminable and Interminable" (1937), Freud talks about three impossible professions in which one can be certain of an unsatisfactory outcome: government, education, and psychoanalysis (SA Supplementary volume, p. 388).[18] If we look at this from our biased perspective, it is obvious that all three crucially involve the voice at their core. They are the professions of the voice, and perhaps it is the cumbersome element of the voice which makes them impossible in the first place. From another angle they appear to be impossible because they all involve transference, and maybe there is a close tie between the two: the voice may well function as the kernel or the lever of transference, as the transferential voice, and maybe transference is but another name for the mechanism of the enactment of the letter by the voice which we have been examining.

We have been considering the first profession, government, with some of the paradoxes of the politics of the voice. I have only briefly touched upon the second, the voice in education, a book with many long chapters which would need much closer scrutiny; but I want to provisionally finish, somewhat abruptly, on the note of "the voice as the pivot of analysis." Indeed, psychoanalysis is also one of those things which can be carried out only *viva voce*, in the living voice, in the living presence of the analysand and the analyst. Their tie is the tie of the voice (analysis by writing, or even by telephone, will never do). But whose voice? The patient, the analysand, is the one who has to present his or her associations, anything that comes to his or her mind, in the presence of the analyst. So the patient is (in principle) the principal or, at the limit, the sole speaker; the dubious privilege of the emission of the voice belongs to him or her. The analyst has to keep silent, at least in principle and the great majority of the time. But here a curious reversal takes place: it is the analyst, with his or her silence, who becomes the embodiment of the voice as the object. She or he is the personification, the embodiment, of the voice, the voice incarnate, the aphonic silent voice. This is not His Master's Voice, not the voice of a command or of the superego, but, rather, the impossible voice to which one has to respond. It is the voice which does not say anything, and the voice which cannot be said. It is the silent voice of an appeal, a call, an appeal to respond, to assume one's stance as the subject. One is called upon to speak, and one would say anything that happens to come into one's mind to interrupt the silence, to silence this voice, to silence the silence; but perhaps the whole process of analysis is a way to learn how to assume this voice. It is the voice in which the linguistic, the ethical, and the political voice join forces, coinciding in what was the dimension of pure enunciation in them. They are knotted together around that pivotal kernel of the object voice, of its void, and in response to it our fate as linguistic, ethical, political subjects has to be pulled to pieces and reassembled, traversed, and assumed.

CHAPTER 6

FREUD'S VOICES

We have been pursuing our object voice from a number of different angles, but it is perhaps time for a "return to Freud," to his own theory of the voice, if such a thing exists at all.

The object "voice" started its career in psychoanalysis, on the stage and in the limelight, with the work of Lacan. He was the one who paid due attention to the voice, which up to then seemed not to have been quite heard, or reduced to whispers, although it was implicated in all the crucial steps of psychoanalysis. He promoted it to the status of the proper object of psychoanalysis, one of the paramount embodiments of what he called *objet petit a* (embodiment hardly being a suitable term), and this he saw as his key contribution to psychoanalysis. To the list of objects inherited from Freud, Lacan notoriously added two new ones, the gaze and the voice, and it looked as if the two newcomers suddenly took precedence and came to serve as model objects (models for that which, by definition, has no model). But although a new slogan, "the gaze and the voice," was quickly coined, it seems that all gazes were fixed on the gaze, both in Lacan's own work and in a host of commentaries, while not all ears were open to the voice, which failed to get a proper hearing. Redressing the balance is a risky business, for I suspect that it is the psychoanalytic fate of balance to be fatally out of balance.

But the story of the voice in psychoanalysis did not start with Lacan, and once we are armed with retrospective knowledge, it seems very strange that it was not heard earlier. The voice was put into the very cradle of psychoanalysis, so to speak, as it is after all in its nature to accompany the cradle. For the story of the voice, once we focus on it, is no sideshow, and not confined to the off-stage voices, the backstage murmurs, or the prompters. It is at the very heart of the psychoanalytic endeavor, although for a long time it has functioned as the story of voices addressed from the center-stage to the off-stage, *à la cantonade*, voices delivered to an unknown recipient, *à bon entendeur salut* (Lacan 1979, p. 208), with greetings to the one who will hear them, like messages in a bottle—and the voice in the bottle is not a bad image for our purpose. Delivered *à la cantonade*, like infants' voices, they were delivered *à Lacan*, to the one who was able to hear them. These voices are many, and they figure so centrally that I am tempted to say: in the beginning was a voice. In the beginning of psychoanalysis, that is, for the voice is a prime candidate for genesis of all sorts—the creation of the universe to start with, as we have seen.

Anecdotally, Freud proclaimed himself to be particularly recalcitrant to music. It is something he readily admits he does not understand; he lacks susceptibility and responsiveness to it; he declares his ignorance and lack of competence in that domain. We cannot quite take his word for it, for his musical references, if not abundant, are still curiously numerous enough, and show no lack of acquaintance (for a detailed list, see Lecourt 1992, pp. 219–223). He refers most often to Mozart, but also to Bizet's *Carmen*, Wagner's *Master-Singers*, Beethoven's *Fidelio*, to Offenbach, and so on—mostly, it is true, to opera. In the analysis of one of his crucial dreams in *The Interpretation of Dreams*, the "revolutionary" dream about Count Thun, we come across Freud humming to himself Figaro's "Cavatina" from *Le Nozze di Figaro* on the platform of a railway station, after seeing by coincidence the Austrian Prime Minister;[1] we discover from the letters that he used to hum arias from *Don Giovanni* to his dog, and so on. Should we see his dismissal of his musical abilities as a denegation? Doth he protest too much?

At the beginning of his piece on "The Moses of Michelangelo" (1914) he pleads for indulgence, for in matters of art he declares himself a mere amateur, trying to solve the mystery of the effect it has on him. He goes on to say:

> works of art do exercise a powerful effect on me, especially those of literature and sculpture, less often of painting. This has occasioned me, when I have been contemplating such things, to spend a long time before them trying to apprehend them in my own way, i.e. to explain to myself what their effect is due to. Wherever I cannot do this, as for instance in music, I am almost incapable of obtaining any pleasure. Some rationalistic, or perhaps analytic, turn of mind in me rebels against being moved by a thing without knowing why I am thus affected and what it is that affects me. (PFL 14, p. 253)

Can we discern in these lines a certain anguish, or even panic, in front of something which threatens to enthrall him, flood him, make him lose his analytic stance and distance? The distance he can maintain with literature and the visual arts? There is a certain paradox in the quote: he is susceptible to literature and sculpture, but he can maintain his distance and analyze how they work; while music does not touch him, but also does not allow for a distance—should he surrender to its charm, it would engulf him like a black hole. A good thing, then, that he has no ear for music, because if he had he would have to listen to it, which would be awful.[2]

Yet his incapacity to appreciate music, whatever may lie at its origin, is perhaps to his advantage: it makes him immune to a particular and most common way of dealing with the voice, the way of its aesthetic appreciation and veneration—the highest rampart against the object voice, as we have seen. His immunity to its aesthetics and its seductive Sirens' song has its counterpart in a great susceptibility for listening to voices in another register, and for hearing the voice precisely where the friend of the Italian opera is hearing-impaired.

If we take Freud under the auspices of the voice, we can see that his voices are many and of very different kinds. We would search in vain for a particular theory of the voice in Freud; he stumbles upon voices in a vast variety of contexts, at many crucial moments, and deals with them in enlightening ways, but these do not add up to a single consistent pattern; rather, they leave us with clues, enigmas, and threads to pursue. Here I will leave aside the two most obvious and frequently discussed instances: hearing voices in psychosis, and the voice of the superego, which I have dealt with briefly already. I will keep to a more elementary level, and try to see how coming to terms with the voice may lie at the bottom of the basic insights of psychoanalysis. I will follow, in three steps, the voice in fantasy, the voice in desire, and the voice in drives. The voice as an excess, the voice as a reverberation, and the voice as silence.

We can start with a provisional and simplified dividing line where the question of the voice can act as the discriminating factor: on the one hand there is the unconscious, such as it is unfolded in the three grand volumes of *The Interpretation of Dreams* (1900), *The Psychopathology of Everyday Life* (1901), and *Jokes and Their Relation to the Unconscious* (1905)—works that inaugurate the twentieth century, and forcefully represent the discovery of psychoanalysis. If the unconscious can be unfolded, this is only because it speaks, its voice can be heard, and if it speaks, this is because it is ultimately itself "structured like a language," as Lacan will attempt to cut this very long story very short half a century later. On the other hand, with the *Three Essays on the Theory of Sexuality* (1905), there is a change of scenery, a different setting, and the stage is suddenly held in sway by heroes of another kind, the drives, and their remarkable feature is that they are silent, *stumm*, mute, says Freud. They don't speak at all, they go about their business in silence—they don't quite keep their mouths shut, not in the case of the oral drive, but if the mouth is opened, it is not in order to speak. (Eating or speaking—Deleuze will dwell insistently on this dilemma, to which we will return.)

When the drives themselves are later divided, when Freud draws the line between the libido on the one hand and the death drive on the other—the divide which will preoccupy and trouble him through much of his later life—it will again be a divide by means of the voice: "We are driven to conclude that the death drives are by their nature mute and that the clamor of life proceeds for the most part from Eros" (PFL 11, p. 387). So in that revised view, the drives still don't speak, although they make a lot of noise, they provide the clamor of life—but only the libido, Eros, whereas its counterpart, the mysterious death drive, keeps silent, invisible and inaudible, albeit omnipresent. Both drives are always intertwined, inserted in each other; they always act together in various combinations, so that the silence of the death drive is the accompanying silent shadow of the clamor of life, its reverse.

THE CLICK

But let us start with the first part of the divide, the unconscious where "it speaks," where speech is the medium of unconscious desire, where, according to the Lacanian dictum, "the unconscious is structured like a language." So where is the voice in all this? The voice which is precisely the element which eludes the signifier and cannot be pinned down by its logic, which is the rest, the leftover of the signifying operation? Is there a voice of the unconscious as opposed to language structure? I can tentatively start with the formula that language itself appears not to be quite structured like a language. There is the element of the voice which disturbs it, prevents it from quite being language; there is a voice like a foreign body which eludes language and at the same time drives it, as it were.

Let us take an example, a curious case that Freud called "A Case of Paranoia Running Counter to the Psychoanalytic Theory of the Disease" (1915). Briefly, there is this beautiful young lady, who is at a certain point convinced by the entreaties of her fellow employee to engage in an affair with him. So she comes to his apartment for the first time, in a state of great nervousness and excitement. But: ·

> Lying partly undressed on the sofa beside her lover, she heard a noise like a click or beat. She did not know its cause, but she arrived at an interpretation of it after meeting two men on the staircase, one of whom was carrying something that looked like a covered box. She became convinced that someone acting on instructions from her lover had watched and photographed her during their intimate tête-à-tête. (PFL 10, p. 154)

The prospect of lovemaking was interrupted by a mysterious sound, a noise, a click, a knock, a beat, a tick. Its origin is unknown, and her lover, when asked, dismisses it as trivial—the old clock ticked, perhaps. The strange noise then acquired a huge importance in retrospect, it was suddenly encircled by a retroactive interpretation, a paranoiac construction, a fantasy which provided it with a meaning and a framework: the poor girl saw herself as the victim of persecution, a conspiracy orchestrated by her lover—it was the click of a camera in order to take embarrassing photos of her, and anything her lover can later say in his defense only proves his guilt all the more. The tiny noise, the inexplicable tick, is like a grain of desire, a small provocation which triggers off massive consequences. And to start with we could say: in the unconscious it doesn't only speak, it ticks, and perhaps there is no ça parle without a ça cliquète. Desire ticks (like the infernal machine?).

So how is the contingent and insignificant external noise linked with the unconscious? How can it become the object of a fantasy, which then animates the subject from the most intimate interior? Freud's account contains two elements. First:

> I do not believe that the clock ever ticked or that there was any noise to be heard at all. The woman's situation justified a sensation of a knock or beat in her clitoris. And it was this that she subsequently projected as a perception of an external object. (ibid., pp. 155–156)[3]

Could there be a simple answer to the intriguing question "What makes women tick"? We can easily see that we are on suspicious ground here, where Freud rather enacts the role assigned to him by the feminist critique—the role of someone who imposes his own male fantasies about feminine sexuality on the hapless woman, so that he may be unwittingly providing an answer to another question, namely, "What makes men tick?" Yet, with all this skepticism in mind, there is at the same time a compelling credibility to what he is saying: the strange loop, the tie between inner and outer, the short circuit between the external contingency and the intimate, the curious match of the click and the inner sexual arousal. The click comes at the most inappropriate moment, it prevents the happy continuation, it is *der Störer der Liebe*, the disturber of love (PFL 14, p. 353), as Freud says in another context, when discussing the dimension of the uncanny. It is the moment of derailment of desire, a structural moment when something which upsets and interrupts the course of desire toward its fulfillment actually defines and drives the desire itself. The click, the tiny tick, the stumbling block of desire, makes the object appear, and quite independently of particular notions of physiology and male projections it produces a paradigmatic situation: the short cut between the inner and outer ticking provides the clue to "what makes desire tick."

But there is more and stranger to come. Hearing the click in that context evokes the stereotypical primal fantasy.

> Among the store of unconscious phantasies of all neurotics, and probably of all human beings, there is one which is seldom absent and

which can be disclosed by analysis: this is the phantasy of watching sexual intercourse between the parents. I call such phantasies . . . "primal phantasies.". . . The accidental noise was thus merely playing the part of a provoking factor which activated the typical phantasy of overhearing which is a component of the parental complex. Indeed, it is doubtful whether we can rightly call the noise "accidental.". . . Such noises are on the contrary an indispensable part of the phantasy of listening [*Belauschungsphantasien*], and they reproduce either the sounds which betray parental intercourse or those by which the listening child fears to betray itself. (ibid., p. 154)

The situation of the patient would thus be a displaced reenactment of a paradigmatic fantasy which is constructed entirely around the kernel of the voice, the grain of an inexplicable noise, a mysterious sound, which can appear even with the tiniest click. At the origin of fantasy there is a traumatic kernel materialized by the voice, the noise—we should allow full latitude here to a sonority not pertaining to language.

The essential feature is the double nature of this sound—it is on the one hand what one hears, which manifests the enigmatic activity of the Other by which one is spellbound, awestruck, mesmerized; and at the same time the sound that one might produce oneself and which could betray us in front of the other, disclose our existence to the Other, reveal our hideaway, where we are the guilty witness of something we shouldn't witness: a "too-much" has been manifested, revealed by the voice, and we fear disclosing "too much" of ourself by our own noise. The subject is petrified in anguish and becomes one with the sound, the sound heard and the sound emitted, he or she is caught between two sounds which can ultimately be seen as one and the same object. (We can all remember the striking scene from Lynch's *Blue Velvet*.) The sound heard raises the question of the mystery in the other—"What makes the Other tick?"—which is immediately translated into one's own mystery—"What makes me tick?," "Can the Other hear me ticking?," so that both sounds, both voices, both tickings, both questions, are amalgamated into one object, the object of terror, the object of anguish, the object of an enigma. The object which is sonorous, and appears as the kernel of subjectivation. The enigma in the Other is that excess which actually makes the Other the Other at all, it is what bestows otherness on it, it is the sound which betrays the excess of an unfathomable enjoyment, and the position of the trapped subject shows how the enjoyment of the Other immediately raises the question of one's own enjoyment. In Dora's analysis, when the same problem occurs,[4] Freud says: "Children, in such circumstances, divine something sexual in the uncanny sounds [das unheimliche Geräusch] that reach their ears. Indeed, the movements expressive of sexual excitement lie within them ready to hand, as innate pieces of mechanism" (PFL 8, pp. 116–117). If there were innate pieces, then the problem would be far less serious: for the whole difficulty is that the subject confronting this enigma is left without clue or guidance.

I can mention here, at least in passing, that Jean Laplanche's enterprise to rehabilitate, as it were, the theory of seduction is located in this particular constellation. There was a line of criticism of Freud which attacked him for allegedly suppressing the evidence of sexual child abuse as the main cause of hysteria, and replacing it with innocuous fantasies. Hysteria presented itself in rather spectacular forms which seemed like effects without a proper cause, and the trauma of seduction seemed to provide the missing cause, while Freud's abandoning of the theory of seduction seemed to put the blame on women themselves again. Laplanche's argument is that seduction, or a traumatic sexual exposure of the child, is indeed at the bottom not only of all hysteria but also of any subject formation. There is always a mysterious overinvestment to which the child is subjected, there is an excess of passion displayed in relation to the child as well as in relations between adults, an excess in the Other that the child witnesses and that amounts to a traumatic mystery which triggers off the process of subjectivation. What is driving the Other, what makes it enjoy, how do I fit into all this? The most standard and stereotypical version of this is Lauschphantasie, the fantasy of overhearing.[5] So seduction is not "all in the mind," but at the same time it is also not simply attributable to external causality—the new causality of fantasy is precisely the encounter between the two.

From our biased angle, the most interesting part is the role played by the voice, the mysterious sound-object, which is the paramount sign of that excess in the Other; it compresses the enigma of the Other while being simultaneously the telltale sign of the excess in the subject—there is, as it were, an overlapping of two excesses. This is where Freud sees the cornerstone on which he hopes to build a new theory of hysteria and a new model of human psychic life. He keeps coming back to the topic over and over again in his correspondence with Fliess and the early writings on the etiology of hysteria.

> The missing piece in the hysteria puzzle which I could not find has turned up in the form of a new source from which an element in unconscious production flows. I refer to the hysterical phantasies which, I now see, invariably go back to things heard in early infancy and only subsequently understood. The age at which such knowledge is acquired is remarkably early—from six to seven months onwards! (April 6, 1897; Freud 1977, p. 193)[6]

A month later:

> The phantasies arise from things *heard* but only understood *later*. . . . They are defensive structures, sublimations and embellishments of the facts, and at the same time serve the purpose of self-exoneration. . . . I now see that all three neuroses, hysteria, obsessional neurosis and paranoia, share the same elements. . . . But the break-through into consciousness, the compromise or symptom-formation, is different in each case. (May 2, 1897; ibid., p. 196)

In "Draft L," dated the same day: "[The phantasies] are related to things heard in the same way as dreams are related to things seen. For in dreams we hear nothing, but only see" (ibid., pp. 197–198).

This series of quotes is from the time when Freud is struggling hard, in his communication with Fliess, to delineate the basic concepts and mechanisms, but we can find many more, and Freud remained remarkably faithful to this particular insight throughout his work right up to his last paper, *An Outline of Psychoanalysis* ([1938] 1940).[7]

The basic insight points in one direction: first, the voice, the noise, things heard, are at the core of the formation of fantasy; a fantasy is a confabulation built around the sonorous kernel, it has a privileged relationship to the voice, as opposed to dreams which are, supposedly, visual, as if the two modes of psychic functioning required two different types of object. The primal fantasy is built around the voice, while the stuff that dreams are made of are images, even though the clue to them is retained by words—this poses the tricky problem of voice and language in dreams, which we must leave aside. Second, and most important, there is a temporality, a specific time-loop, which Freud never tires of mentioning: *the time-lag between perception and understanding*. There is a voice which constitutes an enigma and a trauma because it persists without being understood, there is a time of subjectivation which is precisely the time between hearing the voice and understanding it—and this is the time of fantasy. The voice is always understood *nachträglich*, subsequently, retroactively, and the time-loop of the primal fantasy is precisely the gap between hearing and making sense of what we hear, accounting for it. As in Lacan's graph of desire, where sense emerges on the retroactive vector (Lacan 1989, pp. 303, 306, 315), only here the retroactive loop takes its time, years pass before "the quilting point" makes its appearance. In the meantime fantasy steps in, like a protracted provisional quilting point, and the subject's position is the counterpart of the voice not yet understood. Fantasy functions as a provisional understanding of something which eludes understanding.[8]

Lacan used the parable of the three prisoners to develop his idea of a logical time, three logical times which match the temporality of the parable (1966, pp. 197–213): there is *l'instant de voir*, the instant of seeing—for our purposes *l'instant d'écoute*, the instant of hearing—followed by a protracted *temps pour comprendre*, the time to understand, which is eventually terminated by *le moment de conclure*, the moment of conclusion, where the solution finally appears. The time of fantasy is situated in the time for understanding, between the initial and the final moment: it is the defense against the excessive nature of the initial moment, it frames the voice and underpins it with fiction, it emerges in the place of understanding, instead of understanding, as a stand-in for understanding before the concluding moment when the true sense will finally be revealed, and there will no longer be any need for fantasy.

But the trouble is that the moment for a proper understanding never arrives; it is as if it were infinitely deferred. The time between hearing and understanding is precisely the time of construction of fantasies, desires, symptoms, all the basic structures which underlie and organize the vast ramifications of human enjoyment. But once this mechanism is in place, there is never a point where one could say, with clear objectivity and equanimity, with calm composure: "So this is what it was all about, it was my parents having sex. That's all right then, everything is under control, things make sense; this is, after all, what parents are supposed to do by definition, if they didn't do it they wouldn't have been parents in the first place (at least, not in Freud's day); I can see clearly now, there is no need for trauma, *the world is back in joint again.*" There is an inherent impossibility of ever uttering this— or I suppose if someone did say it, it would be a clear case of psychosis. Say this, or some equivalent, and "the end of civilization as we know it" would follow: our world would be seriously out of joint.

When the subject does finally understand, at the supposed moment of conclusion, it is "always-already" too late, everything has happened in between: the new understanding cannot dislodge and supplant fantasy—on the contrary, it necessarily becomes its prolongation and supplement, its hostage. The true sense, the proper sense, is always preceded by the fantasmatic sense which sets the stage, takes care of the scenery, so when the supposed lead actor finally appears, he is framed: no matter what he says, the stage has been set and the setting overdetermines his words. The advent of adequate understanding is the advent of the most implausible and preposterous fantasy of all: that there could be a neutral objective understanding of "sexuality," of enjoyment, of that excess; that we could treat it with the proper distance, dispassionately, supposedly in a scientific language, preferably in Latin.[9] But there is no proper measure, no middle way of moderation, no level-headedness. We can see that the most technical, meticulously accurate and factual description of "sexual activities" actually appears as the most delirious of all: impartial objectivity immediately coincides with delirium.

When the infant hears, he should not be able to understand anything; when the adult understands, he should not be traumatized; but both these extremes are impossible: the non-understanding is being derailed, and the understanding does not put it back on track. The subject is always stuck between voice and understanding, caught in the temporality of fantasy and desire. In the simplified retroactive perspective, there is "the object voice" in the beginning, followed by the signifier which is a way of making sense of it, of coming to terms with the voice. But we can see from this simple little scheme that the signifier is always taken hostage by fantasy, it is "always-already" inscribed in its economy, it always emerges as a compromise-formation. There is a temporal vector between the voice (the incomprehensible, the traumatic) and the signifier (the articulation, the rationalization), and what links the two, in this precipitating and retroactive temporality, is fantasy as the juncture of the two (which Lacan, in his algebra, marks precisely as $\mathcal{S} \lozenge a$, the juncture between the subject of the signifier and the object).

We saw how sense, when it makes its appearance, instead of dissipating fantasy, only prolongs it. This no doubt sheds some light on Lacan's somewhat enigmatic slogan "*On ne comprend que ses fantasmes,*" "One understands only one's own fantasies." Indeed, understanding is fatally implicated in and entwined with recognition, with finding again (*wiederfinden*, says Freud)—finding the lost clue, finding oneself—finding what one has always known, reducing the unknown and the foreign to the well-known, known since time immemorial. *Einleuchten*, another word of Freud's: to be enlightened by seemingly finding what appeared to be lost, to find what one always-already knew, to be persuaded by seeing the light, with the effect of "Yes, this is it," or—which comes down to the same thing—"Yes, this is me"—and this is the telltale mark, the sure sign of fantasy. Understanding is finding oneself in fantasy, reestablishing its framework to accommodate more and more, enlarging it, not dissipating it, not traversing it—but traversing it is the point where psychoanalysis should lead. So the analytic process would be contrary to understanding, a dissipation of understanding. Knowledge, le savoir, and what Lacan called l'enseigne-ment, teaching, are at the opposite end of fantasy; it is a matter of con-struction, and ultimately of matheme, letters which are precisely meaningless, which are regulated by an automatism of their own, and are, in their literality, the vehicles of the transmission of knowledge. They introduce into knowledge what eludes understanding, the point of anchorage epitomized by matheme. Hence proper knowledge about sex—not its fantasmatic understanding—would be presented precisely by the notorious formulas of sexuation—we could read them as the counterpart, at the opposite end, of that uncanny incom-prehensible noise by which we have been unsettled, and which we couldn't figure out.

LALANGUE

Let us now pursue the voice from a very different angle: the voice in the formations of the unconscious, which, according to Lacan's very elementary thesis, are but the formations of the signifier. So where would the location of the voice be, given the dichotomy, the opposi-tion between the voice and the signifier? To put it roughly, and in a simplified way, words, insofar as they serve as "raw material" for un-conscious processes, are treated as sonorous objects. What counts in them is their particular sonority, resonance, echoes, consonances, re-verberations, contaminations. We can take only the simplest of them, the slip of the tongue, and we need only glance briefly through The Psychopathology of Everyday Life[10] to appreciate "the sonorous setting" of the unconscious.

Freud's study of slips of the tongue, the most important category of a larger class of parapraxes (the word invented by Strachey for Fehl-leistungen), is preceded by a work by Meringer and Mayer, "Slips in Speak-ing and Reading" (Versprechen und Verlesen, 1895). The two authors make a rough classification of the slips and put them into five main cate-gories: transpositions; pre-sonances or anticipations; post-sonances or preservations; contaminations; and substitutions. All these cate-gories are but elaborations of one simple fact: the surface similarities of sound, the fact of homonymy. Words, quite contingently, sound alike, to a greater or lesser degree, which makes them liable to contamination; their mutual sound contacts can transform them, distort them, be it by retention, the inertia of certain sounds, their momentum by which they influence what follows, or by anticipation of certain sounds which influence what precedes them, or by various modes of substitution. In this contamination a new formation is born—a slip, which may sound like nonsense but produces the emergence of another sense.

To take two examples from hundreds: a patient says: "One thing must be granted to [my family]: they all possess *Geiz* [greed, avarice]—I meant to say *Geist* [cleverness, spirit]" (PFL 5, p. 106). To explain this innocuous-looking pun, one could write a whole book;[11] the sound connection establishes the relationship between spirit and avarice, everything is encompassed in that span. The second example: "Es war mir auf der *Schwest* . . . *Brust* so schwer" (ibid., p. 125), "It lay so heavily on my breast." You could think that the anticipated last word simply contaminated a previous one, but Freud is quick to point out the connection to *Bruder und Schwester*, brother and sister, and speculates about the implication of *die Brust der Schwester*, the sister's breast, and the possible fantasy behind it to which the chance encounter of sounds gave an opportunity to come to light.

Sound contaminations can be produced metonymically, on the axis that Saussure called *in praesentia*, by the sounds which are present in the current signifying chain; or the present words may be conflated with absent ones, on the axis *in absentia*, with those that are merely in the speaker's mind (Saussure actually called that axis by a Freudian name, the axis of associations, and included in it homonyms, chance sound similarities). Meringer and Mayer called the absent words surrounding the present ones "'floating' or 'wandering' speech images" which dwell "beneath the threshold of consciousness" (p. 98; quoted by Freud). The clue to this hidden paradigmatic chain lies only in the speaker, but in a speaker whose psychology is entirely delivered up to the intricacies of language sounds. The floating and wandering words are drifting and fluttering around the present chain, waiting for their moment, the opportunity suddenly to come to light. These floating signifiers, in a minimalist sense, are there at all times, lurking in ambush in vast quantities. All these mechanisms are, of course, closely akin to the processes of dream-work described as condensation and displacement, and to those of jokes, so that all three books are organized around the same basic insight, although they approach it from different angles.

It is as if we had a certain miniature version of our preceding scenario, only in reverse: there is a speech which makes sense, and in that horizon of sense-making there is suddenly a disturbance, the intrusion of the voice, the sound, which functions as a disruption of which we cannot make sense. The element of the voice, in the form of contingent and senseless co-sonance, unexpectedly runs amok and produces nonsense, which in the second step turns out to be endowed with an unexpected sense emerging from it. In the setting of understanding—that is, of fantasy—an intruder appears as a foreign body, and its strangeness depends precisely on the element of voice/sound, as opposed to signification. With the formation of fantasy, there was a protracted time-loop; years could pass between the senseless sound and the retroactive understanding; the long time vector provided the framework of fantasy as a makeshift arrangement before the advent of meaning—but nothing is more permanent than makeshift arrangements and temporary measures, which, once established, show a steadfast perseverance and inertia. But here we have a time-loop which happens in an instant, like a flash of lightning, an instantaneous invention, which is gone the moment it is produced. The nonsense emerges from contingent sound encounters, and with it another sense, which can manifest itself only for a moment because of that co-sonance, through the momentary resounding, then it is gone. It is gone despite the interpretation which tries to provide it with a framework of sense, the horizon of understanding; or rather, it evaporates through the interpretation which consists of pinning it down to a particular sense, naming its meaning, reducing its nonsense, but loses it precisely by endowing it with a positive content—as if it existed properly only in that instant, if indeed this can be called existence at all.

The first point that follows from this concerns the relationship between language and the unconscious: the unconscious may well be structured like a language, but language treated in a most peculiar way. We will start with the useful formula proposed by Jacques-Alain Miller, which delineates the Lacanian notion of the voice as that part of the signifier which does not contribute to making sense (Miller 1989, p. 180). The signifier is a mere bundle of differences, it has no positive trait or identity of its own—so it is either different and therefore distinct, or indistinct and therefore indifferent. The whole trick of Saussurean phonology is, after all, to deprive phonemes of any sonorous substance—but reverberations, the contagion of sounds, co-sonances, treating words as sound objects, all this is a very different matter. It is based on similarities, sounding alike, echoes, resemblances, correspondences, all of which stand at the opposite end of the differential logic; they are like a contingent parasite appended to the signifier. In order to sound alike, they have to sound in the first place—that is, be endowed with positive features—but those features are not differential, they may be hard to distinguish, we can never tell how much similarity is enough: does "Ananas" sound like Hammerschlag, to take Freud's example from his specimen dream of Irma's injection?[12] Are anagrams really there, as Saussure tried to prove by examining the bulk of classical Latin poetry at great length, or are they a figment of Saussure's imagination? The trouble is that they are always there, and start proliferating the moment we look for them. There are degrees and shades of similarity, infinite nuances, a moment of the undecidable, as opposed to differentiality, which is always clear-cut— something is either different, and hence linguistically relevant, or indistinguishable, and hence irrelevant. The material realization is indifferent to the signifier, but not at all indifferent to the voice value.

There is a beautiful spot in one of Freud's dreams, reported in *The Interpretation of Dreams*:

> In a confused dream of my own of some length, whose central point seemed to be a sea voyage, it appeared that the next stopping place was called "Hearsing.". . . "Hearsing" was a compound. One part of it was

derived from the names of places on the suburban railway near Vienna, which so often end in "ing": Hietzing, Liesing, Mödling (Medelitz, *"meae deliciae,"* was its old name—that is *"meine Freud"* ["my delight"]). The other part was derived from the English word "hearsay." (PFL 3, 406)

Hearsing, as opposed to *hearsay,* "hearsing" along with hearsay, inserted into hearsay—what an economical description of the way the signifier works in the unconscious.[1] The element of singing in saying, that which does not contribute to signification, is the stuff that enables the flash of the appearance of the unconscious. Analysis is always based on "hearsay"—what else does the analyst do but hear people say?—but the point is that inside the hearsay one should lend an ear to hearsing, *to give hearsing a hearing.* "Hearsing" in "hearsay" is the point where the voice takes over: what seemed to be a mere leftover of signification imbues the very process of signification. But by the same gesture, interpretation also runs the risk of losing it the moment it squeezes it back into the mold of the signifier, as one necessarily does by endowing it with meaning. "Hearsing" is the lever of analytic interpretation, the special way in which it treats "hearsay," but also its counterpart, since interpretation runs into re-signification, while "hearsing" eludes it.

The word as a signifier, the word as a sound object: how do we think them together? Are the two logics simply external, differentiality versus similarity and heterogeneity of sounds? Distinctiveness versus co-sonance? Necessity versus contingency? The notorious arbitrariness of the signifier is the source of necessity; this is the whole point of Saussure, its differentiality is binding and compelling, whereas sounds and voices are purely contingent, their logic is erratic and unpredictable. Lacan's concept for dealing with this is *lalangue* (Lacan in Mitchell and Rose 1982 *passim*). The English translation could not come up with anything better than llanguage, to keep the same sound image, for *lalangue* is a pun, the concept of what in language makes puns possible, and the very word *lalangue* is the first specimen of its kind. *Lalangue* is not language taken as the signifier, but neither is it conceiving language simply under the auspices of sound echoes. It is, rather, the concept of their very difference, the difference of the two logics, their split and their union in that very divergence: a difference which is not the difference of differentiality, but a difference in their very incommensurability. They are not outside each other, but they do not coincide either. I am almost tempted to say (to use Deleuzian parlance) that there are two series, the series of signifiers and the series of voices which do not contribute to signification, and the two series differ precisely on the basis of their points of convergence, of crosscuts, intersections, where the sound conflation functions as the break of signification and at the same time the source of another signification, their amalgamation serving as the point of their divergence.

We can say that in Lacan's early work, where we find the adage "the unconscious is structured like a language," the starting point is the logic of the signifier—his concept of the subject as $, *sujet barré*, the subject without qualities rooted in a lack (that is, the subject without roots), follows from there. He treated the other logic, the "voice value," in the framework of the signifier, as a paradox of its logic. One consequence of this was the stark dichotomy between the signifier and the object, the object presenting the heterogeneous moment of enjoyment "beyond" language, ungraspable by the signifier, although a result of its intervention. Indeed, one of his famous slogans ran: "*jouissance* is forbidden to him who speaks as such [*la jouissance est interdite à qui parle comme tel*]" (Lacan 1989, p. 319). But with the concept of *lalangue* (in *Encore* and after) this external opposition, as it were (though it was never simply external), became the internal split of language as such. It is as if the object, the object voice, and hence enjoyment, became integrated into the signifier, but integrated in such a way that their divergence is what drives *lalangue*. The antinomy of the signifier and the voice, which we have been pursuing from the outset, thus turns into the inner divergence which precludes the separation of signifier versus voice, with the consequence that we can no longer isolate the signifier as the basis of "it speaks." There is a twist in *Encore* where it seems that "*ça parle*," "it speaks," is displaced or replaced by "*ça jouit*," "it enjoys," so that enjoyment becomes the inner element of speech itself—it inundates speech, yet without engulfing it; it invades it in such a way that the logic of difference constantly intersects with the logic of similarities and reverberations, to the point where the former can no longer be isolated as a sphere on its own ("the symbolic").

Lalangue means that there is enjoyment in speech, not the proscribed object beyond it, that every sense is always *jouis-sens, le sens joui*, in another pun: the element of enjoyment in the very process of making sense. So it would follow that "the unconscious is structured like a language" is now replaced by another slogan, "the unconscious is structured like *lalangue*," which displaces the starting point altogether. If the first formula required the antinomy of signifier versus voice, then the second takes them on the same level, as belonging to the same surface, the surface of a Moebius strip: proceeding on the surface of the signifier, we find ourselves on the surface of the voice (and vice versa); the two are placed on the same surface separated merely by its inner torsion. We do not have to cross a border, yet they are not simply the same; their coincidence would disable language, and language now appears as nothing but the torsion leading from one to the other. We have seen that there is no linguistics of the voice, merely the linguistics of the signifier. But Lacan's second answer would be that there is not even a linguistics of the signifier but, rather, something he called *linguisterie*, to do justice to the erratic nature of *lalangue*.

Looking back, we can see that the ghost of *lalangue* was haunted structuralism from the outset. The easiest and most spectacular demonstration is perhaps the title of the series of lectures that Roman Jakobson delivered in New York during the war, one of the mythical birthplaces of structuralism. Jakobson was offered a chair in general linguistics, and he started by giving "six lectures on sound and sense," to explain some basic tenets of structural linguistics on the whole and phonology in particular. Lévi-Strauss was part of the enthusiastic audience, and he later testified that he was a changed man after hearing this revelation, so that the encounter with Jakobson's phonology was at the core of his own project.

The six lectures were published only in 1976, under the title *Six leçons sur le son et le sens*, duly prefaced by Lévi-Strauss. The title, in its deceptive simplicity, economically epitomizes the fate of structural-ism. The English version, *Six Lectures on Sound and Meaning* (published by MIT in 1978), of course ruins it all in its very accuracy. On the face of it, the title goes straight to the core of the problem: how do we make sense with sounds? How do we make sounds make sense? The con-nection between sound and sense is what defines language, and phonology was a revolutionary tool to explain its mechanism and its operation—baffling by virtue of its elegant simplicity of explanation, by its deductive rigor of demonstration, inspiring Lévi-Strauss to see in phonology the lever which could endow human sciences with the very strictness which until then seemed to have been the privilege of the natural sciences.[13]

But listen to it again—I mean listen, not read: *Six leçons sur le son et le sens.* Jakobson spent half of his illustrious linguistic career reflecting not only on standard matters of linguistics, but on his pet subject of poetics. For him, the question "How do sounds make sense?" must be enlarged by and translated into another question, "How does lan-guage produce poetic effects?" Language is never just about making sense, but on the way to making sense it always produces more than the sense catered for, its sounds exceed its sense. The elementary proof of this is the wording of the title: with Jakobson, there can cer-tainly be no coincidence that we find the alliteration of "s" repeated four times at the beginning of words, once in the middle and once at the end; and no coincidence about the pun on "leçons" and "le son"—it all gets lost in the English translation. The title was made with "alliteration's artful aid" (to quote another pun coined by Churchill). Certainly sounds make sense, but at the same time the title demon-strates that there is an excess of sounds over sense, there is a sound-surplus which does not make sense, it is there just like that, for the fun of it, for the beauty of it, for the pleasure of it. For what does allitera-tion mean? Is there a meaning that could be assigned to it? It is as if the title contained a hidden message beyond the straightforward one—not beyond, but in the very same place. The title announces six les-sons, but there is a seventh lesson to be drawn from the title itself.

The title points in two different directions. On the one hand, on the level of meaning, it paves the way for phonology, that is, a treatment of linguistic sounds which deprives them of their phonic substance and reduces them to purely differential entities. But on the other hand, on the level of the phonic substance, sounds are not to be reduced, but to be maintained, elaborated; their music can be heard, they can make sound echoes, they can reverberate, they can be the material of an art of sounds apart from their sense-making properties. The sounds of the title are not the phonologically relevant sounds, they produce an irrelevant surplus in the currency of sense, a frivolous addition, a supplement to the primary function of language. They are like parasites of phonemes—strange parasites, for phonemes are supposed to be fleshless, bloodless, and boneless (in Jakobson's own words), whereas the sounds of the title are endowed with sonorous flesh and blood, like a bodily parasite on a bodiless creature.

Perhaps I am reading too much into this, but I suppose that Jakobson, an admirer of Lewis Carroll, could not have been unaware of the famous slogan from *Alice*: "Take care of the sense, and the sounds will take care of themselves" (Carroll 1986, p. 121). The line is put into the mouth of the Duchess who, when she says it in the book, demonstrates the very opposite, for she most glaringly disregards the sense of what has gone before and, rather, displays the senseless part of making sense; and surely that was not the line that Lewis Carroll ever followed himself, fortunately for us. And there is a glaring contradiction in the line itself, for it is coined on the English proverb "Take care of the pence, and the pounds will take care of themselves." So the line is made possible not by the sense it is supposed to convey, but by following the sound pattern of a mold, the strangely coercive quasi-automatism presented by proverbs (I am tempted to say that, on the whole, proverbs make more sound than sense). The line is most apposite for Jakobson's title: take care of the sense—that is, reduce the voice to phonemes, discrete differential units, if you want to make sense—and the sounds will take care of themselves—that is, there will be a surplus not catered for, you will utter more than you intended, the sounds will exceed your meaning, the uninvited intruders which seem mysteriously to carry a sense of their own, independently of what you wanted to say.

It is here that we can draw a provisional demarcation line between hearing and listening, and between meaning and sense. To be brief: hearing is after meaning, the signification which can be linguistically spelled out; listening is, rather, being on the lookout for sense, something that announces itself in the voice beyond meaning. We could say that hearing is entwined with understanding—hence the French double meaning (*double entendre!*) of *entendre, entendement*, being both hearing and understanding, intellect—that is, reducing the heard to the meaningful, reducing the audible to the intelligible; while listening implies an opening toward a sense which is undecidable, precarious, elusive, and which sticks to the voice. Sense, apart from making a makeshift link to the Deleuzian use of the word in *The Logic of Sense*, also alludes to the other use of sense: that of the five senses, of the sensual (to say nothing of the sensitive and the sensible). The equivoque of sense and sense (the sense of hearing) is, I suppose, structural; it is already encapsulated in the "sound and sense" formula, which could also be read as "sense and sense."

For Jakobson, what does not contribute to meaning, the erratic nature of *lalangue* on which he keeps stumbling, is then taken as the material for poetic effects; it functions as the source of repetitions, rhythms, rhymes, sound echoes, metric patterns—all the complex panoply that produces the enchantment of poetry. *Lalangue* for him is the source of an aesthetic effect which stands apart from the referential or informational function of language; it is its side-effect, which can then present the problem of establishing another kind of codification than the linguistic one. Poetics turns into the search for another set of codes which would bear not on the necessary, as do the linguistic codes, but on the contingent. Inevitably the sounds start to make sense themselves, another kind of sense than words do, an additional sense, a surplus-sense, and this is the bonus of poetry—as if first the sound echoes were the bonus of "taking care of the sense," and then another meaning emerges as the bonus of "taking care of the sounds." Even with pure nonsense poetry, it is very difficult not to see sense in it—the best proof is no doubt the immense host of interpretations and commentaries surrounding probably the most famous nonsense poem of all, "Jabberwocky" in *Alice* (see Carroll and Gardner 1986, pp. 191–197), proving that nonsense makes more sense than normal sense; it is far from absent; rather, there is too much of it.

So one way of taming, as it were, the notion of *lalangue* is to make it a matter of aesthetic pleasure. This is again a way of losing it, despite Lacan's great fascination in that period with Joyce, the author of *lalangue* if ever there was one. It is true that poetry relies on the same mechanisms as those of the unconscious, but the effect that psychoanalysis is after is not that of aesthetic fascination, but that of knowledge. All the talk about the poetics of the unconscious is surely off the mark. It is very significant that Lacan, in *Encore*, proceeds in two correlative moves: he introduces two concepts whose correlation he never explains, *lalangue* and *mathème*, but both are based on that in the signifier which does not contribute to making sense—the object in the signifier, as it were, the object within the signifier, once under the auspices of the surplus-voice (*lalangue*) and once under the auspices of the letter, the senseless letter of the matheme (hence the formulas of sexuation, and so on). I am almost tempted to make use of the Hegelian infinite judgment here: to claim the speculative identity of the two seemingly opposite extremes, so that the pure voice can ultimately be epitomized by the letter, the matheme. It is easy to be thrilled by the poetics of *lalangue* and its infinite echoes; it is more difficult to see that there is the thorn of the dead letter, of a "mathematical" formula which cuts short the endless thrill and refers it back to knowledge.[14] Both are the extreme consequences drawn from the basic axiom of all Lacan's early work: that the unconscious is structured like a language—consequences which, I think, eventually turn this premise upside down.

If the "hearsing" element is ubiquitous, if the floating sounds are always there as erratic and infinite potentialities, why are some realized, while the vast myriad are not? Why are only few chosen, and why those few rather than others? There seems to be a Leibnizian problem: we need a sufficient reason to get from potentiality to actuality. Leibniz's God examined all the potentialities, and from the choice of all possible worlds created only this one, no doubt wisely choosing the best (Voltaire notwithstanding). So who chooses among the infinite sound correspondences? They are not enough on their own, they lack sufficient reason, there has to be a principle which makes them stop floating. No doubt there are laws governing sound contaminations, "but by themselves these laws do not seem to me to be sufficiently effective to disturb the process of correct speaking" (PFL 5, p. 124). Freud's name for that principle is unconscious desire.

But what is its status? Is it a preexistent independent entity, only waiting for its chance to make its entry? Evidently there is no lack of occasions. But that would make unconscious desire something separate and detached from language, an independent tendency which would use language as its means and material in order to "express" itself. Where would it originate? It would appear as the Leibnizian *principium reddendae rationis*, the principle of sufficient reason, providing a sufficient reason for slips, dreams, symptoms—all that seems precisely to lack a sufficient reason, those tiny cracks of contingency which do not possess a firm foundation and appear as a pure surplus, an excess without a covering. We could formulate the problem of the neurotic in Leibniz's terms: everything has a sufficient reason—except me, except my slip, my symptom, my suffering, my enjoyment. How can I ever justify my existence? An impossible task in the universe of the sufficient reason. Can unconscious desire serve as the name for the sufficient reason of all that lacks a sufficient reason? Could we see in it a *ratio* examining all potential slips and wisely choosing the best one?

It is obvious that the link between language and desire is far more delicate and intimate; their intertwining cannot be disentangled. Desire emerges through and is maintained by contingent encounters, this part of the voice in the signifier, and there is no way of extricating it from that web as an independent agency, of placing it somewhere outside language from where it could regulate the particular instances of slips as their cause. A strange loop in causality takes place here, where desire is as much the effect of the slip as its cause. It emerges only through the slip as its effect and, in a circular loop, retroactively becomes its cause; it creates its anteriority, it is readable only in retrospect, it does not preexist somewhere else from where it could manipulate the language and use it as a means for its particular purposes. Ultimately it coincides with the erratic nature of language itself, with its sound echoes and reverberations, its co-sonances. It does not spring from some profundity of unconscious urges; rather, all those urges have to be interpreted as the retroactive effects of something utterly superficial, the contingent resounding of voices in the signifier, as the fold, the wrinkle, the fold of language (to use the excellent Deleuzian word), its excrescence.

Freud often insists that we should not mistake the latent thoughts that the analysis unearths under the manifest content for the unconscious desire itself, *in persona*—those latent thoughts pertain to the preconscious, often something unpleasant, but not foreign to consciousness.[15] It even seemed that the point of analysis was to make conscious those latent thoughts one is unaware of. But desire does not reside in those thoughts themselves, its locus is, rather, between the two, in the very surplus of distortion (*Entstellung*) of the manifest in relation to the latent—the distortion which cannot be accounted for by latent thoughts; they never present sufficient reason for it by themselves. It resides in the form, not in the content, but the stuff of that form is precisely the surplus of "the voice in the signifier." So the sense of interpretation would then ultimately reside not in providing meaning, in reducing the contingency by displaying the logic which lies behind it, but, rather, through the very act of establishing it, in showing this contingency.

> Interpretation is not limited to providing us with the significations of the way taken by the psyche that we have before us. This implication is no more than a prelude. It is directed not so much at the meaning as towards reducing it to the non-meaning of the signifiers, so that we may rediscover the determinants of the subject's entire behavior—not in its significatory dependence, but precisely in its irreducible and senseless character *qua* chain of signifiers. (Lacan 1979, p. 212)

SILENCE

To provide space for the voice: if this is the objective of psychoanalysis, then it is most tangible in the third and most paradoxical of Freud's voices, which is silence. Freud describes the drives as mute, silent, and the silence we will be pursuing is closely related to the drives. Silence does not entail just stillness, peace, an absence of sounds—in its proper sense it is the other of speech, not just of sound, it is inscribed inside the register of speech where it delineates a certain stance, an attitude—even more, an act.[16] For silence to emerge, it is not enough just not to make any noise, and the act of the analyst hinges very much on the nature of silence.

Silence seems to be something extremely simple, where there is nothing to understand or interpret. Yet it never appears as such, it always functions as the negative of the voice, its shadow, its reverse, and thus something which can evoke the voice in its pure form. We could use a rough analogy to start with: that silence is the reverse of the voice just as the drive is the reverse side of desire, its shadow and its "negative."

There are many kinds of silence, and perhaps we can group them for our purposes following Lacan's three registers: the symbolic, the imaginary, and the real. There is symbolic silence to start with, silence as something which ultimately defines the symbolic as such. The symbolic, at its minimum, is reducible to an alternation of presence and absence—already with Saussure the definition of the signifier as a merely differential and oppositional entity entails that language can not only use the opposition between various distinctive traits, but rely on the opposition between something and nothing, the presence of a trait and its absence.[17] The absence of an ending, in grammar, functions itself as a "zero ending," which does the job just as well as an ending at hand; the omission as such functions as a signifier in its own right. If all elements are differential, then the zero-point of difference is the difference between something and its absence, so the absence is itself part of the structure, manifesting the negative nature of the signifier. We have to hear silence, for example, as the absence of a phoneme, in order to get the meaning, so symbolic silence represents the specificity of the symbolic order as such, its structuring principle. The alternation of presences and absences is the very rhythm of the symbolic, its inner condition, and as such it contributes to meaning as much as phonemes.

In the heroic times of structuralism, one used to quote Sherlock Holmes's line about "the dog which didn't bark"—the detective deftly took the absence of a sign as a highly meaningful sign, and only in the symbolic order can something absent refer to something just as well as something present. In structuralism, the dog that doesn't bark bites. The place of a sign, designating its absence, is itself part of the sign, on the same level with it. If there have been many discussions of the relation between the mark and its inscription, the same follows for the relation between the voice and its silence, the silence being an element of the voice, the voice seized in its minimal differentiality.

On a broader level of discourse, a whole "pragmatics of silence" can follow from there, which would explore various uses of silence for "communication" and its efficacy as an inner element of speech. Silence as the simple absence of speech can acquire the highest meaning, it can be taken as a sign of superior wisdom. Silence can be a most telling answer which refers the speaker back to her question and its presuppositions, but it can also be a sign of ignorance, the highest easily mingling with the lowest. "Silence is golden," and *si tacuisses, philosophus mansisses* ("had you kept silent, you would have remained a philosopher," where the silent wisdom of the philosopher appears as the counterpart of the dog that didn't bark).

The pragmatics of silence can be made into a system—even more, promoted to an art, which was done in the time of the flourishing Enlightenment by Abbé Dinouart in his pamphlet *L'art de se taire* ([1771] 2002), *The Art of Keeping Silent*. We can take a brief look at this, just for fun. Dinouart, a fervent supporter of the Church, saw the art of silence in the first place as a weapon against the flood of speech inundating the Enlightenment century. This massive overflow fueled by mere reason was for him but jabber, a gibberish which threatened to undermine the validity of the spiritual and the authority of faith—and we can certainly not accuse the poor Abbé of paranoia. Can one dam this deluge by silence, and thus enable the return of old values? For him, speech is a matter of reason and understanding, but what transcends reason can take place only in silence. Yet silence is an art, it is not easy at all, it does not come naturally: "in order to be silent well, it is not enough to shut one's mouth and not speak: then there would be no difference between man and animals, which are mute by their nature" (Dinouart 2002, p. 38). Silence requires great effort; it implies an ethics whose first principle is: "We must not interrupt the silence unless we have something to say which is better than silence" (ibid., p. 39). Silence would thus be the measure of sense, but can any word be measured against this yardstick? Can we then speak at all? Anything we could say weighs too little against the backdrop of silence.

But Dinouart does not push his ethics so far; rather, it is an ethics of the good measure, of moderation, of weighing one's words and choosing the right moment. The second principle states: "There is a time for silence, just as there is a time for speech" (ibid.). Silence is the choice of *kairos*, the good moment for speech which endows speech with proper authority. So the art of silence is part of rhetoric; it is an art of how to influence the addressee all the better, and already the old rhetoreticians have proposed rhetorical silence to add to their bag of tricks. Silence works as the efficient support which endows the few chosen words with their proper weight.

Dinouart offers a whole phenomenology of silence and its effects, enumerating ten kinds of silence. Briefly: (1) a prudent silence (a prudent man knows when to keep silent and when to speak); (2) a contrived silence (used to confuse the other and hide one's thoughts); (3) a compliant silence (so as not to infuriate the other, and keep out of trouble); (4) a mocking silence (expressing criticism and ironical distance); (5) a spiritual silence (conveying a spiritual openness and presence of mind); (6) a stupid silence (displaying spiritual obtuseness); (7) an approving silence (showing approbation and consent); (8) a contemptuous silence (showing disdain and coldness); (9) a moody silence (with people who depend on their temper); and (10) a political silence ("of a prudent man who controls himself, behaves cautiously, who is not always open, who doesn't say all he thinks, . . . who doesn't always answer clearly, yet without compromising the rights of truth, so as not to be found out") (Dinouart 2002, pp. 42–47).

Dinouart's pragmatics of silence is suspended between two poles: on the one hand there is calculation: how to achieve the greatest effect by silence, and thus use it as an instrument or a weapon; on the other hand there is an ethics of self-control—to learn to be silent is to learn to restrain oneself, to learn the art of self-possession, while speech always delivers us to the powers of the other; a speaking man "belongs less to himself than to others" (ibid, p. 40). There is no contradiction between the two: only a man who exerts complete self-control will be able really to influence others. The good Abbé was an excellent practitioner of his own ethics: it didn't take many words, just a short pamphlet, to ensure his place in history.[18]

If the pragmatics of silence is firmly rooted in silence as a part of discourse, symbolic silence, it also reaches by one of its ramifications something we could call imaginary silence. Silence can indicate the highest wisdom, and its extension can be a "mystic silence," a silence of the universe which can overwhelm and enthrall the observer, a vision of supreme harmony, the oceanic feeling that Freud talks about in *Civilization and Its Discontents*, cosmic peace. There are no voices to be heard, and for that very reason the silence speaks in an unalloyed presence, for voices would spoil the equilibrium, the alternation would bring imbalance. Silence functions as saturated with the highest sense, the mirror which reflects the inner and the outer in a perfect match. It is the silence not of a lack but of a supposed plenitude.

But the reverse of this overwhelming silence is epitomized by Pascal's famous sentence "*Le silence éternel des espaces infinis me fait peur,*" "The eternal silence of infinite spaces terrifies me." Pascal's exclamation expresses a feeling which no doubt pertains to modernity, and stands far apart from mystical silence. It stands at the epistemological break of modern science (ironically Pascal, the great theologist, contributed to the invention of the first calculating machine, and has given his name to a computer program). It is the silence of the universe which has ceased to speak, which is no longer the expression of the supreme sense, of harmony, of God's wise plan. It is the universe which has stopped making sense, and this subtraction of sense coincides with the advent of modern science. (Could one coin a phrase: science and silence?) This silence is neither the imaginary overwhelming nor the symbolic pulsation. The silence of the new universe does not mean anything, it does not make sense, and in this absence of sense it inspires Pascal's anxiety. It is correlative to the advent of the letter of matheme, which is equally deprived of sense.

The silence of the drives has to be read against that background: it is not a silence which contributes to sense, and this is its most disturbing feature; it presents something we can call silence in the register of the real. It does not tell us anything, but it persists—this is another feature of the drives: they insist as a constant pressure, they keep coming insistently and stupidly back to the same place, the locus of their silent satisfaction. There is nothing natural in the silence of the drives—this is not the muteness of some natural life, it does not pertain to some organic or animal base; on the contrary, the drives present a nature denatured, they are not a regression to some originary unsurpassed animal past which would come to haunt us, but the consequence of the assumption of the symbolic order. They get hold of the organic functions and corrupt them, so to speak—they abolish the natural functions of the organs and turn them into extensions of a phantom organ (hence Lacan's myth of lamella); they behave like parasites which derail the organic from its natural course, but their parasitism takes support from an excess produced by the invasion of the symbolic into the body, the intrusion of the signifier into the corporeal. What do the net of signifiers, this abstract and negative differential matrix, and the body have in common? The simplest clue is offered by the topology that we have detected in different realms: their intersection is the drive, which does not simply pertain to either the signifier or the organic; it is placed at the point of their "impossible" juncture. We used this topology to establish the proper locus for the voice, but it is emblematic for the location of the drive: all drives pertain to that realm of intersection, neither the structure nor the body, but not something external to them either; it lies at their core and keeps them together. Freud, in a famous adage, wrote that the interpretation of dreams was "the royal road to a knowledge of the unconscious activities of the mind" (PFL 4, p. 769)—I would add: to the unconscious "structured like a language"—and we can extend this by saying that the voice, this excrescence of language, is the royal road to the drives, the part which "doesn't speak."

Freud ascribed silence to only half of the drives, those that he summed up by the death drive, while the other half was summed up by the libido, bearer of all the "clamor of life." This entailed the rather mythical (and I think misleading and unfortunate) dualism of Eros and Thanatos as two cosmic principles constantly intertwined in an eternal struggle. But if one of the contenders is very clamorous, then the most salient feature of the other is that it is silent—this trait constantly recurs under Freud's pen—and since it cannot be heard and positively perceived, scientifically observed, many of Freud's followers (let alone critics) could not follow him there. They implied that in raising this highly speculative hypothesis (and Freud readily admits its speculative, even mythological nature)[19] Freud may be hearing voices. Hearing voices in that most improbable but tenacious and insidious way which is hearing a silence. How can one possibly observe this silence? Is Freud just following his fixed idea, like those saints and madmen who were assigned a mission by hearing a voice? Only his mission came from hearing a silence?

So how can we hear this silence? What difference can it make? Can we put it to use? Apart from theoretical speculation, does it have any practical consequences? Here we can propose a simple thesis: the silence of the drives is closely connected to the silence of the analyst. Psychoanalysis, in its elementary form, places side by side an analysand who speaks—the only rule being that he or she should freely say anything that comes to mind—and an analyst who keeps silent. An analogy may be useful here: we have seen how Socrates turned himself into the agent of his own daemon, his inner voice, applying the same relation to others as his daemon did to him; the analyst's stance, in a different register, consists in turning himself into the agent of a voice which coincides with the silence of the drives, by assuming this silence as the lever of his position, thus turning the silence into an act.

We have seen that *lalangue* ultimately points to a dimension where "the voice in the signifier" becomes a vehicle of enjoyment, so that speech appears as a process where signifier and enjoyment amalgamate in the infinity of sound reverberations and puns which form the texture of the unconscious. Silence seems to be at the extreme opposite end to this, and indeed the function of the analyst's silence is to interrupt this process, to bring it to a halt, to introduce a break, a gap in that flow, in this production of meaning which coincides with the production of *jouis-sens*. There is a point where the poetry of the unconscious falls on the deaf ears of the analyst. If the analyst's first function was to lend an ear to *lalangue*, to act as its addressee and the recipient of its messages beyond meaning, to listen to its sense, then his second function is the opposite: to cut short the endless poetry of the unconscious, the infinite flow of free associations, the constant slippage of enjoyment and sense. In the first role he was the interpreter deciphering the coded messages, even if he avoided the trap of simply reducing them to meaning, but in the second he embodies the limit of interpretation.

The second role, although seemingly at a maximum distance, is but the flip side of the first. It is already inscribed in the very outset of the analytic situation, in its minimal features, for the moment words are proffered in the presence of this silent other, a simple and striking effect sets in: words are suddenly transposed into a dimension where they start to sound strange and hollow; the moment the analysand hears his or her own voice against the backdrop of that silence, there is a structural effect which we could call *the dispossession of the voice*, its expropriation (*ex-proprius*—it is deprived of its proper nature). It ceases to be the asset of self-presence and auto-affection (all that could form the basis of phonocentrism). The freedom of "saying no-matter-what" is suddenly transposed into its opposite; the opposite motion sets in the very moment one starts using this freedom, the predicament where the analysand would gladly say anything to cover this silence, but to no avail. We can see our voice-scenario in its last version:

in the midst of the universe of speech there is a break introduced by silence, by this deaf voice, which dispossesses all other voices and disrupts the universe of sense.

The initial supposition of the beginning of analysis is placed under the banner of what Lacan called "the subject supposed to know." The analysand does not embark on analysis in order to listen to silence, but on the assumption that there is a supposed knowledge behind it, a knowledge that supposedly holds the clues to his or her symptoms, the keys to their meaning and their (dis)solution. Without this supposition of knowledge held by the Other, which is the lever of transference, analysis could never begin. So the analyst is placed in the realm of the Other supposingly holding the knowledge which will offer a guarantee to help the analysand out of his or her troubles, a guarantee that all nonsense will make sense, and this structural illusion underlies the "free associations" and induces the patient to address his or her speech to the analyst in the first place. But what, then, is the connection between the Other, with the supposition of its knowledge, and the silence of the drives?

In one of his (rather rare) reflections about the voice in the seminar on anxiety (June 5, 1963), Lacan argues for his tenet that the object voice has to be divorced from sonority. He makes a curious excursion into the physiology of the ear; he talks about the cavity of the ear, its snail-like shape, *le tuyau*, the tube, and goes on to say that its importance is merely topological, it consists in the formation of a void, a cavity, an empty space, of "the most elementary form of a constituted and constituting void [*le vide*]" (Lacan 2004, p. 318), like the empty space in the middle of a tube, or of any wind instrument, the space of mere resonance, volume. But this is but a metaphor, he says, and continues with the following rather mysterious passage:

> If the voice, in our sense, has an importance, then it doesn't reside in it resonating in some spatial void. The simplest emission of the voice in what is linguistically called its phatic function—which is supposed to be on the simplest level of establishing a contact, although it concerns something quite different—resonates in the void which is the void of the Other as such, *ex nihilo*, so to speak. The voice responds to

what is said, but it cannot be responsible for it [*La voix répond à ce qui se dit, mais elle ne peut pas en répondre.*] In other words: in order for it to respond we have to incorporate the voice as the alterity of what is said [*l'altérité de ce qui se dit*]. (ibid.)

How do we make sense of this? If there is an empty space in which the voice resonates, then it is only the void of the Other, the Other as a void. The voice comes back to us through the loop of the Other, and what comes back to us from the Other is the pure alterity of what is said, that is, the voice. This may be the original form of the famous formula that the subject always gets his own message back in an inverted form: the message that one gets back in response is the voice. Our speech resonates in the Other and is returned as the voice— something we did not reckon on: the inverted form of our message is its voice which was created from a pure void, *ex nihilo*, as an inaudible echo of pure resonance, and the non-sonorous resonance endows what is said with alterity. The void produces something out of nothing, albeit in the form of an inaudible echo. We expect a response from the Other, we address it in the hope of a response, but all we get is the voice. The voice is what is said turned into its alterity, but the responsibility is the subject's own, not the Other's, which means that the subject is responsible not only for what he or she said, but must at the same time respond for, and respond to, the alterity of his or her own speech. He or she said something more than he or she intended, and this surplus is the voice which is merely produced by being passed through the loop of the Other. This, I suppose, is at the bottom of this rather striking dispossession of one's voice in the presence of the silence of the analyst: whatever one says is immediately countered by its own alterity, by the voice resounding in the resonance of the void of the Other, which comes back to the subject as the answer the moment one spoke. This resonance expropriates one's own voice; the resonance of the Other thwarts it, scoops it out, although it is but an echo of subject's own words. The speech is the subject's own, but the voice pertains to the Other, it is created in the loop of its void. This is what one has to learn to respond for, and respond to.[20] And this is how the Other of the symbolic order, to which the analyst lends his support, is transformed into the agent of the voice: the silence makes that in the Other the voice emerges. One could express this economically in Lacanian algebra: from A to a. Resonance is the locus of voice—voice is not a primary given which would then be squeezed into the mold of the signifier, it is the product of the signifier itself, its own other, its own echo, the resonance of its intervention. If voice implies reflexivity, insofar as its resonance returns from the Other, then it is a reflexivity without a self—not a bad name for the subject. For it is not the same subject which sends his or her message and gets the voice bounced back—rather, the subject is what emerges in this loop, the result of this course.

The entire process of analysis thus turns into a trajectory guided by the voice. We have already seen that the voice is the very medium of analysis, and that the only tie between analyst and patient is the vocal tie. The analyst is hidden, like Pythagoras, outside the patient's field of vision, adding another turn of the screw to Pythagoras' device: if with Pythagoras the lever was the acousmatic voice, then here we have *an acousmatic silence*, a silence whose source cannot be seen but which has to be supported by the presence of the analyst. All three modalities of Freud's voices are gathered together and come into play.

First, the speech addressed to that Other acquires the form of *lalangue*: the Other is supposed to hear precisely "the voice in the signifier," the coded message pertaining not to the speaker's intention but to its slip, the constant slipping of the signifier on the voice; to hear the "hearsing" in the "hearsay." This is the stuff of unconscious formations and the work of desire, and the analyst, as the hearer, returns the message back to the sender—the message articulated in the signifiers is returned as the voice, that is, the language is returned as *lalangue*. Second, the interpretation of these formations eventually leads to their rooting in fantasy, where desire got its bearings in the first place by coming to terms with a traumatic kernel, in Freud's scenario epitomized by the voice that the fantasy tried to neutralize and endow with sense. The infinite proliferation of unconscious formations and their interpretation is countered by their reduction to a minimal core of fundamental fantasy.[21] Third, if the analyst's silence served as the backdrop for the flourishing of *lalangue* and its infinite interpretation, it is also something which keeps bringing it to a halt and sets a limit to it. The analyst is the agent of the Other, but not merely as "the subject supposed to know"—at the same time (and we cannot separate the two) it is the Other in which the voice resonates and "takes place," the support of the alterity of the voice, the place where the voice takes the value of event, of a break.

This is where "returning the message in its inverted form" acquires its final destination: the returned message is merely the voice of pure resonance; or, in other words, *the message of desire is returned as the voice of the drive.* But this is not a voice one could isolate in itself, independently of the other two; it is not the black hole of a mute enjoyment engulfing the subject, speech, desire, sense—should we try to take this voice directly as an object, as a goal, we would inevitably miss it. The problem of the drives is that they can never be taken directly as the supposed place of enjoyment; "it" does not enjoy the way we would want to—this is the whole predicament of analysands—yet "it" can be tackled, if only by the long road of "working through" the voice and the loop of the Other.

The last stage of this trajectory would be the passage from the position of the analysand to that of the analyst: it is a way of remaining faithful to this experience, to this event, to this voice, by assuming its position, by representing the very object voice. To respond to the voice and respond for it is the starting point of analytic discourse, and its point is to keep the space open for this break in the continuity of "bodies and languages." This is one way of looking at what Lacan called *la passe* as the outcome of analysis: how to turn the impasse of confronting this voice into a *passe,* a new opening.[22]

CHAPTER 7

KAFKA'S VOICES

Let us take as a provisional starting point the question of immanence and transcendence in Kafka, which can easily cause confusion and is but an avatar of the relation between internal and external that we have been pursuing. In brief, there is a whole line of interpretation which maintains that the predicament of Kafka's universe can best be described in terms of the transcendence of the law. Indeed, it seems that the law is inaccessible to Kafka's "heroes": they can never find out what it says, the law is an ever-receding secret, even its very existence is a matter of presumption. Where is the law, what does it command, what does it prohibit?[1] We are always "before the law," outside its gates, and one of the great paradoxes of this law is that it prohibits nothing, but is itself prohibited; it is based on a prohibition of the prohibition, its prohibition itself is prohibited.[2] We can never get to the locus of prohibition—if we could do that, then we would be saved—or so it seems. The transcendence of the law, on this account, epitomizes the unhappy fate of Kafka's subjects, and the only transcendence in Kafka's world is the transcendence of this law which seems like an unfathomable, ungraspable deity, a dark god emitting obscure oracular signs; we can never figure out its location, purpose, logic, or meaning.

On closer inspection, however, this elusiveness of the transcendent law reveals itself to be a mirage: it is a necessary delusion, a perspectival illusion, for if the law always escapes us, this is not because of its transcendence, but because it has no interior. It is always deferred from one instance to another, from one office to the next, because it is nothing but this movement of deferral, it coincides with this perpetual motion of evasion. The unfathomable secret behind some closed door, behind some inscrutable façade, is no secret at all—there is no secret outside this metonymical movement, which can be seen as coinciding with the movement of desire. If the law has no interior, it has no exterior either: we are always-already inside the law, there is no outside of the law, the law is pure immanence, "the unlimited field of immanence instead of infinite transcendence," to quote Deleuze and Guattari (1975, p. 79), since this second account has been made justly famous by their book on Kafka, one of the most influential recent readings.

So what on the first account appeared as pure transcendence is on the second account seen as pure immanence. On the first account we are always-already and irretrievably excluded; on the second we are always included and there is no transcendence, we are trapped in the immanence of the law which is at the same time the immanence of desire. Do we have to decide between the two, join one camp or the other? Are the two accounts irreconcilable? Although the second reading is no doubt far more useful and effectively dissipates the misunderstandings advanced by the first, it still perhaps does not quite cover what is at stake in Kafka. By promoting the dimension of pure immanence it perhaps eludes, reduces, and avoids a paradox: the paradox of the emergence of a transcendence at the very heart of immanence, or, rather, of the way immanence always doubles itself and intersects with itself. Or, to put it another way: there might be no inside, there might be no outside, but the problem of intersection remains.

Lacan, to my knowledge, never mentions Kafka in his published work, but we do find a couple of passing references in his unpublished seminars, and one of these bears directly on our point. In his seminar on "Identification" (Seminar IX, 1961/62), Lacan develops his use of topology for the first time at some length. He takes the "image" of a torus and sees the problem of the subject's desire in topological terms, translating his dictum that "the subject's desire is the desire of the Other" into the problem of establishing a communication, a passage between two tori, that of the subject and that of the Other. This requires an invention of a certain topological model where the curvature of the space would establish a link between the inside and the outside. He talks about an irreducible analogy which is "impossible to exclude from what [for the subject] is called interior and exterior, so that the one and the other pass into each other and command each other" (session of March 21, 1962). Looking for such a topological model, he has recourse to Kafka, giving a particular reference to Kafka's brilliant story "The Burrow," one of his last.[3] The complicated architecture of the burrow, with its labyrinthine passages and its true and false entries, the problem of hiding and escape, of passing from interior into exterior— all this gives the perfect paradigm for what Lacan is looking for. The burrow is the place where one is supposed to be safe, neatly tucked inside, but the whole story shows that in the most intimate place of shelter one is thoroughly exposed; the inside is inherently fused to the outside. But this structure does not relate only to architectures and space organization, it concerns "something which exists in the most intimate of organisms," their internal organization and their relation to the outside. Indeed, the man appears to be "the animal of the bur-row, the animal of the torus," and Kafka's recourse to animality—one of his favorite devices, to which we will return—thus hinges on a minimal pattern which links the human being as an "animal" organ-ism to the social and the symbolic. The one passes into the other in a curved space where they can be neither opposed nor collapsed.[4]

The immediate connection between "animality" and the law, so cen-tral to Kafka, is also the cornerstone of Agamben's endeavors, and in particular of his reading of Kafka, where "bare life" and the law appear as the front and the flip side of the same thing, although Agamben approaches this by a very different route. In his reading of the famous parable, the gate of the Law is always open, the doorkeeper doesn't prevent the man from the country from entering, yet the man finds it impossible to enter through the open door. The openness itself im-mobilizes, the subject stands awestruck and paralyzed in front of the open door, in a position of exclusion from the law, but an exclusion which is precisely the form of his inclusion, since this is how the law holds him in sway. "Before the law" one is always inside the law, there is no place before the law, this very exclusion is inclusion.

Exclusive inclusion or inclusive exclusion is the way in which Agamben, as we have seen, describes the structure of sovereignty: it is the point of exception inscribed in the law itself, the point which can suspend the validity of laws and proclaim the state of emergency. At the opposite end of the sovereign we have its inverse figure, the con-verse point of exception, which is *Homo sacer*: bare life excluded from the law in such a way that it can be killed with impunity, yet without entering the realm of sacrifice. Being outside the law, his bare life exposed to be killed with impunity, *Homo sacer* is exposed to the law as such in its pure validity. The state of emergency is the rule of law in its pure form—precisely the excess of validity over meaning (*Geltung ohne Bedeutung*, to use the expression from Gershom Scholem's correspondence with Walter Benjamin in the 1930s), the suspension of all laws and therefore the institution of the law as such. We could say: Kafka's is the literature of the permanent state of emergency. The subject is at the mercy of the law beyond all laws, without any defense; he can be arbitrarily stripped of all his possessions, including his bare life. The law functions as its own permanent transgression. Kafka's heroes are always *Homines sacri*, exposed to the pure validity of the law which manifests itself as its opposite. Kafka has turned *Homo sacer* into the central literary figure, thus displaying a certain shift in the functioning of the law which took place at the beginning of the twentieth century, and inaugurated a new era, with many drastic consequences which would define that century.

Agamben proposes an optimistic reading, as it were, of the parable "Before the Law," precisely at the point where most interpreters see merely the defeat of the man from the country. It is true that the man never manages to get into the Law, he dies outside the gate and, while dying, learns that this gate was reserved only for him. Yet the last sentence reads: "This gate was made only for you. I am now going to shut it [*Ich gehe jetzt und schließe ihn*]" (1995, p. 4). But if the very openness of the law is the pure form of its closure and of its unqualified validity and power, then the man succeeded in a most remarkable feat: he managed to attain closure. He managed to close the door, to interrupt the reign of pure validity. The closed door, in this reading, is a chance of liberation: it sets the limit to pure immanence. Admittedly, he was successful only at the price of his own life, so that the law is interrupted only when he is dead—one reading would be: the law has no power over the dead alone, one doesn't stand a chance while one is alive. Still, there is a prospect of closure, of invalidating the law if only one persists long enough. Was the man from the country so naive or so shrewd? On the one hand he was very timid, he let himself be subdued very quickly, he was easily diverted from his initial intention, instantly intimidated. On the other hand, however, he displayed incredible obstinacy, persistence, and determination. It was a struggle of exhaustion: it is true that they managed to exhaust him entirely with the open door, yet in the end he was the one who exhausted the law. If one is prepared to persist to the end, one can put an end to the validity of the law.

This seems like a desperate strategy; but what other strategies are there in this impossible predicament? If there is always some way out of the closure, there seems to be none out of the openness. This is why Kafka is generally misperceived as the depressing author of total closure with no exit, but this is also where the solution of pure immanence does not quite offer a good answer. In what follows I will examine three strategies which offer an exit, as it were, and they are all connected with the instance of the voice—precisely as a point of a paradox.

Why the voice? What places the voice in a structural and privileged position? The law always manifests itself through some partial objects, through a glimpse, some tiny fragment one unexpectedly witnesses and which, in its fragmentation, remains a mystery; by morsels; by servants, doorkeepers, maids; by trivia, by trash, the detritus of the law. This massive validity without meaning is epitomized by partial objects, and those are enough for the construction of fantasies; they suffice to capture desire. And among those there is the voice, the senseless voice of the law: the law constantly makes funny noises, it emits mysterious sounds. The validity of the law can be pinned to a senseless voice.

When the land surveyor K. arrives in the village beneath the castle, he takes lodgings in an inn, and is eager to clarify the nature of his assignment. He was sent for, he was summoned, and he wants to know why, so he calls the castle—he uses a recent invention, the telephone. But what does he hear on the other end of the line? Just a voice which is some kind of singing, or buzz, or murmur, the voice in general, the voice without qualifications.

The receiver gave out a buzz of a kind that K. had never before heard on a telephone. It was like the hum of countless children's voices—but yet not a hum, the echo rather of voices singing at an infinite distance—blended by sheer impossibility into one high but resonant sound that vibrated on the ear as if it were trying to penetrate beyond mere hearing. (Kafka 1997, p. 27)

There is no message, but the voice is enough to stupefy him; he is suddenly paralyzed: "In front of the telephone he was powerless." He is spellbound, mesmerized. This is just one example chosen at random among many.

The intervention of a voice at this juncture is crucial and necessary, since the voice epitomizes at best validity beyond meaning, being structurally placed at the point of the exception. The law can remain the law only insofar as it is written, that is, given a form which is universally at the disposal of everyone, always accessible and unchangeable—but with Kafka one can never get to the place where it is written to check what it says; access is always denied; the place of the letter is infinitely elusive. The voice is precisely what cannot be checked, it is ever-changing and fleeting, it is the non-universal *par excellence*, it is what cannot be universalized. We have already seen that the voice is structurally in the same position as sovereignty, and can put the validity of the law into question: the voice stands at the point of exception, the internal exception which threatens to become the rule, and from this point it displays a profound complicity with bare life. The emergency is the emergence of the voice in the commanding position, its concealed existence suddenly becomes overwhelming and devastating. The voice is precisely at an unplaceable spot simultaneously interior and exterior to the law, and hence a permanent threat of the state of emergency. And with Kafka the exception has become the only rule. The letter of the law is hidden in some inaccessible place and may not exist at all, it is a matter of presumption, and we have only voices in its place.

ULYSSES

K. is spellbound by the voice emanating from the castle down the telephone, as the wanderer is spellbound by the song of the Sirens. What is the secret of that irresistible voice? Kafka offers an answer in his short story "The Silence of the Sirens" ("Das Schweigen der Sirenen"), written in October 1917 and published in 1931 by Max Brod, who also provided the title. In this story the Sirens are irresistible because they are silent, yet Ulysses nevertheless manages to outwit them. Here we have the first strategy, the first model of escape from the unstoppable force of the law.

"To protect himself from the Sirens Ulysses stopped his ears with wax and had himself bound to the mast of his ship" (1995, p. 430). The first sentence is already one of Kafka's wonderful opening *coups de force*—like, for example, the opening paragraph of his novel *America*, where we see his hero, Karl Roßmann, arriving by boat in New York harbor, admiring the Statue of Liberty, with her sword rising high up to the sun. We almost do not notice, but where is the sword in the Statue of Liberty? Here we have Ulysses stopping his ears and tied to the mast, while in the legend it was the oarsmen who had their ears stopped with wax, while Ulysses was tied to the mast. There was a division of labor—indeed, the very model of the division of labor, if we follow the argument that Adorno and Horkheimer developed in *The Dialectic of the Enlightenment* (2002). There is a sharp division between those who are doomed to be deaf and to work, and those who listen and enjoy, take pleasure in art, but are helplessly tied to the mast. This is the very image of the division between labor and art, and this is the place to start scrutinizing the function of art, in its separation from the economy of work and survival—that is, in its powerlessness. Aesthetic pleasure is always pleasure in chains, it is thwarted by the limits assigned to it, and this is why Ulysses confronting the Sirens is so exemplary for Adorno and Horkheimer.

Kafka's Ulysses combines both strategies, the aristocratic and the proletarian one; he takes double precautions, although we all know that this is useless: the song of the Sirens could pierce any wax, and true passion could break any chains. But the Sirens have a weapon far more effective than their voice: their silence, that is, the voice at its purest. The silence which is unbearable and irresistible, the ultimate weapon of the law. "And though admittedly such a thing has never happened, still it is conceivable that someone might possibly have escaped from their singing; but from their silence certainly never" (p. 431). We cannot resist silence, for the very good reason that there is nothing to resist. This is the mechanism of the law at its minimal: it expects nothing of us, it does not command, we can always oppose commands and injunctions, but not silence. Silence here is the very form of the validity of the law beyond its meaning, the zero-point of voice, its pure embodiment.

Ulysses is naïve: he childishly trusts his devices, and sails past the Sirens. The Sirens are not simply silent; they pretend to sing: "He saw their throats rising and falling, their breasts lifting, their eyes filled with tears, their lips half-parted," and he believed they were singing, and that he had escaped them and outfoxed them, although their singing was unstoppable. "But Ulysses, if one may so express it, did not hear their silence; he thought they were singing and that he alone did not hear them" (p. 431). If he knew they were silent, he would be lost. He imagines that he has escaped their power by his naive cunning, and in the first account we are led to suppose that it was his naivety that saved him.

Yet the truth of the story is perhaps not in Ulysses' naivety at all: "Perhaps he had really noticed, although here the human understanding is beyond its depths, that the Sirens were silent, and held up to them and to the gods the aforementioned pretense merely as a sort of shield." The shrewd and canny Ulysses, the sly and cunning Ulysses— Homer most often accompanies his name by one of those epithets. Is his ultimate slyness displayed by putting up an act of naivety? So in the second account he outwits them by pretending not to hear that there is really nothing to hear. They were going through the motions of singing; he was going through the motions of not hearing their silence.

We could say that his ruse has the structure of the most famous Jewish joke, the paragon among Jewish jokes, in which one Jew says to another at the railway station: "If you say you're going to Krakow, you want me to believe you're going to Lemberg. But I know that in fact you're going to Krakow. So why are you lying to me?"[5] So by extension we could imagine the Sirens' reaction: "Why are you pretending that you don't hear anything when you really don't hear anything? Why are you pretending not to hear when you know very well there is nothing to hear? You pretend so that we'll think you don't hear anything, while we know very well that you really don't hear anything." The Jewish joke is Ulysses' triumph, he manages to counter one pretense with another. In the joke the first Jew, the one who simply told the truth about his destination, is the winner, for he managed to transfer the burden of truth and lie onto the other one, who could reply only with a hysterical outburst. We are left with the same oscillation as in our story: was the truth-teller so naive or so shrewd? This is exactly the question which remained in the air with the man from the country dying on the threshold of the Law. Ulysses' strategy is perhaps not unrelated to the strategy of the man from the country: Ulysses counters pretense with pretense; the man counters deferral with deferral, exhaustion with exhaustion—he manages to exhaust the exhaustion, to bring an end to the deferral, to close the door.

This does not work with the Sirens. To be sure, they are defeated: "They no longer had any desire to allure; all they wanted was to hold as long as they could the radiance that fell from Ulysses' great eyes" (p. 431). Were they suddenly seized by a yearning for the one who managed to get away? "If the Sirens had possessed consciousness they would have been annihilated at that moment. But they remained as they had been; all that had happened was that Ulysses had escaped them" (p. 432). They have no consciousness, all their behavior is going through the motions, they are automata, they are inanimate, they are machines imitating humanity, cyborgs, and this is why their defeat cannot have any effect. This one has escaped, but that cannot dismantle the mechanism.

So can we fight the law by turning a deaf ear to it? Can we just pretend not to hear its silence? This is no simple strategy, it defies human understanding, says Kafka, it boggles the mind. It takes supreme cunning, yet does not introduce a closure of the law. Ulysses was an exception, and everybody else is the rule.[6]

THE MOUSE

Let us now turn to another strategy which again has the voice at its kernel—this time a voice which is put in a position from which it could counter the voice, or the silence, of the law. "Josephine the Singer, or the Mouse Folk" ("Josefine die Sängerin oder das Volk der Mäuse") is actually the last story Kafka ever wrote, in March 1924, a couple of months before his death. By virtue of being the last, it inevitably invites us to read it as his testament, his last will, the *point de capiton*, the quilting point, the vantage point which will shed some ultimate light on his work, provide a clue which will illuminate, with finality, all that went before. And it is no doubt ironical that this clue, this suture, is provided not only by a voice but by the tiniest of voices, a minute microscopic squeak,[7] and we cannot resist taking this minuscule peep as the red thread that could retroactively enlighten Kafka's obscurity.

There is the vast question of Kafka's multiple uses of the animal kingdom, which are so prominent in his work—Deleuze and Guattari dwell upon this at some length. There is, most notoriously, the becoming-animal of Gregor Samsa, which features, among other things, his voice, the incomprehensible chirping sounds which come out of his mouth when he tries to justify himself in front of the chief clerk. "'That was no human voice,' said the chief clerk . . ." (p. 98), it is the signifier reduced to a pure senseless voice, reduced to what Deleuze and Guattari call pure intensity. The general question can be put in the following way: is animality outside the law? The first answer is: by no means. Kafka's animals are never linked to mythology, they are never allegorical or metaphorical. There is the justly famous line by Deleuze and Guattari: "Metamorphosis is the contrary of metaphor" (Deleuze and Guattari 1975, p. 40),[8] and Kafka is perhaps the first utterly non-metaphorical author.

Animal societies, the mice and the dogs[9] (to which we will come in a moment), are organized "just like" human societies,[10] which means that animals are always denaturalized, deterritorialized animals; there is nothing precultural, innocent, or authentic about them.

Yet on the other hand they nevertheless represent what Deleuze and Guattari call *la ligne de fuite*, a certain line of flight. The becoming-animal of Gregor Samsa means his escape from the mechanism of his family and his job: a way out of all the symbolic roles he had assumed. His insecthood is at the same time his liberation. Metamorphosis is an attempt to escape, albeit a failed one. But there is a double edge to this: we can read the becoming-animal on the first level as becoming that which the law has made out of subjects, that is, creatures reduced to bare animal life, the lowest kind of animality represented by insects, the crawling disgusting swarm to be decontaminated, the non-sacrificial animality (the insect is the anti-lamb) which evokes the bare life of *Homo sacer*. The law treats subjects as insects, as the metaphor has it, but Gregor Samsa destroys the metaphor by taking it literally, by literalizing it; thus the metaphor collapses, the distance of analogy evaporates, and the word becomes the thing. But by fully assuming the position of bare life, reduction to animality, a *ligne de fuite* emerges—not as an outside of the law but at the bottom of the full assumption of the law. Animality is endowed with ambivalence precisely at the point of fully realizing the implicit presupposition of the law.

Josephine's voice presents a different problem: the emergence of another kind of voice in the midst of a society governed by the law; a voice which would not be the voice of the law, though it may seem impossible to tell them apart. Josephine's voice is endowed with a special power in the midst of this entirely unmusical race of mice.[11] So what is so special about Josephine's voice?

> Among intimates we admit freely to one another that Josephine's singing, as singing, is nothing out of the ordinary. Is it in fact singing at all? . . . Is it not perhaps just piping [whistling, *pfeifen*]? And piping is something we all know about, it is the real artistic accomplishment of our people, or rather no mere accomplishment but a characteristic expression of our life. We all pipe, but of course no one dreams of making out that our piping is an art, we pipe without thinking of it, indeed without noticing it, and there are even many among us who are quite unaware that piping is one of our characteristics. . . . Josephine . . . hardly rises above the level of our usual piping. . . ." (p. 361)

Josephine merely pipes, whistles, as all mice constantly do, albeit in a less accomplished manner than the others. "Piping is our people's daily speech . . ." (p. 370), that is, speech minus meaning. Yet her singing is irresistible; this is no ordinary voice, though it is indistinguishable from others by any of its positive features. Whenever she starts singing—and she does so in unpredictable places and times, in the middle of the street, anywhere—a crowd immediately gathers and listens, completely enthralled. So this very ordinary piping is suddenly elevated to a special place, all its power stems from the place it occupies, as in Lacan's definition of sublimation: "to elevate an object to the dignity of the Thing" (Lacan 1992, p. 112). Josephine herself may well be convinced that her voice is very special, but it cannot be told apart from any other. This is 1924, ten years after Duchamp displayed his *Roue de bicyclette* (1913), the ordinary bicycle wheel, this art object which, mysteriously, looks exactly like any other bicycle wheel. As Gérard Wajcman puts it, Duchamp invented the wheel for the twentieth century.[12] There is an act of a pure *creatio ex nihilo*, or rather, *creatio ex nihilo* in reverse: the wheel, the object of mass production, is not created out of nothing; rather, it creates the nothing, the gap that separates it from all other wheels, and presents the wheel in its pure being-object, deprived of any of its functions, suddenly elevated to a strange sublimity.

Josephine's voice is the extension of the ready-made into music. All it does is introduce a gap, the imperceptible break that separates it from all other voices while remaining absolutely the same—"a mere nothing in voice" (p. 367). This can start anywhere, everywhere, at any time, with any kind of object: this is the art of the ready-made, and everything is ready-made for art. It is like the sudden intrusion of transcendence into immanence, but a transcendence which stays in the very midst of immanence and looks exactly the same, the imperceptible difference in the very sameness. Her art is the art of the minimal gap, and this is the hardest nut to crack.

> To crack a nut is truly no feat, so no one would ever dare to collect an audience in order to entertain it with nut-cracking. But if all the same one does do that and succeeds in entertaining the public, then it can-

not be a matter of simple nut-cracking. Or it is a matter of nut-cracking, but it turns out that we have overlooked the art of cracking nuts because we were too skilled in it and that this newcomer to it first shows us its real nature, even finding it useful in making his effects to be rather less expert in nut-cracking than most of us. (pp. 361–362)

So any voice will do to crack the nuts, provided it can create nothing out of something. Her genius is in having no talent, which makes her all the more a genius. An accomplished trained singer would never have pulled off this feat.

Josephine is the popular artist, the people's artist, so the people take care of her as a father takes care of his child, while she is persuaded that she is the one who takes care of the people; when they are "in a bad way politically or economically, her singing is supposed to save" them, and "if it doesn't drive away the evil, at least gives us strength to bear it" (p. 366). Her voice is a collective voice, she sings for everybody, she is the voice of the people, who otherwise form an anonymous mass. "This piping, which rises up where everyone else is pledged to silence, comes almost like a message from the whole people to each individual" (p. 367). In a reversal, she embodies the collectivity and relegates her listeners to their individuality. Her oneness is opposed to the collectivity of people—they are always treated *en masse*, they display uniformity in their reactions, despite some minor divergences of opinion, and their commonsensical opinion is rendered by the narrator (*Erzählermaus*, as one commentator put it), the bearer of the doxa.[13] They are non-individuals, while she, at the other end of the scale, is the exceptional one, the elevated individuality who stands for, and can awaken, the lost individuality of others.

But in her role as artist she is also the capricious prima donna; there is the whole comedy of her claims for her rights. She wants to be exempt from work, she requires special privileges, work allegedly harms her voice, she wants due honor to be paid to her services, she wants to be granted a place apart. She "does not want mere admiration, she wants to be admired exactly in the way she prescribes" (p. 362). But the people, despite their general esteem for her, do not want to hear about any of this, they are cold in their judgment—they respect her, but want her to remain one of them. So there is the whole charade of the artist who is not appreciated as she deserves, she does not get the laurels that she thinks belong to her, she puts up a preposterous act of genius not understood by her contemporaries. Out of protest she announces that she will cut down on her coloratura—this will teach them a lesson—and maybe she does, only nobody notices. She keeps coming up with all sorts of whims, she lets herself be begged, and only reluctantly gives in. There is the comedy of hurt narcissism, megalomania, an inflated ego, the high mission of the artist's overblown vocation. So one day she indeed stops singing, firmly believing that there will be some huge scandal, but nobody gives a damn, everybody goes about their business as usual, without noticing a lack—that is, without noticing the lack of a lack, the absence of the gap.

> Curious, how mistaken she is in her calculations, the clever creature, so mistaken that one might fancy she has made no calculations at all but is only being driven on by her destiny, which in our world cannot be anything but a sad one. Of her own accord she abandons her singing, of her own accord she destroys the power she has gained over people's hearts. How could she ever have gained that power, since she knows so little about these hearts of ours? . . . Josephine's road must go downhill. The time will soon come when her last notes sound and die into silence. She is a small episode in the eternal history of our people, and the people will get over the loss of her. . . . Perhaps we shall not miss so very much after all, while Josephine . . . will happily lose herself in the numberless throng of the heroes of our people, and soon, since we are no historians, will rise to the heights of redemption and be forgotten like all her brothers. (p. 376)

Despite her vanity and megalomania, people can easily do without her, she will be forgotten, no traces of her art will be left—this is not a people of archivists, and besides, there is no way one could store, collect, archivize her art, which consists purely in the gap.

So this is the second strategy: the strategy of art, of art as the nonexceptional exception, which can arise anywhere, at any moment, and is made of anything—of ready-made objects—as long as it can provide them with a gap, make them make a break. It is the art of the minimal difference. Yet the moment it makes its appearance, this difference is bungled by the very gesture which brought it about, the moment this gesture and this difference become instituted, the moment art turns into an institution to which a certain place is allotted and certain limits are drawn. Its power is at the same time its powerlessness, the very status of art veils what is at stake. Hence the whole farce of the egocentric megalomania and misunderstood genius which occupies the major part of the story. Josephine wants the impossible: she wants a place beyond the law, beyond equality—and equality is the essential feature of the mouse-folk, equality in tininess, in their miniature size (hence her claims to greatness are all the more comical). But at the same time she wants her status as exception to be legally sanctioned, symbolically recognized, properly glorified. She wants to be, like the sovereign, both inside and outside the law. She wants her uniqueness to be recognized as a special social role, and the moment art does this, it is done for. The very break it has introduced is reduced to just another social function; the break becomes the institution of the break, its place is circumscribed, and as an exception it can fit very well into the rule—that is, into the rule of law. As an artist who wants veneration and recognition she will be forgotten, relegated to the gallery of memory, that is, of oblivion. Her voice, which opens a crack in the seamless continuity of the law, is betrayed and destroyed by the very status of art, which reinserts it and closes the gap. At best it can be a tiny recess: "Piping is our people's daily speech, only many a one pipes his whole life long and does not know it, where here piping is set free from the fetters of daily life and it sets us free too for a little while" (p. 370).

Just for a little while, but by setting us free, it only helps us to bear the rest all the better. The miniature size of the mouse is enough to open the gap, but once it is instituted and recognized, its importance shrinks to the size of the mouse, despite its delusions of grandeur. It is the voice tied to the mast, and the oarsmen, although they may hear it in the flash of a brief recess, will continue to be deaf. Thus we do not end up with Kafka's version of Ulysses but are stuck with Ulysses *tout court*—or, rather, with the Adorno and Horkheimer version. Josephine's sublime voice will finally be *den Mäusen gepfiffen*, as the German expression has it (and this German phrase may well be at the origin of the whole story), that is, piped to the mice, piped in vain to someone who cannot understand or appreciate it—not because of some mass obtuseness, but because of the nature of art itself. We could say: the art is her mousetrap. So the second strategy fails, it is ruined by its own success, and the transcendence that art promised turned out to be of such a nature that it could easily fit in as one part of the division of labor; the disruptive power of the gap turned out to accommodate the continuity all too well.

THE DOG

Let us now consider a third option. "Investigations of a Dog" ("Forschungen eines Hundes"), written in 1922 (two years before Kafka's death) and published in 1931, the title again provided by Max Brod, is one of the most obscure and most bizarre among Kafka's stories—and that is saying something—apart from being one of the longest. Here we have a dog who lives a normal dog's life, like everybody, and is suddenly awakened from this life by an encounter with seven rather special music-producing dogs.

> Out of some place of darkness, to the accompaniment of terrible sounds such as I had never heard before, seven dogs stepped into the light . . . they brought the sound with them, though I could not recognize how they produced it. . . . At that time I still knew hardly anything of the creative gift for music with which the canine race alone is endowed, it had naturally enough escaped my but slowly developing powers of observation; for though music had surrounded me as a perfectly natural and indispensable element of existence ever since I was a suckling, an element which nothing impelled me to distinguish from the rest of existence . . . ; all the more astonishing, then, indeed devastating, were these seven great musical artists to me. (p. 281)

To start with, the situation is similar to that of Josephine's singing: music is everywhere in dogs' lives, the most run-of-the-mill thing, utterly inconspicuous, and it takes "great musical artists" to single it out, that is, to produce the break. But there is a twist:

> They did not speak, they did not sing, they remained generally silent, almost determinedly silent; but from the empty air they conjured music. Everything was music, the lifting and setting down of their feet, certain turns of the head, their running and their standing still, the positions they took up in relation to one another . . . , [their] lying flat on the ground and going through complicated concerted evolutions. . . . (ibid.)

Where does the music come from? There is no speaking, no singing, no musical instruments. It just came from nowhere, from the empty air, *ex nihilo*. Music was everywhere in dogs' lives, ready-made, but this one was just created out of nothing. We have seen that Josephine's problem was to create a nothing out of something, *creatio ex nihilo* in reverse, *creatio nullius rei*, but here it is even better: their problem is how to create nothing out of nothing, the gap of nothing which encircles the ready-made object made out of nothing. There we have the great wonder: the ready-made nothing. The ready-made nothing is epitomized by the voice without a discernible source, an acousmatic voice. It is like the voice as pure resonance that Lacan talks about in *Anxiety* in the passage we have examined above.

The seven dogs' voices come out of a pure void, they spring up from nothing, a pure resonance without a source, as if the pure alterity of the voice had turned into music, music that pervades anything and everything, as if the voice of this resonance has got hold of all possible points of emission. The resonance of the voice functions not as an effect of the emitted voice but as a cause, a pure *causa sui*, but one which, in this self-causality encompasses everything. It is as if the pure void of the Other started to reverberate in itself in the presence of those great musicians, whose art consisted merely in letting the Other resonate for itself.

The hapless young dog is overwhelmed:

> the music gradually got the upper hand, literally knocked the breath out of me and swept me far away from those actual little dogs, and

> quite against my will . . . my mind could attend to nothing but this blast of music which seemed to come from all sides, from the heights, from the deeps, from everywhere, surrounding the listener, over-whelming him, crushing him, and over his swooning body still blowing fanfares so near that they seemed far away and almost in-audible . . . the music robbed me of my wits. . . . (p. 282)

This experience entirely shatters the young dog's life, it is the start of his quest, his investigations. His interest in all this is not artistic at all, there is no problem of the status of this voice as art, as with Josephine; his interest is an epistemological one. It is the quest for the source, the attempt to gain knowledge about the source of it all. One of Josephine's endeavors is to preserve the dimension of the child in her art, in the midst of that race of mice which is both very childish and prematurely old at the same time—they are like children infused with "weariness and hopelessness" (p. 369), and Josephine's voice is like preserving their childhood against their economy of survival, against the always premature adulthood. But the young dog is at the very op-posite end of this; he decides that "there are more important things than childhood" (p. 286). *Es gibt wichtigere Dinge als die Kindheit* (Kafka 1996, p. 420): this is one of Kafka's great sentences, it should be taken as a motto, or indeed as a most serious political slogan. A political slo-gan in our time of a general infantilization of social life, starting with the infantilization of infants, a time which loves to take the despicable opposite line: that we are all children in our hearts, and that this is our most precious possession, something we should hold on to. There are more important things than childhood: this is also the slogan of psy-choanalysis, which indeed seems to be all about retrieving child-hood, but not in order to keep this precious and unique thing, but to give it up. Psychoanalysis is on the side of the young dog who decides to grow up, to leave behind "the blissful life of a young dog," to start his investigations, turn to research, pursue a quest.

This quest takes a strange and unexpected turn. The question "Where does music come from? Where does the voice come from?" is immediately translated into another question: "Where does food come from?" The mystery of the incorporeal resonance of the voice is without further ado transformed into the mystery of a very different kind, of the most corporeal kind imaginable. The voice is a resonance from nowhere, it does not serve any purpose (Lacan's definition of enjoyment), but food is at the opposite end, the most elementary means of survival, the most material and bodily of elements. It is the question about a mystery where there does not seem to be any mystery; the dog sees a mystery where nobody else sees any; the simplest and the most palpable thing suddenly becomes endowed with the greatest of secrets. A break has happened, from nowhere, and he wants to start his inquiries with the simplest things. In a few sentences, in a few lines, we go from the enigma of song to the enigma of food—the stroke of Kafka's genius at its best, in a passage which is completely unpredictable and completely logical at the same time.

Once he starts asking questions, there is no end to mystery. What is the source of food? The earth? But what enables the earth to provide food? Where does the earth get food from? Just as the source of the law was an enigma which we could never solve, so is the source of food an ever-elusive enigma. It seems as though food, pure materiality and immanence, will suddenly point to the transcendence, if only it is pursued far enough. So the dog goes around asking other dogs, who all seem quite unconcerned by such self-evident trivialities; nobody would dream of taking such banal inquiries seriously. When he asks them about the source of food, they immediately assume that he must be hungry, so instead of an answer they give him food, they want to nourish him, they want to stuff his mouth with food, they counter his questioning by feeding him.[14] But the dog's mouth cannot be stuffed, he is not put off that easily, and he gets so involved in his investigation that he eventually stops eating. The story has many twists and turns that I cannot go into, all of them illuminating and strangely wonderful; I will just jump to the last section.

The way to discover the source of food is to starve, as in "A Hunger Artist" ("Ein Hungerkünstler"), the story written in the same year—not the starving artist, which is a common enough phenomenon, but someone who has elevated starvation to an art. The starvation, as it turns out, is his ready-made, since his secret is that he actually really dislikes food. His art is not adequately appreciated, just like Josephine's, and this is why the hunger artist will die of hunger. But the dog is no artist, this is not the portrait of the artist as a young dog; this dog is a would-be scientist and he is starving on his quest for knowledge, which almost brings him to the same result. But at the point of total exhaustion, when he is already dying (like the man from the country), there is salvation, salvation at the point of the "exhaustion of exhaustion." He vomits blood, he is so weak that he faints, and when he opens his eyes there is a dog which appears from nowhere, a strange hound standing in front of him.

There is an ambiguity—is this last part a hallucination of the dying dog? Or, even more radically, is this the answer to Hamlet's question "But in that sleep of death, what dreams may come"? Is this last section a possible sequel to "Before the Law," the dreams that may come to the man from the country at the point of his death? Is it all a delusion, the glimpse of salvation only at the point of death? Salvation only at the price that it does not have any consequence? But Kafka's describing this delusion, his pursuing it to the end, bringing it to the point of science, to the birth of science from the spirit of a delusion on the threshold of death: this is all the consequence that is needed, something that affects the here and now, and radically transforms it.

The dying dog tries at first to chase away the apparition of the hound (is it a ghost which intervenes at the end, as opposed to the other one which intervened in the beginning?). The hound is very beautiful, and at first it even appears that he is trying to pay court to the starved dog; he is very concerned about the dying dog, he cannot let him be. But all this dialogue is but a preparation for the event, the emergence of song, the song again coming from nowhere, emerging without anyone's will.

> Then I thought I saw something such as no dog before me had ever seen. . . . I thought I saw that the hound was already singing without knowing it, nay, more that the melody separated from him, was floating on the air in accordance with its own laws, and, as though he had no part in it, was moving toward me, toward me alone . . . the melody, which the hound soon seemed to acknowledge as his, was quite irre-

sistible. It grew stronger; its waxing power seemed to have no limits, and already almost burst my eardrums. But the worst was that it seemed to exist solely for my sake, this voice before whose sublimity the woods fell silent, to exist solely for my sake; who was I, that I could dare to remain here, lying brazenly before it in my pool of blood and filth. (p. 314)

The song again appears from nowhere, it starts from anywhere, from a void, it is separated from its bearer, it is only *post festum* that the hound steps in to assume it, acknowledge it as his. And this song is directed toward the starving dog alone, it is for his ears only, the impersonal call which addresses only him personally, just as the door of the Law is reserved only for the man from the country. It is like the pure voice of a call, just like the irresistible call of the law, like its irrepressible silence, only this time the very same call as its opposite, the call of salvation.

So this voice from nowhere introduces the second break; the dog suddenly recovers on the threshold of death, the voice gets hold of him and instills new life in him, he who could not move cannot but jump up now, resurrected, the born-again dog. And he pursues his investigations with redoubled force, he extends his scientific interest to canine music. "The science of music, if I am correctly informed, is perhaps still more comprehensive than that of nurture" (pp. 314–315); the new science he is trying to establish encompasses both his concerns, the source of food and the source of the voice; it combines them into a single effort. The voice, the music, like the pure transcendence, and food as the pure immanence of the material world: but they share common ground, a common source, they are rooted in the same kernel. The science of music is held in higher esteem than the science of nurture, it reaches the sublime, but this is precisely what prevents it from penetrating "deeply into the life of the people," it is "very esoteric and politely excludes the people" (p. 315). It has been erroneously posited as a separate science, different from that of nurture; its power was powerless by virtue of being relegated to a separate realm. This was Josephine's unhappy fate: her song was separated from food, art was pitted against survival, the sublime was her mousetrap, just as being immersed in nurture was the unhappy fate of all the rest. Just as the science of nurture has to lead through star-vation, so the science of music refers to silence, to "*verschwiegenes Hun-dewesen*," the silent essence of the dog, the essence that, after the experience of the song, can be discovered in any dog as its true na-ture. For penetrating this essence, "the real dog nature," the path of nurture was the alternative and simpler way, as it seemed, but it all boils down to the same thing—what matters is the point of intersec-tion. "A border region between these two sciences, however, had al-ready attracted my attention. I mean the theory of incantation, by which food is called down [*Es ist die Lehre von dem die Nahrung herabrufenden Gesang*]" (p. 315; Kafka 1996, p. 454). The song can call down, *herabrufen*, the food: the source of food was mistakenly sought in the earth, it should have been sought in the opposite direction. The voice is the source of food that he has been seeking. There is an overlapping, an intersection between nourishment and voice. We can illustrate it yet again with the intersection of two circles, the circle of food and the circle of the voice and music. What do we find at the point where they overlap? What is the mysterious intersection? But this is the best defi-nition of what Lacan called *objet petit a*. It is the common source of both food and music.

Food and voice—both pass through the mouth. Deleuze keeps coming back to that over and over again. There is an alternative: either you eat or you speak, use your voice, you cannot do both at the same time. They share the same location, but in mutual exclusion: either in-corporation or emission.

> Any language, rich or poor, always implies the deterritorialization of the mouth, the tongue and the teeth. The original territoriality of the mouth, the tongue and the teeth is food. By being devoted to the ar-ticulation of sounds, the mouth, the tongue and the teeth are deterri-torialized. So there is a disjunction between eating and speaking. . . . To speak . . . is to starve. (Deleuze and Guattari 1975, pp. 35–36)

By speech mouth is denaturalized, diverted from its natural function, seized by the signifier (and, for our purposes, by the voice which is but the alterity of the signifier). The Freudian name for this deterritorialization is the drive (if nothing else, it has the advantage of sparing us that terrible tongue-twister, but its aim is the same). Eating can never be the same once the mouth has been deterritorialized—it is seized by the drive, it turns around a new object which emerged in this operation, it keeps circumventing, circling around this eternally elusive object. Speech, in this denaturalizing function, is then subjected to a secondary territorialization, as it were: it acquires a second nature with its anchorage in meaning. Meaning is a reterritorialization of language, its acquisition of a new territoriality, a naturalized substance. (This is what Deleuze and Guattari call the extensive or representational function of speech, as opposed to the pure intensity of the voice.) But this secondary nature can never quite succeed, and the bit that eludes it can be pinned down as the element of the voice, this pure alterity of what is said. This is the common ground it shares with food, that in food which precisely escapes eating, the bone that gets stuck in the gullet.[15]

So the essence of the dog concerns precisely this intersection of food and voice, the two lines of investigation converge; from our biased perspective they meet in the *objet petit a*. So there would have to be a single science; the dog, on the last page, inaugurates a new science, he is the founding dog of a new science—although by his own admission he is a feeble scientist, at least by the standards of the established sciences. He could not pass

> even the most elementary scientific examination set by an authority on the subject . . . the reason for that can be found in my incapacity for scientific investigation, my limited powers of thought, my bad memory, but above all in my inability to keep my scientific aim continuously before my eyes. All this I frankly admit, even with a certain degree of pleasure. For the more profound cause of my scientific incapacity seems to me to be an instinct, and indeed by no means a bad one. . . . It was this instinct that made me—and perhaps for the sake of science itself, but a different science from that of today, an ultimate science [*einer allerletzten Wissenschaft*]—prize freedom higher than everything else. Freedom! Certainly such freedom as is possible today is a wretched business. But nevertheless freedom, nevertheless a possession. (pp. 315–316)

This is the last sentence of the story. The last word of it all, *le fin mot* as *le mot de la fin*, is freedom, with an exclamation mark. Are we not victims of a delusion, should we not pinch ourselves, is it possible that Kafka actually utters this word? This may well be the only place where Kafka talks about freedom in explicit terms, but this does not mean that there is unfreedom everywhere else in his universe. Quite the opposite: freedom is there at all times, everywhere, it is Kafka's *fin mot*, like the secret word we dare not utter although it is constantly on our mind. A freedom that might not look like much, that might actually look wretched, but it is there at all times, and once we spot it there is no way of going away from it, it is a possession to hold on to, it is the permanent line of flight turned into the permanent line of pursuit. And there is the slogan, the program of a new science which would be able to treat it, to take it as its object, to pursue it, the ultimate science, the science of freedom. Kafka lacks the proper word for it, he cannot name it—this is 1922—but he had only to look around, to examine the ranks of his Jewish Austrian compatriots.

Of course—psychoanalysis.

INTRODUCTION *CHE BELLA VOCE!*

1. "I don't hear well" was the famous line uttered by Milošević at a mass rally in Belgrade in 1989; it quickly turned into a proverb, and started to epitomize the core of the Yugoslav crisis. In this further inversion, it is not the "subjects" but the Leader who is hearing-impaired, precisely when he is confronted with *vox populi*. But the voice of the people, in those circumstances, was pressing not for human rights and civil liberties, but for harsher measures and repressive action against "the enemies," so the truth of the line is that he heard only too well, and very selectively turned a deaf ear. This extension of our story quickly demonstrates that the voice and hearing are also at the core of politics—I will come back to that.

2. To acknowledge a personal debt I must, in the rich store of literature, single out Slavoj Žižek, who has used the story recurrently, from *The Sublime Object of Ideology* (1989) to *The Puppet and the Dwarf* (2003), where it provided the title.

3. One can find an extensive and most entertaining history of this chess-playing machine in Tom Standage's remarkable book *The Turk* (2002), from which I draw some information here. With all his vast number of references, Standage, curiously, never mentions Benjamin.

4. As it turned out, when the machine was finally examined in 1840, there was enough space for a normal adult person and no need for a dwarf, a hunchback, or a child, despite appearances. The idea of a human dwarf inside is almost as old as the automaton itself; it was promoted by Thicknesse, Decremps, Böckmann, and Racknitz in the 1780s, then forcefully by

Robert Willis in the 1820s, and so on. The automaton finished its days in a fire in Philadelphia in 1854.

5. Poe was well aware of this; he dealt with Kempelen in another piece, "Von Kempelen and his Discovery," where Kempelen is ascribed another astounding invention: how to make gold out of lead, the dream of alchemy come true. If the first piece takes the scientific approach based on factual observation, then the second is entirely Borgesian: it mixes fact with fiction, and emulates factual narrative to the point where one cannot tell the two apart.

6. This comes from *Briefe an eine deutsche Prinzessin über verschiedene Gegenstände aus der Physik und Philosophie*, 1761 ("Letters to a German princess on various topics in physics and philosophy"). The very title gives a rather picturesque presentation of the Enlightenment framework, where one of the greatest scientists of the time tries to enlighten the sixteen-year-old Friederica Charlotte Louisa, daughter of the Brandenburg prince. If, according to Kant's famous dictum, "Enlightenment is mankind's exit from its self-incurred immaturity," then it appears that those to be enlightened are in the first place not the immature uneducated masses, but the monarchs and the rulers.

7. For the pioneering efforts of Christian Gottlieb Kratzenstein (who won the prize), Christoph Friedrich Hellwag, Abbé Mical, and others, see Felderer 2002, on whom I mostly rely for this history.

8. This was the year of Mozart's *The Magic Flute*, and we can recall Mozart's own fascination with mechanical musical instruments and automata, for example, the pieces for mechanical organ K. 594, K. 608, and K. 616, commissioned by Count Deym, as well as the use of "mechanical" bells in *The Magic Flute* itself. The "mechanically produced sublime" was obviously in the air.

9. "You are my friend—I love you with all my Heart—Leopold the Second—Roman Emperor—always Augustus—daddy, mummy, my wife, my husband, the king, let's go to Paris." We have the report of a Mr. Windisch, *Lettres de M. Charles Gottlieb deWindisch sur Le joueur d'échecs de M. De Kempelen* (Basel, 1783), quoted by Parret 2002, p. 27.

10. I should also add that Charles Babbage saw the chess automaton in 1819, and was so impressed by it that the pursuit of its enigma led him to the construction of the first computing machine. See Standage 2002, pp. 138–145.

11. The problem of the synthetic production of the human voice turned out to be a very hard nut to crack, and had to wait for the electronic age for a satisfactory solution. After the efforts of Helmholtz, D. C. Miller, C. Stumpf, J. Q. Stewart, R. Paget, and many others, it was only in 1939 that H. Dudley, R. Riesz, and S. S. A. Watkins constructed a machine they called a

Voder (Voice Demonstrator), which was shown at the World's Fair in New York.

CHAPTER 1   THE LINGUISTICS OF THE VOICE

1. "The medium is the message"—this notorious slogan should perhaps be twisted in such a way that the message of the medium pertains to its voice.

2. The French can use a handy pun with the expression *vouloir dire*: the voice "wants to say," that is, it means, there is a *vouloir-dire* inherent in the voice. Derrida has made a great case for this in one of his earliest and best books, *La voix et le phénomène* (1967b), where, to put it briefly, his analysis of Husserl pinpoints the voice as the "*vouloir-dire*" of the phenomenon.

3. See Miller: "*tout ce qui, du signifiant, ne concourt pas à l'effet de signification*" (1989, p. 180). For the present purposes, I am leaving aside the difference between meaning and sense, to which I will come later.

4. John the Baptist himself refers this qualification to another point in the Bible (Isaiah 40: 3), but the examination of that point implies that the famous saying, *vox clamantis in deserto*, looks like the result of erroneous punctuation.

5. Could we go so far as to say that John the Baptist plays the same role, in relation to Christ, as Kempelen's vocal machine does in relation to the thinking machine? That John the Baptist is the hidden theological voice-dwarf of the Word?

6. But if the voice precedes the Word, and enables its Meaning, then in the second step the point of the manifestation of the Word is that it becomes flesh. The material element which had to be obliterated spectacularly reappears as the manifestation of the Word, in the guise of the flesh of ideality itself.

7. "*In the language itself, there are only differences.* Even more important than that is the fact that, although in general a difference presupposes positive terms between which the difference holds, in a language there are only differences, *and no positive terms.* . . . the language includes neither ideas nor sounds existing prior to the linguistic system, but only conceptual and phonetic differences arising out of that system" (Saussure 1998, p. 118).

8. Imagine someone reading the evening news on TV with a heavy regional accent. It would sound absurd, for the state, by definition, does not have an accent. A person with an accent can appear in a talk-show, speaking in her own voice, but not in an official capacity. The official voice is the voice devoid of any accent.

9. "For what is science but the absence of prejudice backed by the presence of money?" (Henry James, *The Golden Bowl*).

10. As opposed to the voice of the Kempelen machine, which was uncanny by being "human, all too human" in its lack of precision.

11. *Pausaníou pausaménou*—Plato is making a pun in Greek, using the similarity of sounds, and the rhetoricians he ironically refers to are no doubt the sophists, where sophistry, much to Plato's horror, appears as the kind of thinking based not only on meaning and ideas, but on the erratic nature of homonyms, puns, wordplays, and so on—all that Lacan will sum up in his concept of *lalangue*, and is very relevant to our topic of the voice. I will come back to it at some length. For the best account of it, I can only refer the reader to Barbara Cassin's remarkable book *L'effet sophistique* (Paris: Gallimard, 1995).

12. To make a quick slide from Plato to Lubitsch: in *That Uncertain Feeling*, a film made in 1941, we have one of those brilliant Lubitsch openings. A woman comes to an analyst because she has hiccups. To start with there is just a woman and a voice-symptom, the involuntary voice which condenses all her troubles, and which she doesn't dare to call by name. It seems indecent, it doesn't become a lady, it is too trivial, so she describes her trouble as follows: "It comes and it goes. When it comes I go, and when I come it goes." "The ego and the id," one is tempted to say, where hiccups appear as "it," no doubt the id which carries away the subject and condenses her being. And you will certainly not be able to interpret Lubitsch if you don't know why Merle Oberon has hiccups.

13. See Lacan 1966, p. 679; 1994, p. 188; for extensive elaborations on the scream, see the unpublished seminar *Problèmes cruciaux pour la psychanalyse* (1964/65); also in *Identification* (1961/62). See also Poizat 1986, pp. 144–145; 1991, pp. 204–205; and 1996, pp. 191–192.

14. Arthur Janov's *The Primal Scream* (1970) immediately became a bestseller, soon to be followed by *The Primal Revolution* (1972), *The Primal Man* (1976), and so on, and by a movement which, in the 1970s, promised to revolutionize psychotherapy. All that was needed was allegedly to regress to the deepest layer of oneself, to find one's way to the origin of it all in the scream, thus liberating oneself from the repression of culture and the symbolic torment, and finally breathe freely, with the freedom of the infant. If psychoanalysis was from the outset "the talking cure," then Janov's last book title continues to announce: *Words Won't Do It*.

15. See the beginning of the Rome Discourse: "all speech calls for a reply. I shall show that there is no speech without a reply, even if it is met only with silence, provided that it has an auditor: this is the heart of its function in analysis" (Lacan 1989, p. 40).

16. "For the unconditional element of demand, desire substitutes the 'absolute' condition: this condition unties the knot of that element in the proof of love that is resistant to the satisfaction of a need. Thus desire is

neither the appetite for satisfaction, nor the demand for love, but the difference that results from the subtraction of the first from the second, the phenomenon of their splitting (*Spaltung*)" (Lacan 1989, p. 287). The voice is precisely the agent of this split. We could compress this to a simple formula: desire is demand minus need. See also *Identification*: "the Other will endow the scream of need with the dimension of desire" (May 2, 1962).

17. I think it is in bad taste to quote oneself, but here I must make an exception, and cite our book on the opera (Slavoj Žižek and Mladen Dolar, *Opera's Second Death*, New York and London: Routledge 2002) where this is scrutinized at greater length.

18. "the horror of castration has set up a memorial to itself in the creation of this substitute. . . . It remains a token of triumph over the threat of castration and a protection against it" (PFL 7, p. 353).

CHAPTER 2   THE METAPHYSICS OF THE VOICE

1. In French *la conscience* can mean both "consciousness" and "conscience." I think it is quite obvious that what is meant in this context is "consciousness," not "conscience," as the English translation has it. In his analysis of Husserl, Derrida reduces it to a slogan: "The voice *is* consciousness" (1967b, p. 89).

2. There is a more banal experience which demonstrates this: hearing one's own voice on tape always (or at least initially) fills one with horror and displeasure. One may well obtain narcissistic pleasure by looking at one's image in the mirror, but listening to one's recorded voice is unpleasant— the gap this introduces into "hearing oneself speak" is enough to disrupt narcissism; there is always something uncanny about it.

3. Among many formulations, here is a lesser known but very clear one: "under the form of i(a) my image, my presence in the Other, is without a rest. I cannot see what I lose in it. This is the sense of the mirror stage. . . . The object *a* is what is lacking, it is not specular, it cannot be seized in the image" (Lacan 2004, pp. 292, 294).

4. This is also why music is treated in a very different way from painting, which poses interminable problems of imitation, copies, mimesis, and so on.

5. For Aristotle's analogous views on the modes, see Aristotle 2001, *Politics* VIII, 1340b. A little further on (1342b 2–7), however, he takes issue with that particular passage in the *Republic* concerning the Phrygian mode.

6. See also: "It will further be necessary to make a rough general distinction between two types of songs, those suited for females and those suited for males, and so we shall have to provide both with their appropriate scales and rhythms; it would be a dreadful thing that the whole tune or rhythm

of a composition should be out of place, as it will be if our various songs are inappropriately treated in these respects" (Plato 1978, *Laws* VII, 802e).

7. Aristotle will have to deal with the same problem. The liberal studies, with music in the highest place of honor, are quintessential to education; they are "proper for a freeman to acquire, but only in a certain degree, and if he attend to them too closely, in order to attain perfection in them, the evil effects will follow" (Aristotle 2001, *Politics* VIII, 1337b 15–17). Curiously, most of Book VIII of *Politics* is devoted to music as a means of education.

8. For a detailed account, see Poizat's remarkable book on sacred music, *La voix du diable* (1991). I draw a lot of the information in this section from this source.

9. Quoted in O'Donnell's commentary on *Confessions* (Augustine 1992), vol. III, pp. 218–219).

10. For Hildegard, who has become a rather fashionable figure, see Peter Dronke, *Women Writers of the Middle Ages* (Cambridge: Cambridge University Press, 1984); Barbara Newman, *Sister of Wisdom* (Aldershot, UK: Scolar Press, 1987); Sabina Flanagan, *Hildegard of Bingen* (London: Routledge, 1989); and Régine Pernoud, *Hildegarde de Bingen* (Paris: Éditions du Rocher, 1994). None of these books quite does justice to her musical work.

11. The project was presented to the Convention on the eighteenth Brumaire, year II of the Revolution: another memorable eighteenth Brumaire which preceded its more famous counterpart by seven years. Marx's theory could thus be extended: Napoleon's *coup d' état* was itself already a repetition, quite in accordance with Plato's view that musical changes prefigure social ones. Only for Plato, they heralded decadence, whereas here they were the harbinger of a dictatorship which was supposed to put an end to decadence.

12. François-Joseph Gossec (1734–1829) acquired his musical knowledge and some glory as a court composer. In 1766 he became Prince Condé's *intendant de la musique*, and in 1774 *maître de musique* at the Royal Academy, then the founder and first director of the *École royale de chant*. After the Revolution he was music inspector, and one of the principal holders of musical authority in France for a quarter of a century. In 1816, after the downfall of Napoleon and the restoration, he was summarily sacked for his allegiance to revolutionary ideas, so he died in great poverty and entirely forgotten. Among his numerous works are *Hymne à Jean-Jacques Rousseau, Hymne à l'Être Suprême, Hymne à la liberté, Chant du 14 juillet,* and so on. His Requiem is still performed sometimes.

13. For lack of space, I cannot venture here into the fascinating realm of the history of castrati, their rise within the Catholic Church in the sixteenth century, their quasi-angelic demeanor which seemingly dissociates the enjoyment of the voice from sex, their massive presence in the opera, their incredible vogue that lasted some three centuries, their gradual decline

until they were confined to the Sistine Chapel; finally their banning, only in 1903, by Pope Leo XIII. (See Balzac's short story "Sarrazine," rendered famous by Barthes.) They raise in the most immediate way the question of the relation between voice and castration, a rather too obvious and hence trivial demonstration of the structural tie between castration and the object in psychoanalysis (see, for example, Lacan's graph of desire, where voice and castration are to be found at parallel and analogous points: Lacan 1989, p. 315). The best accounts so far of the history of castrati are probably Patrick Barbier, *Histoire des castrats* (Paris: Grasset, 1989), and Hubert Ortkemper, *Engel widerWillen* (Berlin: Henschel, 1993).

14. Shofar is also used on a number of other ritual occasions carefully scrutinized by Reik. On July 27, 1656, Spinoza heard the sound of shofar accompany the formal text of excommunication read by the priest.

15. This constellation is by no means limited to Judaism or Christianity. Some version of it appears in almost all ancient mythologies where the bond between voice and creation, and specifically between voice and the foundation of a primeval Law, seems to be a commonplace:

Considerable information about the nature of music and its role in the world is provided by the myths of creation. Each time that the genesis of the world is described with some precision, the acoustic element intervenes at the decisive moment of action. Whenever a deity manifests the will to give birth to itself or to another deity, to bring forth the sky and the earth or the man, it emits a sound. . . . The source from where the world emanates is always an acoustic source. (Schneider 1960, p. 132)

Schneider cites several diverse instances taken from a variety of ancient and "primitive" cultures, and convincingly demonstrates the necessary link between the voice, religion, and the basic social rituals, the umbilical cord between the voice and a rudimentary social bond.

16. We must bear in mind that for Lacan, *passage à l'acte* is sharply opposed to *acting out*. It is difficult to find a good English equivalent.

17. The whole section of *Encore* from which this passage is taken actually bears the title "God and the *jouissance* of The Woman."

18. "The woman relates to S($Å$), which means that she is already doubled, and is not all . . . the supreme Being . . . is situated in the place, the opaque place of the *jouissance* of the Other—that Other which, if she existed, The Woman might be" (Lacan quoted in Mitchell and Rose 1982, pp. 152, 153).

CHAPTER 3　THE "PHYSICS" OF THE VOICE

1. "*Elles sont, ces vérités, des corps incorporels, des langages dépourvus de sens, des infinis génériques, des suppléments inconditionnés. Elles deviennent et demeurent suspendues, comme la*

conscience du poète, 'entre le vide et l'événement pur'." The quote is from the circulated manuscript version of *Logiques des mondes.*

2. There is no mention of a curtain in Diogenes; its source is to be found in Iamblichos, *De vita Pythag.,* 72, 89.

3. This theatrical invention precedes more than a century another philosophico-theatrical stroke of genius, Plato's cave, which also features extensively the problem of the acousmatic voice and attributing it to an origin: "Don't you think [the prisoners] would believe that the shadows passing in front of them were talking whenever one of the carriers passing along the wall was doing so?" (Plato 1997, *Republic,* 515b). So the assignment of voices to creatures is inherently based on a make-believe.

4. ". . . seeing no one, Dorothy asked, 'Where are you?' 'I am everywhere,' answered the Voice, 'but to the eyes of common mortals I am invisible'" (Baum 1995, p. 110).

5. "It is manifest that behind the so-called curtain which is supposed to conceal the inner world, there is nothing to be seen unless *we* go behind it ourselves, as much in order that we may see, as that there may be something behind there which can be seen" (Hegel 1977, p. 103).

6. The formula was made famous by Octave Mannoni's seminal paper "Je sais bien, mais quand même," in Mannoni 1969. For the best commentary, see Pfaller 2002.

7. Merleau-Ponty, at a certain moment in the complex argument of *The Phenomenology of Perception,* poses the phenomenon as *la chose intersensorielle,* an intersensorial thing (1978, p. 366), a combination of several senses: "If a phenomenon . . . offers itself only to one of my senses, it turns into a phantom, and it will come close to real existence, only if . . . it is capable of speaking to my other senses, as e.g., a hard wind which becomes visible only by agitating the landscape" (p. 368). There is a simple mechanism of "phantomatization" often used in cinema: deprive the image of the sound or the sound of the image, and the cut-off half will acquire a phantom-like dimension, it will become oneiric or surreal, as if the missing half has lent its power to the present one. Where coordination fails, where the seen and the heard do not match, a phantom appears (if we leave aside other senses). Phenomenon, on the other hand, is the "coincidence," the encounter of the gaze and the voice, the seen and the heard, that which shows itself (*phaino,* which Heidegger links with *phos,* light) and what is said (*logos*) and heard. Hence all the program of phenomenology. If one part is missing, phenomenology risks turning into phantomology.

8. "It seems rather that when the fetish is instituted some process occurs which reminds one of the stopping of memory in traumatic amnesia. As in this latter case, the subject's interest comes to a halt half-way, as it were;

it is as though the last impression before the uncanny and traumatic one is retained as a fetish" (PFL 7, p. 354).

9. See Adorno: "What was then in expressionism, with which the young Schönberg has a lot in common, called the scream, is not only something that eludes communication by renouncing the habitual articulation of sense, but objectively also a desperate attempt to reach those who no longer hear" (1973, p. 286).

10. This is also why formulas like those proposed by Barthes—*le grain de la voix*, the grain of the voice, "the materiality of the body speaking its mother tongue," "the body in the singing voice," and so on (Barthes 1982, pp. 238, 243)—will never do. The problem is that the voice cannot be pinned to a body, or be seen as an emanation of the body, without a paradox.

11. Lacan actually uses the English distinction between the aim and the goal, indiscernible in the French *le but*.

Here we can clear up the mystery of the *zielgehemmt*, of that form that the drive may assume, in attaining its satisfaction without attaining its goal. . . . When you entrust someone with a mission, the aim is not what he brings back, but the itinerary he must take. The aim is the way taken. The French word *le but* may be translated by another word in English, goal. . . . If the drive may be satisfied without attaining what . . . would be the satisfaction of its end . . . , it is because . . . its aim is simply this return into circuit. . . . The *objet petit a* is not the origin of the oral drive. It is not introduced as the original food, it is introduced from the fact that no food will ever satisfy the oral drive, except by circumventing [circling around] the eternally lacking object. (Lacan 1979, pp. 179–80)

. . . in the profound relation of the drive, what is essential is that the movement by which the arrow that sets out towards the target fulfils its function only by really re-emerging from it, and returning on to the subject. (p. 206)

12. We could say that the problem with singing— and, by extension, music— is that it tries to turn the aim into the goal, it takes the object of the drive as the object of immediate enjoyment, and precisely for that reason misses it. Its aesthetic pleasure reinserts enjoyment into the boundaries of the pleasure principle.

13. I am drawing here on "The History of Nipper and His Master's Voice," <http://danbbs.dk/~enikoest/nipper.htm>, and giving just a brief summary of this site.

14. A bit further on Lacan makes another comment on this,

the ambiguity of the two levels, that of the natural function of the lure and that of *trompe-l'oeil*. If the birds rushed to the surface on which Zeuxis had deposited his dabs of color, taking the picture for edible grapes, let us observe that the success of such an undertaking does not imply in the least that the grapes were admirably reproduced, like those we can see in the basket held by Caravaggio's *Bacchus* in the Uffizi. If the grapes had been painted in this way, it is not very likely that the birds would have been deceived, for why should the birds see grapes portrayed with such extraordinary verisimilitude? There would have to be something more reduced, something closer to the sign, in something representing grapes for the birds. But the opposite example of Parrhasios makes it clear that if one wishes to deceive a man, what one presents to him is the painting of a veil, that is to say, something that incites him to ask what is behind it. (pp. 111–112)

15. One should go even further, and talk about "ontological shame"—a term magisterially developed by Joan Copjec.

16. Orpheus, as opposed to the Sirens, yields authority to the Other and tries to elicit the Other's mercy through his voice, while the Sirens, the depositories of the voice as authority, are merciless.

17. This casts some light on Lacan's formula for the drive in the graph of desire, $\$ \lozenge D$ (1989, pp. 314–315), the subject confronted with the demand, with that excess of demand which sticks to the voice.

CHAPTER 4   THE ETHICS OF THE VOICE

1. Bernard Baas (1998) is a very useful guide here; I will follow in his footsteps, adapting them to my own agenda. See also Baas 1990.

2. "Take Socrates. The inflexible purity of Socrates and his *atopia* are correlative. Intervening, at every moment, there is the demonic voice. Could one maintain that the voice that guides Socrates is not Socrates himself?" (Lacan 1979, p. 258.)

3. Conscience coincides with the voice, although a few pages earlier Rousseau established the following premise: "I don't deduce these rules from the principles of high philosophy, but I find them at the bottom of my heart where nature has inscribed them in indelible letters" (1969, p. 594). But the invisible letter of nature is powerless without the voice as its only true expression.

4. This condemnation of "the voices of passion," *les voix des passions*, may appear to be at odds with the thrust of Rousseau's argument in *Essay on the Origin of Languages* (1761), namely that the voice of passion was precisely the primordial stuff of language, the happy initial state where language coincided with singing, the state which was lost when passions were divorced from it, and language, uprooted from its natural soil, could become an instrument of corruption. But the contradiction is only apparent: those primordial passions which were one with language were also one with the natural propensity to morality, and this community of passions and

morals in the natural voice is what both ethics and music should endeavor to recover. Hence Rousseau's intense preoccupation with music (including his charming opera *Le devin du village*, still occasionally performed). So for Rousseau there is an ethical mission to music—to make passions and morals sing with one voice—and we could also say the reverse: that there is a musical mission to ethics.

5. The question of the power of reason emerges in the *Critique of Practical Reason* in the guise of *Triebfeder*, the driving force of reason (and we should note the peculiar tie with *Trieb*, the Freudian drive). The moral law in its pure formality lacks power to determine the will, it needs a driving force which Kant finds in a paradoxical feeling, respect (*die Achtung*) for the moral law. He takes this respect to be the only *a priori* and non-pathological feeling, which is not of empirical origin, but produced by the law itself. We could argue that respect for the moral law holds the same structural place in Kant's argument as the voice of reason. For the best comment on this, see Zupančič 2000.

6. He goes on: "The nature of reason is a guarantee that afterwards it will not fail to give man's emotional impulses and what is determined by them the position they deserve. But the common compulsion exercised by such a dominance of reason will prove to be the strongest uniting bond among men and lead the way to further unions" (ibid.). So reason is expected to be a generous enlightened dictator which will wisely allow his subjects some leeway. Like a new incarnation of Frederick the Great, the hero for so many Enlightenment thinkers, and in particular Kant's great idol?

7. "If I cannot bend the higher powers, I will move the infernal regions."

8. The *New Introductory Lectures on Psychoanalysis* were written in 1932 and actually published in December 1932, a month before the official date of publication and less than two months before Hitler's seizure of power.

9. "The moral law, looked at more closely, is simply desire in its pure state" (Lacan 1979, p. 275). See also:

the moral imperative is not concerned with what may or may not be done. To the extent that it imposes the necessity of a practical reason, obligation affirms an unconditional "Thou shalt." The importance of this field derives from the void that the strict application of Kantian definition leaves there. Now we analysts are able to recognize that place as the place occupied by desire. Our experience gives rise to a reversal that locates in the center an incommensurable measure, an infinite measure, that is called desire. (Lacan 1992, pp. 315–316, *passim*)

"And when the law is actually there, desire doesn't hold, but only because the law and the repressed desire are one and the same thing, this is just what Freud has discovered" ("Kant avec Sade," in Lacan 1966, p. 782).

10. "I propose then that, from an analytical point of view, the only thing which one can be guilty of is of having given ground relative to one's desire" (Lacan 1992, p. 319). For all this, I cannot do better than refer the reader to the excellent account given by Alenka Zupančič (2000).

11. See Baas 1998; Agamben 1991 ("the Voice manifests the event of language as time, if thinking is the experience of language which in every sentence, in every word experiences the very event of language—it thinks, in other words, being and time in their coincidence in the Voice. . . ." [p. 175]).

12. See Derrida:

> Heidegger, after evoking the voice of being, notes that this voice is silent, mute, non-sonorous, without a word and originally aphonic (*die Gewähr der lautlosen Stimme verborgener Quellen*). The voices of origins cannot be heard. This is the rupture between the original sense of being and the word, between meaning and voice, between the voice of being and *phone*, between the call of being and the articulated sound. This rupture, which at the same time affirms the basic metaphor and casts doubts about it by displaying its metaphorical shift, demonstrates Heidegger's position in relation to the metaphysics of presence and logocentrism. It is part of metaphysics and transcends it. Yet it cannot be divided. (Derrida 1967b, p. 34)

13. I must add that the "ethics of the voice" does not exhaust the ethical tradition. In one of the greatest books on ethics—with the most economical title, *Ethics*—Spinoza does not have recourse to the voice of consience (but he does a few times mention *morsus conscientiae*, the bite of conscience, perhaps deeming audition too slight for what is at stake). Spinoza is both the most radical metaphysician and, for that very reason, someone who exhibits many traits which separate him from all the standard images—no wonder Heidegger has nothing to say about him.

14. This formula is taken from Zupančič 2000, p. 164, to which I am greatly indebted also for the arguments that follow. See also Baas 1998, p. 196 and *passim*.

15. "The source of its compulsive character [of the super-ego] which manifests itself in the form of a categorical imperative" (PFL 11, p. 374); "As the child was once under a compulsion to obey its parents, so the ego submits to the categorical imperative of its super-ego" (ibid., p. 389); "The super-ego . . . may then become harsh, cruel and inexorable against the ego which is in its charge. Kant's categorical imperative is thus the direct heir of the Oedipus complex" (ibid., p. 422); and so on.

16. "Two things fill the mind with ever new and increasing wonder and awe . . ." (Kant 1993, p. 169). In this, the best-known quote from Kant, we find *Bewunderung und Ehrfurcht*, which could also be translated as "admiration and consternation," "worship and trepidation"—in short, highly pathological entities by Kant's own standards, as opposed to *Achtung*, respect.

17. There is what Eric Santner, in his excellent book (2001), has called "undeadness" and "surplus-animation," the animation which sustains the vicious circle of transgression and guilt, undeadness as opposed to life.

18. With shofar, the vocal remnant of the primal father is turned into a ritual and public seal of the law, its underside thus recognized, sustained, and utilized for "common good." Such a neat division, however, can never quite work without some residue—we will come back to this. As for the relation between law and superego in Judaism and Christianity, see Žižek 2003; Santner 2001.

19. As Jean-Michel Vives put it succinctly: "Voice without law leads to lethal [mortifère] enjoyment, law without voice remains a dead letter" (quoted by Poizat 2001, p. 143).

20. From this angle we could tackle the status of the voice in psychosis, something I cannot deal with here. If the superego functions as the shadow and the supplement of the law, if it operates in and through this division, this yields some variant of the "neurotic" mechanism. But if the voice supplants the Other and immediately "makes the law," then it entails the dramatic consequences we can witness in psychosis. Lacan scrutinized psychosis under the heading of "the foreclosure of the name of the father"—and we could say that the foreclosed "name of the father" returns in the Real precisely as the voice.

CHAPTER 5   THE POLITICS OF THE VOICE

1. By a strange coincidence, perhaps the two best-known books of political philosophy at the end of the twentieth century, two discoveries of the last decade, both start off with a discussion of this passage: Jacques Rancière's *La Mésentente* (1995, pp. 19–25; 1998) and Giorgio Agamben's *Homo sacer* (1997, pp. 15–19). Both were published in 1995 in their French and Italian originals.

2. To quote some of Agamben's own examples: Foucault's *le grand renfermement* functions as "the closure of the outside"; it includes a part of the population by excluding them and exposing them to "special treatment"—thus they are not outside the social, but at the point where the social mechanisms are manifested most explicitly. The crucial and general mechanism of *the ban* excludes someone, a category, a group of people, from the law, and thus defines the validity of the law by including/excluding its outside. "The outlaw" is subject to the law in its pure form.

3. We can recall how making fun of the legal profession was one of the highlights of Enlightenment comedy. Take, for example, the court scene in Beaumarchais's *Figaro*.

4. The central role of the immediacy of the voice caused many legal problems with the introduction of sound recording and then video into the courtroom (in Germany, for example, video was admitted in 1998). In most countries those records, as a rule, are still seen as secondary to the written protocol supervised by the judge. To say nothing of the fact that radio or TV transmission of court proceedings is ruled out—among other considerations, it would dissipate the illusion, the legal fiction, of the immediacy of the voice as the locus of justice.

5. "To vote" stems from Latin *votum, voveo*, meaning a wish, a pledge, and has no relation to *vox*, voice.

6. There is a grand operatic example of this: the opening scene of Moussorgsky's *Boris Godunov* revolves entirely around the problem of the acclamation of the monarch.

7. See Poizat 2001, pp. 236 ff. and *passim* for a comprehensive account of the adage as well as its connection to elections. Alcuin's letter states: "According to divine laws one has to lead the people, not to follow it. . . . One shouldn't listen to those who say *Vox populi, vox Dei*, since the tumultuous zeal of the people always borders on madness" (p. 238).

8. In a gesture which is like a counterpoint to this, Hegel's monarch accomplishes and enacts the rational legality not by his voice but by his signature, a senseless written sign which renders the law effective. The monarch is the constitutive exception inscribed within the realm of the law, reduced to the mere signifier, the signature, a pure performative act without a meaning. This was Hegel's wager: to include the point of exception and thus to neutralize it, to enact the realm of reason through the exception at its center. The point of this strategy was to reduce the exception to a senseless letter, still universally available and verifiable, a zero-point of universality, as opposed to the totalitarian ruler pinned to the voice. For the difference between the two, see Žižek 1993, pp. 174–193.

9. For much of what follows I am again indebted to Alenka Zupančič (2003, pp. 168–169). See also Poizat 2001, pp. 169–172.

10. It is rather significant that this scene was the first time cinema audiences actually heard Chaplin's voice, since he had many misgivings before espousing the "talking movies."

11. "In this society the king doesn't address the listeners who are his subjects directly and loudly. His voice is always quiet, grave, low. Every time the sovereign pauses, an assistant in charge of repetition amplifies and transmits loudly the royal words to the public. But this human amplifier is not limited to mechanical reproduction of the words of the sovereign. It happens that he completes them and modifies their style when reciting them for the audience" (Kawada 1998, p. 12).

12. "The King's body impresses, dominates, stuns, judges and stupefies not so much by the luxury of its appearance or the panegyric allegories, not by the sacred terror of the untouchable sacred flesh stemming from the medieval fables, but by the effect of its voice" (Salazar 1995, p. 289).

13. If the sacred, then only in the sense of the sacred as Agamben presents it in *Homo sacer*, which is an entity precisely outside the sacred and the sacrificial, an opening to the biopolitical.

14. "He is placed at the juncture of *zoe* and *bios*, of the biological and the political body. His person is the place where the one constantly passes into the other" (Agamben 1997, p. 198).

15. This is where some criticism of Lacan is in order. On the last page of *Seminar XI*, he says:

> There is something profoundly masked in the critique of the history that we have experienced. This, re-enacting the most monstrous and supposedly superseded forms of the holocaust, is the drama of Nazism. I would hold that no meaning given to history, based on Hegeliano-Marxist premises, is capable of accounting for this resurgence—which only goes to show that the offering to obscure gods of an object of sacrifice is something to which few subjects can resist succumbing, as if under some monstrous spell. (1979, pp. 274–275)

> The problem of holocaust is not the problem of sacrifice, nor of obscure deities.

16. See Žižek, *Did Somebody Say Totalitarianism?* (2001a).

17. This is but a hint in need of much further elaboration. We can connect it, for example, to Rancière's opposition between police and the political, and between the usual identification and subjectification: "By subjectification I mean the production through a series of actions of a body and a capacity for enunciation not previously identifiable within a given field of experience, whose identification is thus part of the reconfiguration of the field of experience" (Rancière 1998, p. 35).

18. This important text is curiously missing from the PFL edition, so I must for once refer to James Strachey, ed., *The Standard Edition of the Complete Psychological Works of Sigmund Freud* (London: Hogarth Press, 1953–73), vol. 23, p. 249. Freud had used the same idea in his "Preface to August Aichhorn's *Wayward Youth*" (1925 f.), SE 19, p. 273.

CHAPTER 6 FREUD'S VOICES

1. Freud adds self-critically: "It is a little doubtful whether anyone else would have recognized the tune" (PFL 4, p. 300). The tune was, of course, the famous "*Se vuol ballare, Signor Contino,*" with an obvious reference to Count Thun.

2. As in the old joke: Good thing I don't like asparagus, because if I did I would have to eat it, and that would be awful.

3. Freud occasionally comes back to this idea of the connection between the clock and the female genitals, and between ticking and the clitoris in particular. "The ticking of the clock can be equated with the ticking of the clitoris during sexual arousal" (PFL 1, p. 303).

4. Dora was another victim of nocturnal listening: "Dora's symptomatic acts and certain other signs gave me good reasons for supposing that the child, whose bedroom had been next door to her parents', had overheard her father in his wife's room at night and had heard him (for he was always short of breath) breathing hard while they had intercourse" (PFL 8, p. 116). The paramount case is that of the Wolf Man, which I will leave aside.

5. Curiously, the same example is used by Merleau-Ponty in his *Phenomenology of Perception* (1978, p. 215), without reference to Freud, in a phenomenological analysis of understanding.

6. Four years earlier: "I believe I understand the anxiety neuroses of young people who must be regarded as virgins with no history of sexual abuse. I have analyzed two such cases, and the cause was an apprehensive terror of sexuality, against a background of things they had seen or heard and only half-understood; thus the etiology was purely emotional, but still of a sexual nature." (May 30, 1893, Freud 1977, p. 73.)

7. Our attention is first attracted by the effects of certain influences which do not apply to all children, though they are common enough—such as the sexual abuse of children by adults, their seduction by other children (brothers or sisters) slightly their seniors, and, what we should not expect, their being deeply stirred by seeing or hearing at first hand sexual behaviour between adults (their parents) mostly at a time at which one would not have thought they could either be interested in or understand any such impressions, or be capable of remembering them later. (PFL 15, p. 421)

The exclusive focus on hearing is now mitigated by the inclusion of seeing.

8. Here I must refer to the classic paper on the origin of fantasy by Laplanche and Pontalis ([1964] 1985), which still provides an excellent approach to the self-reflexive and circular way in which the fantasy of origin functions as the origin of fantasy as well as the original fantasy, the clue to the emergence of both sexuality and subjectivity.

9. I suppose the symptom of this is that there are no neutral non-marked expressions for sexual parts or actions in any language: they are either vulgar, obscene, featuring a vast florid variety, or else technical and laden with foreign words.

10. This was Freud's most popular work, first published in 1901 in a mere 92 pages, then expanded with each new edition to the final 310 pages in 1924.

11. It so happens that I have written one, available only in Slovene (*On Avarice*, Ljubljana 2002), which could be seen as a long footnote to this Freudian slip.

12. Freud says in a footnote: "I must add that the sound of the word 'Ananas' bears remarkable resemblance to that of my patient Irma's family name [Hammerschlag]" (PFL 4, p. 192). A question of taste?

13. "Phonology cannot help but play the same innovative role with respect to the social sciences that nuclear physics, for example, has played for all the hard sciences" (Lévi-Strauss 1958, p. 39). A vast epistemological program followed from this insight.

14. If the epistemological program of all early structuralism was based on phonology, then a very different kind of epistemology follows from the matheme as the detritus, as it were, of the phonological operation. It links the epistemology underlying psychoanalysis to that of Galilean science: indeed, to physics, which Lévi-Strauss took as an analogy—for the best comment on this I can only refer to the extensive and lucid work of Jean-Claude Milner.

15. "The latent dream-thoughts are the material which the dream-work transforms into the manifest dream. . . . Analytic observation shows further that the dream-work never restricts itself to translating these thoughts into the archaic or regressive mode of expression that is familiar to you. In addition, it regularly takes possession of something else, which is not part of the latent thoughts of the previous day, but which is the true motive for the construction of the dream. This indispensable addition is the equally unconscious wish [desire] for the fulfillment of which the content of the dream is given form." (PFL 1, pp. 261–262.)

16. Lacan proposed, in one of his unpublished seminars, a difference between *sileo*, a simple absence of voice and sound, and *taceo*, which entails an act. See Fonteneau 1999, p. 126.

17. "The language may be content simply to contrast something with nothing" (Saussure 1998, p. 86).

18. Abbé Dinouart (1716–86) was a lot more loquacious as a translator and a compiler of various texts. Apart from this short pamphlet he wrote two further ones: *Le triomphe du sexe* (1749), which caused him some difficulties with the Church, and *L'éloquence du corps* (1754). Sex, body, silence—another unknown precursor of psychoanalysis?

19. "The theory of the drives is so to say our mythology. Drives are mythical entities, magnificent in their indefiniteness. In our work we cannot

disregard them, yet we are never sure that we are seeing the clearly" (PFL 2, p. 127; I have substituted "drives" for "instincts").

20. Baas puts this very well: "The voice is never my own voice, but the response is my own response" (1998, p. 205).

21. Lacan makes an immediate link between the fundamental fantasy and the drive: "after the mapping of the subject in relation to the [object] a, the experience of the fundamental fantasy becomes the drive" (Lacan 1979, p. 273).

22. One of Lacan's key papers on this problem most appropriately bears the title "On Freud's 'Trieb' and the Psychoanalyst's Desire" (Lacan 1966, pp. 851–854), linking the drive to the position of the analyst.

CHAPTER 7   KAFKA'S VOICES

1. See "The Problem of Our Laws":

   Our laws are not generally known; they are kept secret by the small group of nobles who rule us. We are convinced that these ancient laws are scrupulously administered; nevertheless it is an extremely painful thing to be ruled by laws that one does not know. . . . The very existence of these laws, however, is at most a matter of presumption. There is a tradition that they exist and that they are a mystery confided to the nobility, but it is not and cannot be more than a mere tradition sanctioned by age, for the essence of a secret code is that it should remain a mystery. . . . There is a small party who . . . try to show that, if any law exists, it can only be this: The Law is whatever the nobles do. (1995, pp. 437–438)

   All quotes from Kafka's stories are from The Complete Stories (Kafka 1995).

2. See Derrida 1985, p. 122 and passim.

3. "Der Bau," written at the end of 1923 and published after Kafka's death by Max Brod, who also provided the title. The German word is impossible to translate in all its ambiguity. It can mean the process of building, construction; the result of building, the edifice; the structure, the making (of a plant, of a novel . . .); a jail; a burrow, a hole in the ground, a mine. The oscillation is not only between the process and the result (establishing an equivalence between "process" and "structure"), but also between erecting an edifice and digging a hole.

4. There is another passing mention of Kafka in Lacan's seminar "D'un Autre à l'autre" (Lacan 1968/69). In the session of June 11, 1969, Lacan proposes the Trojan Horse, with its empty belly, "the empty set," hiding the dangerous object, as a good model of the big Other, where Troy itself, in extension, appears as "the Kafkaesque castle."

5. This, of course, is one of the grand examples from Freud's book on jokes (PFL 6, p. 161). In the "Index of Jokes" at the end of the volume, this joke is laconically referred to as "Truth a lie (Jewish)," and indeed, as I have tried to argue elsewhere, this joke most economically epitomizes the problem that "Jewishness" presented for Western culture: the indistinguishable character of truth and lie, the fact that they not only look alike but actually coincide, so that "Jewishness" seems to undermine the very ground of the truth-telling capacity of language. This is the very problem with the "Jews": they look exactly like us, just as a lie looks exactly like the truth.

6. Before leaving Ulysses, let me just recall that in the standard iconography Ulysses was transformed into a Christian hero. This goes back to Saint Ambrose, in the fourth century, who depicted Ulysses as a man courageously resisting temptation. So in endless renditions we see him tied to the mast, in a parody of Christ tied to the cross, surrounded by a host of naked girls on the beaches, or the Sirens turned into mermaids; he is sweating and shivering all over, fighting inner struggles, heroically defying temptation, like Saint Anthony; he is the Greek paragon of Christian virtue. And we can easily see that he is indulging in this very Christian form of "surplus-enjoyment," this thwarted—and hence irresistible—form of enjoyment in transgression and culpabilization. For an overview of the multiple uses of the Sirens, see Vic de Donder 1992.

7. The German dictionary offers the expression *das trägt eine Maus auf den Schwanz fort* for a quantity so small that a mouse could carry it on its tail (with all the German ambiguity of the word, tail/penis). There is a rather vulgar expression in Slovene, "the mouse's penis," which means the smallest thing imaginable, one cannot possibly conceive of anything smaller; the mouse's voice is of that order of magnitude. The mouse's penis—a circumlocution for castration? Is Josephine a *castrato*, is this the secret of her voice?

8. "There is no longer a proper sense and a figurative sense, but a distribution of states along the fan of the word. . . . What is at stake is not a resemblance between an animal and a human behavior, and even less a play upon words. There is no longer a man or an animal, since each deterritorializes the other. . . . The animal doesn't speak as a human, but extracts from language the tonalities without meaning. . . ." (Deleuze and Guattari 1975, p. 40.)

9. Here we should also recall the badger from "The Burrow," the story used by Lacan. The badger is the antisocial animal, the solitary digger, the animal of an utter exclusion from society, but from that outside he has to deal all the more with the oppressive and unfathomable big Other.

10. On closer scrutiny, both mice and dogs in many respects strangely resemble the Jews and their destiny, as several interpreters have pointed out,

but I will not go into this: "No creatures to my knowledge live in such wide dispersion as we dogs . . . ; we, whose one desire is to stick together . . . we above all others live so widely separated from one another, engaged in strange vocations that are often incomprehensible even to our canine neighbors . . ." (pp. 279–280). In both cases there is also a metaphor—to live like a dog, poor as a mouse—which is destroyed by its literalization. With mice we should also keep in mind the connection of the German word, *Maus*, with *mauscheln*, with all its connotations in German (a verb derived from Yiddish for Moses, *Mausche*, and meaning to speak Yiddish or Yiddishized German, and by extension to speak in an incomprehensible way, and by further extension secret dealings, hidden affairs, deceit).

11. What Freud and Kafka curiously have in common, apart from the obvious analogies of their Jewish origins and sharing the same historical moment and the space of Central Europe, is their claim that they are both completely unmusical—which made them both particularly susceptible to the dimension of the voice.

12. Wajcman (1998) provides the the best commentary on Duchamp I know of.

13. Kafka, in the manuscript, crossed out four instances where the narrator speaks in the first person—his is the voice of anonymity, and must remain without an "I."

14. I cannot resist the temptation to quote some Lacan here: "Even when you stuff the mouth—the mouth that opens in the register of the drive—it is not the food that satisfies it. . . . As far as the oral drive is concerned . . . it is obvious that it is not a question of food, nor of the memory of food, nor the echo of food, nor the mother's care . . ." (Lacan 1979, pp. 167–168); "the fact that no food will ever satisfy the oral drive, except by circumventing [circling around] the eternally lacking object. . . . The *objet petit a* is not the origin of the oral drive. It is not introduced as the original food, it is introduced from the fact that no food will ever satisfy the oral drive, except by circumventing [circling around] the eternally lacking object" (ibid., p. 180).

15. "This *a* is presented precisely . . . as the object that cannot be swallowed, as it were, which remains stuck in the gullet of the signifier" (Lacan 1979, p. 270).

BIBLIOGRAPHY

Adorno, Theodor W. (1973). *Einleitung in die Musiksoziologie*, in *Gesammelte Schriften*, vol. 14. Frankfurt: Suhrkamp.

Adorno, Theodor W., and Max Horkheimer (2002). *Dialectic of Enlightenment*. Stanford: Stanford University Press.

Agamben, Giorgio (1991). *Le langage et la mort*. Paris: Christian Bourgeois [1982].

Agamben, Giorgio (1997). *Homo sacer*. Paris: Seuil [1995].

Aristotle (2001). *The Basic Writings of Aristotle*. New York: Modern Library.

Assoun, Paul-Laurent (1995). *Leçons psychanalytiques sur le regard et la voix. Vol. 1: Fondements. Vol. 2: Figures*. Paris: Anthropos-Economica.

Attali, Jacques (1977). *Bruits*. Paris: Presses Universitaires de France.

Augustine (1992). *Confessions*. 3 vols. Ed. James J. O'Donnell. Oxford: Clarendon Press.

Baas, Bernard (1990). "Le démon de Socrate," in *Socrate. Perspectives philosophiques—perspectives psychanalytiques*. Strasbourg: Presses Universitaires de Strasbourg, pp. 109–132.

Baas, Bernard (1998). *De la chose à l'objet*. Leuven: Peeters/Vrin.

Badiou, Alain. *Logiques des mondes* (manuscript to be published by Seuil in 2006).

Balmès, François (1997). *Le nom, la loi, la voix*. Paris: Erès.

Barthes, Roland (1982). *L'obvie et l'obtus*. Paris: Seuil.

Baum, L. Frank (1995). *The Wonderful Wizard of Oz*. London: Penguin.

Benjamin, Walter (1987). *Illuminations*. New York: Schocken Books.

Carroll, Lewis, and Martin Gardner (1986). *The Annotated Alice*. Harmondsworth: Penguin.

Castarède, Marie-France (1991). *La voix et ses sortilèges*. Paris: Belles Lettres [1987].

Cavarero, Adriana (2003). *A più voci. Filosofia dell'espressione vocale*. Milan: Feltrinelli.

Cavell, Stanley (1994). *A Pitch of Philosophy*. Cambridge, MA: Harvard University Press.

Chion, Michel (1982). *La voix au cinéma*. Paris: Cahiers du cinéma.

Chion, Michel (1998). *Le son*. Paris: Nathan.

Deleuze, Gilles, and Félix Guattari (1975). *Kafka. Pour une littérature mineure*. Paris: Minuit.

Derrida, Jacques (1967a). *De la grammatologie*. Paris: Minuit / (1976). *Of Grammatology*. Baltimore: Johns Hopkins University Press.

Derrida, Jacques (1967b). *La voix et le phénomène*. Paris: Presses Universitaires de France.

Derrida, Jacques (1972). *La dissémination*. Paris: Seuil.

Derrida, Jacques (1985). "Préjugés, devant la loi," in Jean-François Lyotard, *La faculté de juger*. Paris: Minuit.

Dinouart, Abbé (2002). *L'art de se taire*. Grenoble: Jérôme Millon [1771].

Donder, Vic de (1992). *Le chant de la sirène*. Paris: Gallimard.

Felderer, Brigitte (2002). "Stimm-Maschinen. Zur Konstruktion und Sichtbarmachung menschlicher Sprache im 18. Jahrhundert," in Kittler, Macho, and Weigel, eds. (2002), pp. 257–278.

Fonteneau, Françoise (1999). *L'éthique du silence. Wittgenstein et Lacan*. Paris: Seuil.

Freud, Sigmund (1969–75). *Studienausgabe*. Frankfurt: Fischer (cited as SA).

Freud, Sigmund (1973–86). *The Pelican Freud Library*. 15 vols. Harmondsworth: Penguin (cited as PFL).

Freud, Sigmund (1977). *The Origins of Psychoanalysis. Letters to Wilhelm Fliess*. New York: Basic Books.

Hegel, G. W. F. (1977). *Phenomenology of Spirit*. Trans. A. V. Miller. Oxford: Oxford University Press.

Heidegger, Martin (1973). *Being and Time*. Oxford: Blackwell / (1963). *Sein und Zeit*. Tübingen: Niemeyer.

Heidegger, Martin (1976). *Wegmarken (Gesamtausgabe I/9)*. Frankfurt: Klostermann.

Jakobson, Roman (1960). "Closing Statement: Linguistics and Poetics," in Thomas A. Sebeok, *Style in Language*. Cambridge, MA: MIT Press, pp. 350–377.

Jakobson, Roman (1963). *Essais de linguistique générale I*. Paris: Minuit.

Jakobson, Roman (1968). *Child Language, Aphasia and Phonological Universals*. The Hague and Paris: Mouton [1941].

Jakobson, Roman (1976). *Six leçons sur le son et le sens*. Paris: Minuit.

Jankélévitch, Vladimir (1983). *La musique et l'ineffable*. Paris: Seuil [1961].

Kafka, Franz (1995). *The Complete Stories*. Ed. N. N. Glatzer. New York: Schocken Books.

Kafka, Franz (1996). *Die Erzählungen. Originalfassung*. Ed. Roger Hermes. Frankfurt: Fischer.

Kafka, Franz (1997). *The Castle*. New York: Schocken Books.

Kant, Immanuel (1993). *Critique of Practical Reason*. Ed. and trans. Lewis White Beck. New York: Macmillan.

Kawada, Junzo (1998). *La voix. Étude d'ethno-linguistique comparative*. Paris: Éditions de l'École des hautes études en sciences sociales.

Kittler, Friedrich, Thomas Macho, and Sigrid Weigel, eds. (2002). *Zwischen Rauschen und Offenbarung. Zur Kultur- und Mediengeschichte der Stimme*. Berlin: Akademie Verlag.

Lacan, Jacques (1966). *Écrits*. Paris: Seuil.

Lacan, Jacques (1975). *Les écrits techniques de Freud (Le séminaire, Livre I*, ed. Jacques-Alain Miller). Paris: Seuil [1953/54].

Lacan, Jacques (1979). *The Four Fundamental Concepts of Psycho-Analysis (Seminar XI*, ed. J.-A. Miller). Harmondsworth: Penguin [1964].

Lacan, Jacques (1989). *Écrits: A Selection*. Ed. and trans. A. Sheridan. London: Tavistock/Routledge.

Lacan, Jacques (1991). *Le transfert (Le séminaire, Livre VIII*, ed. J.-A. Miller). Paris: Seuil [1960/61].

Lacan, Jacques (1992). *The Ethics of Psychoanalysis (Seminar VII*, ed. J.-A. Miller). New York: Norton [1959/60].

Lacan, Jacques (1994). *La relation d'objet (Le séminaire, Livre IV,* ed. J. -A. Miller). Paris: Seuil [1956/57].

Lacan, Jacques (2004). *L'angoisse (Le séminaire, Livre X,* ed. J. -A. Miller). Paris: Seuil [1962/63].

Lacan, Jacques. *Identification* (1961/62). Unpublished seminar.

Lacan, Jacques. *Problèmes cruciaux pour la psychanalyse* (1964/65). Unpublished seminar.

Lacan, Jacques. *D'un Autre à l'autre* (1968/69). Unpublished seminar.

La Mettrie, Julien Offray de (1981). *L'homme-machine.* Paris: Denoël-Gonthier.

Laplanche, Jean, and J. -B. Pontalis (1985). *Fantasme originaire, fantasme des origines, origines du fantasme.* Paris: Hachette [1964].

Lecourt, Édith (1992). *Freud et le sonore.* Paris: L'Harmattan.

Lévi-Strauss, Claude (1958). *Anthropologie structurale.* Paris: Plon.

Lévi-Strauss, Claude, and Didier Eribon (1990). *De près et de loin.* Paris: Odile Jacob.

McCallion, Michael (1998). *The Voice Book.* London: Faber & Faber [1988].

Mannoni, Octave (1969). *Clefs pour l'imaginaire; ou L'autre scène.* Paris: Seuil.

Merleau-Ponty, Maurice (1978). *Phénoménologie de la perception.* Paris: Gallimard-TEL [1945].

Miller, Jacques-Alain (1989). "Jacques Lacan et la voix," in Ivan Fonagy et al., *La voix. Actes du colloque d'Ivry.* Paris: La lysimaque.

Mitchell, Juliet, and Jacqueline Rose (1982). *Feminine Sexuality: Jacques Lacan and the École freudienne.* London: Macmillan.

Nancy, Jean-Luc (2002). *À l'écoute.* Paris: Galilée.

Parret, Herman (2002). *La voix et son temps.* Brussels: De Boeck & Larcier.

Pfaller, Robert (2002). *Die Illusionen der anderen.* Frankfurt: Suhrkamp.

Plato (1978). *The Collected Dialogues.* Ed. Edith Hamilton and Huntington Cairns. Princeton: Princeton University Press.

Plato (1997). *Complete Works.* Ed. John M. Cooper. Indianapolis/Cambridge: Hackett.

Plutarch (1949). *Moralia,* vol. III. London: Heinemann and Cambridge, MA: Harvard University Press.

Poe, Edgar Allan (1984). *The Complete Tales and Poems.* Harmondsworth: Penguin.

Poizat, Michel (1986). *L'Opéra ou le cri de l'ange*. Paris: Métailié.

Poizat, Michel (1991). *La voix du diable*. Paris: Métailié.

Poizat, Michel (1996). *La voix sourde*. Paris: Métailié.

Poizat, Michel (2001). *Vox populi, vox Dei*. Paris: Métailié.

Proust, Marcel (2001). *In Search of Lost Time*, vol. 3. Trans. C. K. Scott Moncrieff and T. Kilmartin, revised by D. J. Enright. London: Everyman.

Rabinovitch, Solal (1999). *Les voix*. Paris: Erès.

Rancière, Jacques (1995). *La Mésentente*. Paris: Galilée / (1998). *Disagreement: Politics and Philosophy*. Minneapolis: University of Minnesota Press.

Reik, Theodor (1928). *Das Ritual. Psychoanalytische Studien*. Leipzig, Vienna, and Zurich: Internationaler Psychoanalytischer Verlag (Imago-Bücher).

Rouget, Gilbert (1980). *La musique et la transe*. Paris: Gallimard.

Rousseau, Jean-Jacques (1969). *Oeuvres complètes*, vol. IV. Paris: Gallimard (Bibliothèque de la Pléiade).

Salazar, Philippe-Joseph (1995). *Le culte de la voix au XVIIᵉ siècle*. Paris: Éditions Champion.

Santner, Eric (2001). *On the Psychotheology of Everyday Life: Reflections on Freud and Rosenzweig*. Chicago: University of Chicago Press.

Saussure, Ferdinand de (1972). *Cours de linguistique générale*. Paris: Payot / (1998). *Course in General Linguistics*. Ed. and trans. Roy Harris. London: Duckworth.

Schaeffer, Pierre (1966). *Traité des objets musicaux*. Paris: Seuil.

Schneider, Marius (1960). "Le rôle de la musique dans la mythologie et les rites des civilisations non européennes," in *Histoire de la musique I*. (ed. Roland-Manuel). Paris: Gallimard (Bibliothèque de la Pléiade).

Silverman, Kaja (1988). *The Acoustic Mirror*. Bloomington: Indiana University Press.

Standage, Tom (2002). *The Turk*. New York: Berkeley Books.

Vasse, Denis (1972). *L'ombilic et la voix*. Paris: Seuil.

Vissmann, Cornelia (2002). "Action writing: Zur Mündlichkeit im Recht," in Kittler, Macho, and Weigel (eds.) (2002), pp. 133–151.

Wajcman, Gérard (1998). *L'objet du siècle*. Lagrasse: Verdier.

Žižek, Slavoj (1989). *The Sublime Object of Ideology*. London and New York: Verso.

Žižek, Slavoj (1993). *Tarrying with the Negative*. Durham: Duke University Press.

Žižek, Slavoj (2001a). *Did Somebody Say Totalitarianism?* London and New York: Verso.

Žižek, Slavoj (2001b). *On Belief.* London: Routledge.

Žižek, Slavoj (2003). *The Puppet and the Dwarf: The Perverse Core of Christianity.* Cambridge, MA: MIT Press.

Zupančič, Alenka (2000). *Ethics of the Real.* London and New York: Verso.

Zupančič, Alenka (2003). *The Shortest Shadow: Nietzsche's Philosophy of the Two.* Cambridge, MA: MIT Press.